DEADLY EMBRACE

DEADLY EMBRACE

Pakistan, America, and the Future of the Global Jihad

BRUCE RIEDEL

BROOKINGS INSTITUTION PRESS
Washington, D.C.

Copyright © 2011
Paperback edition copyright © 2012
THE BROOKINGS INSTITUTION
1775 Massachusetts Avenue, N.W., Washington, DC 20036.
www.brookings.edu

The Library of Congress has cataloged the hardcover edition as follows:
Riedel, Bruce O.
   Deadly embrace : Pakistan, America, and the future of the global jihad / Bruce Riedel.
      p.   cm.
   Includes bibliographical references and index.
   Summary: "Explores the long and contentious relationship between the United States and Pakistan since Pakistan's founding with emphasis on events that occurred during the author's thirty-year career with the CIA and on how Pakistan's history and U.S. responses have contributed to the current struggle with terrorism"
—Provided by publisher.
   ISBN 978-0-8157-0557-4 (hardcover : alk. paper)
   1. United States—Foreign relations—Pakistan. 2. Pakistan—Foreign relations—United States. 3. Terrorism—Prevention. 4. Islam and politics—Pakistan. I. Title.
   JZ1480.A57P178 2011
   327.7305491—dc22   2010045328

ISBN 978-0-8157-2274-8 (pbk. : alk. paper)

9 8 7 6 5 4 3 2 1

Printed on acid-free paper

Typeset in Sabon

Composition by Cynthia Stock
Silver Spring, Maryland

Printed by R. R. Donnelley
Harrisonburg, Virginia

To my beloved Elizabeth

CONTENTS

Preface: *The Mystery of Abbottabad*   ix

Preface to the First Edition   xvii

ONE   Understanding Pakistan   1

TWO   Zia's Jihad   17

THREE   Omar's Jihad   36

FOUR   Osama's Jihad   60

FIVE   Global Jihad   86

SIX   Thinking the Unthinkable:
Implications of a Jihadist State in Pakistan   106

SEVEN   Helping Pakistan   119

Key Persons and Timeline   145

Notes   149

Bibliography   165

Index   171

PREFACE
The Mystery of Abbottabad

ON A CLEAR NIGHT in early May 2011, American navy commandos found and killed Osama bin Laden in his hideout in the Pakistani city of Abbottabad. After searching for "high-value target number one" since 1998, the Central Intelligence Agency had finally found the most wanted man in human history. Thorough and careful intelligence analysis had tracked him down to a house in this garrison city that also boasts Pakistan's premier military academy. Abbottabad is just thirty miles north of the country's capital in Islamabad and the nearby military general headquarters in Rawalpindi. It is located on the famous Karakoram Highway that follows the ancient Silk Road from South Asia over the Himalayas and Hindu Kush to China. In American terms it was as if bin Laden were hiding just outside the gate of the U.S. Naval Academy in Annapolis, Maryland, an hour's drive from the White House and the Pentagon.

Abbottabad is named after a British army officer and colonial administrator, Sir James Abbott, who founded the city as a cantonment for the British army in India in January 1853. Abbott fought in the British East India Company's wars against the Sikhs in the middle of the nineteenth century and was very fond of the city he founded. He wrote a poem about it later that included the line "to me the place seemed like a dream." One expert has written that "for the Pakistani military, the image of paradise is the cantonment."

Whether dream or paradise, much about Osama bin Laden's hideout in Abbottabad is still a mystery. The CIA traced him there by following the trail of a Pakistani acting as his courier, Abu Ahmed al Kuwaiti, who had worked with bin Laden in the planning of the 9/11 attacks. Al Kuwaiti was a Pakistani Pashtun tribesman who was born and raised in Kuwait and spoke fluent Arabic and Pashto, so he could move between two cultures easily. In 2010 the intelligence community traced him to Abbottabad and a three-story housing compound that seemed different from most other homes in the city. It was surrounded by an eighteen-foot-high wall topped with barbed wire, had no electronic signatures (phone or Internet), and seemed custom-built to hide someone. Privacy screens and interior walls obstructed vision into the compound from the outside. The children inside were home schooled and the residents burned all of their garbage.

Bin Laden had apparently moved into the house sometime in 2006, and the facility itself had been adjusted and built to its unusual design in 2005 for his use. He was a recluse inside but not isolated from the world. Al Kuwaiti, acting as courier, brought him messages and letters from the outside, and bin Laden dispatched his letters via his courier. After bin Laden's death, the SEAL commandos scooped up scores of documents and computer files. In those were found correspondence from bin Laden to his wives, children, and subordinates such as Ayman Zawahiri. He was very much in charge of his global terrorist empire and kept abreast of plots like the July 2005 London bombing. He was constantly pressing his lieutenants for more terror.

Al Qaeda practiced good tradecraft in concealing its leader's hideout for five years. But he could not hide in Abbottabad without some support network beyond al Kuwaiti. Phone numbers found in the house by the SEAL team suggested that al Kuwaiti was in touch with a Pakistani terrorist group. This was confirmed in June 2011 by the *New York Times*, which reported that al Kuwaiti apparently was in contact with Harakat ul Mujahedin, a terror group created in the 1980s by Pakistan's Inter-Services Intelligence directorate (ISI) to fight India, and it has loyally worked with the ISI for decades. It was at the center of the hijacking of an Indian airliner in 1999, conducted with the assistance of the ISI and al Qaeda. Its leader, Fazlur Rehman Khalil, lives openly in an Islamabad suburb.

The most important mystery, of course, is what the Pakistani army and the ISI knew about bin Laden's hideout. From the day the CIA became focused on Abbottabad, President Barack Obama decided that he could not trust the Pakistanis with information about the hideout. No Pakistani official was given any advance warning about U.S. suspicions or that the United States intended to send commandos to find and either capture or kill him. During months of surveillance of the compound and preparation for the SEAL operation, Pakistan was kept completely in the dark by Obama and his national security team.

It was an extraordinary decision. Since 2001 Pakistani leaders from General and, later, President Pervez Musharraf to today's President Ali Asif Zardari and the chief of army staff General Ashfaq Kayani, who is the real power in the country, had promised again and again to help America fight al Qaeda. Now at the moment of truth, the American president, correctly, judged he could not trust them with the vital information on the location of al Qaeda's top leader. Obama's decision spoke volumes about America's real attitude toward its Pakistani partner. It is a safe bet that had we given the Pakistanis bin Laden's location, he would have escaped.

Abbottabad is not an ordinary city. Pakistan's first military dictator, Field Marshall Ayub Khan, was born near here. It is the home of the Kakul Military Academy, the Pakistani equivalent of West Point or Sandhurst. Several regiments of the army call it home. In December 2006 the first joint Pakistani-Chinese anti-terrorist exercise ever held in Pakistan was carried out in Abbottabad. The choice of the city for such a high-profile event underscores its importance to the military. Some generals retire to its pleasant weather and surroundings. In short, from its founding during the Raj to today it is a military city.

In 2006 the commandant of the Kakul academy was General Nadeem Taj. He had been a close confidant of Musharraf and, in October 1999, had accompanied him on an official visit to Sri Lanka. On their flight home to Pakistan, Nawaz Sharif, then prime minister, fired Musharraf from his job as chief of army staff (COAS). Taj helped Musharraf engineer a coup from the plane and the overthrow of Sharif. Taj was also with Musharraf when he survived an assassination plot in December 2003. For his loyalty he was appointed director general of military intelligence in 2003 and then commandant of Kakul in 2006. So he was the man in charge in the city when bin Laden set up his hideout.

In late 2007 Taj was again promoted, by Musharraf and Kayani, this time to become director general of the ISI, the top intelligence job in the country, replacing Kayani who moved up to be COAS. On Taj's watch the drone campaign to kill al Qaeda leaders in Pakistan was expanded by

President George Bush. But the targets consistently escaped because they were warned of the impending attacks. Since the ISI was given advance notice of drone operations at that time (this policy changed after 2007), it was not hard to determine where the leaks came from. Then in December 2007, while campaigning for office, Benazir Bhutto was assassinated in Rawalpindi. The United Nations investigation later concluded the ISI deliberately destroyed vital forensic evidence that would have assisted in finding those responsible. In 2008 the Indian embassy in Kabul was attacked by the Afghan Taliban, an attack the U.S. determined was ordered by the ISI.

The Bush team was outraged at the ISI's behavior and wanted Taj sacked, but instead he was promoted again by Kayani in October 2008 to be commander of the XXX Corps in the Pakistani army, a key assignment that made him one of the dozen men who control the army. A month later ten Pakistani terrorists attacked the Indian city of Mumbai, killing dozens including six Americans. We now know the attack was planned and partly funded by the ISI during the tenures of Kayani and of Taj as director generals of the intelligence service. The American who helped plan the attack, David Headley, has testified to that in trials in Chicago.

From the moment the SEAL raid became public, Pakistanis have wondered what their army and intelligence services knew about bin Laden's lair. One thing is certain—no one believes President Zardari knew anything about the hideout. He is powerless and clueless about what the ISI is up to. Officially the ISI says it too was clueless and knew nothing. Many Pakistanis find that hard to believe. Three days after the raid, an op-ed in the influential newspaper *Dawn*, entitled "The Emperor's Clothes," noted that "there is a deep, deep sense of unease here. Pakistanis are asking did the army know he was there? They knew. They knew he was there [in Abbottabad]. And they knew they could get away with it."

But we don't really know. Perhaps the ISI was ignorant of bin Laden's whereabouts and negligent in looking for him. Maybe Musharraf, when he headed the government, Kayani, and Taj are just incompetent. They had been warned to look in Abbottabad. In his own memoirs Musharraf wrote in 2006 that his government knew al Qaeda was hiding key leaders in the city. The Afghan intelligence chief, Amrullah Saleh, says he told Musharraf in 2006 in a meeting in Pakistan that bin Laden was hiding in the area around Abbottabad. According to Saleh, in response to the news Musharraf "banged the table and said am I president of a banana republic? How can you tell me bin Laden is hiding in a settled area of Pakistan?" After the SEAL raid Musharraf told the media that he remembered jogging by the house bin Laden was hiding in when he visited the academy.

The question of negligence or complicity about the army's role in bin Laden's hideout is much more than academic. It has grave policy implications. If the army were simply clueless about where al Qaeda's leader was hiding for at least half a decade, then the United States cannot rely on it to fight terror effectively. If the inner circle of al Qaeda's core, sometimes called al Qaeda al Umm, or mother al Qaeda in Arabic, could outfox the ISI so easily then the ISI is a very weak partner.

If, on the other hand, the army or parts of it were complicit in hiding bin Laden for years, it suggests an astonishing degree of duplicity, and this is truly frightening. A complicit army would have been al Qaeda's behind-the-scenes ally in terror for years, maybe all the way back to 9/11. It would be the secret patron of global jihad on a scale almost too dangerous to conceive. We would need to rethink our entire relationship with Pakistan and our understanding of its strategic motives.

If only a part of the army, an errant general perhaps, were complicit, it raises serious questions about the army's cohesion and internal loyalties. Who was the rogue and who knew what he was up to? How many others are there like him, perhaps guarding nuclear weapon depots?

For now we don't know. Rumors abound. A new book on the SEAL mission claims the commandos were told by their commanders that the ISI was involved in hiding bin Laden. The Pentagon, however, denies the author had any access to the team. A senior Pakistani official told me that the contracting firm for the hideout's special construction in 2005 was run by a former ISI officer who did lots of work for the spy agency. The United States government, including Congress, should make answering the question conclusively a very high priority.

But the mystery of bin Laden's curious hideout and who knew he was there may never be answered fully. A Pakistani journalist who wrote extensively about the links between the ISI and jihadists in Pakistan, Syed Saleem Shahzad, was murdered after he began investigating the story. Many believe the ISI killed him. Top Pentagon officials have said he was.

The journalist's death joins many other mysteries in the history of Pakistan. We still don't know who assassinated Pakistan's third dictator, General Zia ul Haq, the man who turned the country forcefully toward Islamist politics and helped godfather the global jihad. We don't know who killed Benazir Bhutto in December 2007.

One thing we do know: since that May evening the bilateral relationship has continued to deteriorate. In September 2011 the Afghan Taliban attacked the American embassy in Kabul, and the chairman of the joint chiefs later publicly accused the ISI of directing the attack. In November a fire fight on the Afghan-Pakistan border led to two dozen Pakistani soldiers losing their lives in NATO airstrikes. The Pakistani ambassador to Washington, Hussain Haqqani, was fired for being too critical of the army and too friendly to the United States. The odds are good it will only get worse. If the CIA finds Zawahiri or other senior al Qaeda terrorists hiding in Pakistani cities, another commando operation is likely. If there is another Mumbai-style attack in India, the ISI will be held responsible by India and war could follow. If there is another massive terror attack inside the United States postmarked Pakistan, there would be pressure for massive retaliation.

At the start of the Obama administration the policy group I chaired for the president recognized the clash between U.S. and Pakistani policies. Then and now Pakistan provides critical sanctuary and support to the Afghan insurgency; the Taliban's leadership meets under Pakistani protection in Quetta in Baluchistan even while our policy is reviewed in the White House Situation Room. With no illusions, the president had tried to reset relations with Pakistan by increasing aid and dialogue while also stepping up drone operations to do what Pakistan would not do on its own to fight terror.

Engagement was and is the right approach, but three years later it needs some reshaping. The generals who run Pakistan have not abandoned their obsession with challenging India, tolerating terrorists at home, seeking a Taliban victory in Afghanistan, and building the fastest growing nuclear arsenal in the world. The civilians elected by the Pakistani people in 2008 have been sidelined and intimidated. Some have been murdered. Pakistan is sliding into a fifth military dictatorship with a façade of civilian rule masking the real power, the corps commanders who run the army. The generals believe their country is invulnerable since they control NATO's essential supply line from Karachi to Kabul and their nuclear weapons deter all foes. Kayani has said America cannot treat Pakistan like Iraq or Libya because it has the bomb.

The army also believes that, with time on the Taliban's side, NATO is doomed to give up in Afghanistan, and the sooner it leaves the region the better for Pakistan. The generals want Americans and Europeans to believe the war is hopeless and not worth the price. They are encouraging the Taliban to speed the withdrawal with spectacular attacks designed to foster defeatism, such as the one on our embassy in September 2011. NATO is now fighting an escalating and dangerous proxy war with Pakistan in Afghanistan.

The United States tried to make Pakistan part of the solution in Afghanistan; now it must try to persevere in the face of its opposition. A containment approach will mean a more hostile relationship. But it should be focused and targeted, not a confrontation with the Pakistani people. Accountability needs to be introduced into our approach to the army and ISI. When we learn an ISI officer is engaged in assisting terror, whether in the Afghan or Indian theaters, we should make it personal. Those ISI officers engaged in helping our enemies should be put on our wanted lists, sanctioned at the United Nations, and, if sufficiently dangerous, hunted down. Sanctioning organizations in Pakistan has not worked in the past but sanctioning individuals has, as A. Q. Khan, the nuclear proliferation agent, can attest. We broke his international empire by making it very personal.

In Afghanistan we should not have false hopes that a political solution is in sight. The Taliban murdered the Kabul government's chief negotiator, former President Burhanuddin Rabbani, in the fall of 2011: an emissary from the Quetta Shura, the Taliban's top leadership council, asked to see him and then blew himself and Rabbani up with a bomb hidden in his turban. That assassination probably buried any hope for a peace agreement in the foreseeable future. If Pakistan decides it wants to help and delivers the Taliban to the bargaining table someday, that should be welcomed but it is very unlikely. The ISI can and will veto any peace efforts with the Taliban it opposes. Rather than counting on ISI help, we need to continue to build an Afghan army that can control the insurgency with long-term NATO assistance and minimal U.S. combat troops. Fortunately, we are doing so now for the first time.

India is critical in all of this. Obama has wisely invested time and capital in building ties to New Delhi, visiting there in November 2010. A strategic dialogue between America and India on Pakistan is essential; and this could focus the Pakistani army's mind more fully on the counterproductive results of its policies and force it to reconsider its strategic plans. The good news is that India and Pakistan are trying to improve trade and transportation links severed in 1947—we should encourage that forward. We should also increase intelligence cooperation against terror targets in Pakistan. India can play an important role in helping Afghanistan, and we should encourage that to happen. And we should persuade India to do more to resolve Kashmiri anger because it is in all our interests.

America and Pakistan have had a tempestuous relationship for decades. For far too long we have banked on the army to protect our interests. Now we need to contain its aggressive instincts, help those who want a progressive Pakistan, and build a regional environment that isolates and fights terror. For the foreseeable future while the Pakistani army determines the country's strategic direction, we will need to contain its ambitions until the political process inside Pakistan produces real civilian rule and a new direction for its foreign policy.

In the chapters that follow I try to explore all these mysteries, policy conundrums, and challenges. I try to shed light on how Pakistan became the most dangerous country in the world and on the role America played and still plays in Pakistani politics. The stakes in Pakistan are enormous. It will soon be the most populous country in the Islamic world and the fifth largest in the world. It has the fastest growing nuclear arsenal in the world and is on track to be the world's third largest nuclear weapons state. Understanding Pakistan is an urgent priority for all Americans.

B. R.
January 2012

PREFACE TO THE FIRST EDITION

IN 1998 I WROTE a memo to President Bill Clinton titled "Pakistan: The Most Dangerous Country in the World." Pakistan had just tested nuclear weapons, and nowhere else on the planet were so many ominous trends colliding in a uniquely combustible way. During subsequent crises with India, Pakistan issued threats of nuclear war (as did India), and today it has the fastest-growing nuclear arsenal in the world, not to mention a long history of proliferating its nuclear technology to other countries. Former foreign minister of Iran Ali Akbar Velayati has confirmed that Pakistan provided his country with its first nuclear centrifuge technology in 1985. By the time President Barack Obama took office in 2009, the fearsome trends had not abated, and he asked me to chair an interagency strategic review of U.S. policy toward Pakistan—a country with which the United States is locked in what is best described as a deadly embrace.

Pakistan became independent in 1947, the first country to be created as a home for Muslims and one that now holds the world's second largest Muslim population, which in another two decades may well become the largest. Although its founder, Muhammad Jinnah, had envisioned a democratic and moderate Islamic nation, within eleven years it was in military hands. Since 1958 it has experienced three military coups and been ruled by four military dictators, one of whom, Zia ul-Haq, was an Islamic militant deserving of the title "fanatic."[1] The challenges for democracy and Islam are more daunting here than anywhere else in the world's Islamic community, or *ummah*.

One reason is Pakistan's alarming role in the global jihadist movement, launched there in the 1980s in reaction to the Soviet invasion of neighboring Afghanistan. It was the brainchild of a Palestinian ideologue named Abdallah Yusuf Mustafa Azzam, who was Osama bin Laden's first partner in *jihad,* the campaign for the defense of Islam. Intent on global jihad, Azzam declared the movement must have a solid foundation, *al qaeda* in Arabic, thereby planting the seeds for the terrorist group that attacked the United States on September 11, 2001.[2]

Under Osama bin Laden's leadership, al Qaeda has become the world's first truly global terrorist movement, attracting followers throughout the ummah, some of whom have committed the most terrible violence of the twenty-first century. As President Obama has rightly pointed out, the United States is today at war with al Qaeda. And as he has also warned, it is not just America that is at grave risk from al Qaeda but the entire world: "If there is a major attack on an Asian, European or African city it's likely to have ties to al Qaeda's leadership in Pakistan."[3]

Pakistan itself has been wracked by terror and militancy in the past few years. From one end of the country to the other, mass casualty attacks occur almost daily. Ironically, many of its terror groups have long-standing ties with the Pakistani army and its intelligence service, making Pakistan both a patron and a victim of the Frankenstein it helped to create, which may eventually destroy it.

Many Pakistanis believe the United States had a large hand in creating this monster. To some extent, they are right. America has been a fickle friend, sometimes acting as Pakistan's closest ally and sharing important secret programs, while at other times moving to isolate and impose sanctions against it. For good reasons and bad, successive U.S. presidents from both parties have pursued narrow short-term interests in Pakistan that have contributed to its instability and radicalization, and thereby created fertile ground for global jihad. How and why this has happened is the subject of this book. It also provides some thoughts on what may come next in the jihad, along with some policy recommendations on how to help Pakistan help itself.

Pakistan's complex behavior and motives are certainly difficult for outsiders—including U.S. presidents—to grasp, especially when they learn that Pakistan has been equally fickle, and also duplicitous, in its relationship with the United States, The facts are often far from clear, and much about Pakistani behavior remains a mystery. What cannot be disputed, however, is that the country lies in a dangerous part of the world, and its internal politics are violent and volatile. The government often tries to pursue multiple agendas and to reconcile competing interests. As a result, notes Maleeha Lodhi, a wise former Pakistani ambassador to the United States, policymaking tends to be "impulsive, chaotic, erratic and overly secretive."[4] To add to this complexity, the most important strategic imperative for the Pakistani national security bureaucracy, especially the army and the intelligence services, is the competition with India. Indeed, many outsiders underestimate the obsession with India in Pakistani life.

Pakistan can be frustrating for Americans as a consequence. Some suggest we should deal with it harshly. One of my former colleagues has suggested we should treat it like "Sherman marching across Georgia during the Civil War" and compel it to do our bidding by force and intimidation.[5] I suggest a different approach based on engagement, red lines, and consistency and constancy.

Observers of Pakistan must also be careful with the terminology they use to describe Pakistani behavior. Jihad, like the word "crusade," for example, means different things to different people, and its meaning has changed over time. The vast majority of Muslims in the ummah rightly regard al Qaeda's interpretation as an aberration from standard usage and one that distorts their religion. Benazir Bhutto, in her last book, *Reconciliation: Islam, Democracy, and the West,* brilliantly quashed the notion that al Qaeda and other extremist Muslim organizations are true defenders of Islam or are following the true path of jihad. To its credit, the Obama administration has carefully avoided terms such as "the war on terror" or "war on Islam," recognizing, as the president's adviser on terrorism John Brennan notes, that "describing our enemies in religious terms lends credence to the lie propagated by al Qaeda that the U.S. is somehow at war with Islam."[6]

I use the terms "jihadist" and "global jihad" in this book to refer to the terrorists' own name for themselves and for the distorted view of jihad central to their ideology. It is impossible to understand al Qaeda or the Taliban without comprehending the meanings they have in mind. Thus my use of their terminology is in no way an endorsement of the terrorist viewpoint, but a means of clarifying the threat they pose.

Pakistan has intrigued me since I first began studying Islam at Harvard University four decades ago. For much of that time, I have been a participant in America's deadly embrace with Pakistan. Since 1991 I have had the honor of working in the White House, advising four presidents on Pakistan. When in March 2007 Tony Lake and Mona Sutphen asked me to join Senator Barack Obama's presidential campaign, I agreed on the spot and served as his South Asia team chief during the campaign and the transition. In January 2009 he asked me to chair the strategic review of the situation in Pakistan and Afghanistan for his new administration.

This book draws on the insights of many Pakistanis, both about their country and about America's relationship with it. Some have risked everything in bold and just causes undertaken with the United States, such as defeating the Soviet Union. Others have taken enormous risks trying to build a democracy in Pakistan. I thank all of them, including those who may disagree with the message of this book. Many Afghans, Indians, and Arabs have also been key sources.

In addition, scores of Americans, including several former ambassadors and chiefs of station, have provided important observations; I thank all of them as well. I recall vividly the day in 1979 when our embassy in Islamabad was overrun by an angry Pakistani mob and Zia ignored our pleas for help—only the bravery of our diplomats and Marines saved the staff that day. Our best have long been called to service in Pakistan, and I am grateful to every one of them.

My colleagues at Brookings are a particularly treasured resource. The staff of Brookings Institution Press and those in foreign policy and at the Saban Center—Vanda von Felbab Brown, Dan Byman, Steve Cohen, Mike O'Hanlon, Martin Indyk, Ken Pollack, and many others—have been helpful time and again. Strobe Talbott and I have traveled to Pakistan together many times, and he has been a role model for me as a diplomat, scholar, and friend. Aysha Chowdhry has been an invaluable research assistant, whose support has encompassed editing and, most important, reminding me that Pakistan's future will be built on its best asset, its young people.

My wife, Elizabeth, has been my inspiration and adviser throughout this project and so much more. She has "lived" Pakistan for the past decade. This book is dedicated to her.

I am, of course, solely responsible for its contents. All statements of fact, opinion, or analysis are those of the author and do not reflect the official positions or views of the Central Intelligence Agency (CIA) or any other office of the U.S. government. Nothing in the following pages should be construed as asserting or implying that any branch of government has authenticated the information herein or endorsed the author's views. This material has been reviewed by the CIA to prevent the disclosure of classified information.

DEADLY EMBRACE

CHAPTER ONE

UNDERSTANDING PAKISTAN

WE WERE ABOARD Air Force One en route to California when I began briefing President Barack Obama on the strategic review of American policy toward Afghanistan and Pakistan he had asked me to do. Seated behind his wood desk in the president's cabin, Obama listened closely, asking many questions. I first summarized the threat assessment.

A syndicate of terrorists now embedded in Pakistan and Afghanistan was planning further attacks on American interests at home and abroad. A prominent member was al Qaeda, the group that changed world history with its attack on New York and Virginia on September 11, 2001. The syndicate also included the Afghan Taliban, which hosted al Qaeda back in 2001; the new Pakistani Taliban, which helped al Qaeda murder former Pakistani prime minister Benazir Bhutto; Lashkar-e-Tayyiba, the group that attacked Mumbai in November 2008, only three months before our flight; and a host of other terrorists.

By the time we landed, I had walked the president through the review's 20 recommendations and some of its 180 proposals for specific actions. The report's chief architects were the two cochairs, Under Secretary of Defense Michelle Flournoy and Special Representative Ambassador Richard Holbrooke, and myself, along with the head of U.S. Central Command (CENTCOM), General David Petraeus, and field commanders in Kabul. It had taken six weeks to shepherd the review through the interagency process and to get input from Pakistanis and Afghans, North Atlantic Treaty Organization (NATO) allies, other nations with soldiers in Afghanistan, and key geopolitical players such as India and Saudi Arabia. National Security Council principals—including Vice President Joe

Biden, Secretary of State Hillary Clinton, Secretary of Defense Robert Gates, National Security Adviser Jim Jones, and others—had also examined it carefully.

As we walked from Air Force One to a waiting Marine helicopter, I drew the president's attention to the review's central conclusion: Pakistan, the birthplace of global Islamic jihad and now its epicenter, had become a crucible of terror and was the most dangerous country in the world. Clearly, it held the key to destroying both al Qaeda and the larger syndicate.

The president's busy schedule in California included an interview on television's *Tonight Show with Jay Leno* in which he talked about getting a dog for his two daughters. Oddly enough, my Blenheim puppy, Nelson, had been sitting on my lap when the president's call came through at my weekend home in Maryland, inviting me to lead the review. It was just five days after he had been sworn in on the Capitol steps, but he was already engaged in what he called the most important national security issue facing the nation.

I had first met Barack Hussein Obama in 2007, when I joined his campaign as a volunteer expert providing advice on South Asian issues and counterterrorism. In July 2008 I accompanied him to the Willard Hotel in Washington, where he had his first substantive encounter with the new Pakistani administration replacing the dictatorship of Pervez Musharraf, represented by Prime Minister Yousaf Raza Gillani. Throughout his conversation with Gillani, I was impressed by Obama's command of the issues and effective style of communication.

Though thrilled at Obama's victory in November 2008, by then I had been retired for two years and was eager to stay out of government. I had joined Brookings Institution's Saban Center for Middle East Policy in Washington, and after almost thirty years with the U.S. Central Intelligence Agency (CIA), I was enjoying the freedom of continuing work in my area of expertise—the Middle East and South Asia—but now as a scholar and teacher. The president urged me to return to government for two months to help reassess American policy on the crisis in South Asia, which was badly in need of attention.

I could not have agreed more. The conflict President Obama had inherited in Afghanistan had turned into the "forgotten war" of the twenty-first century. After a brilliant start in 2001, when the United States and a handful of coalition allies helped the Northern Alliance topple the Taliban's Islamic Emirate of Afghanistan in less than a hundred days, Washington's attention shifted from Afghanistan to Iraq. As a result, it squandered an easy military victory, permitting the foe to recover and make a comeback.

By 2009 the Taliban and its al Qaeda ally had established a secure safe haven across the border in Pakistan and were threatening the stability of the southern and eastern half of Afghanistan. A war that should have ended in 2002 had been rekindled—and was soon being lost. Worse still, the militants were now headquartered in Pakistan, a country facing a severe political crisis that was pushing the state to the brink of failure. Having the fastest-growing nuclear arsenal in the world and being its second largest Muslim country with a population of 180 million, Pakistan seemed poised to become a jihadist enclave.

This was not the first time America had taken its eye off the ball in South Asia. In the 1980s, with the help of Pakistan, the United States had inflicted a crushing defeat on the Soviet Fortieth Red Army in Afghanistan, which was followed by the collapse of the Soviet Union and end of the cold war. But it then focused its attention elsewhere (ironically, much of it on Iraq), leaving Afghanistan to become transformed, not into a stable and friendly nation, but a hostile and fanatic foe eager to host al Qaeda and act as the base for the deadliest attack ever on U.S. soil.

During my thirty years of service at the CIA, Pentagon, and White House, I have had the privilege of advising four presidents on South Asian affairs. This experience has taught me, often the hard way, that the politics of the region are both unpredictable and often inscrutable to an outsider. But America's policies toward Pakistan and Afghanistan must often appear just as inscrutable to South Asians, especially when, for complex reasons, its strategies have aided the foes of democracy and the very enemies Americans are now fighting against there.

My goal in the following pages is to explain this paradox—specifically, to determine why successive U.S. administrations have undermined civil government in Pakistan, aided military dictators, and encouraged the rise of extremist Islamic movements that now threaten the United States at home and abroad. A first step to this end is to recognize that Pakistan, past and present, remains shrouded in mystery, with key events in its development related to conspiracy and unsolved assassinations. A second step is to examine U.S. relations with Pakistan during the first two and a half decades of its independence, bearing in mind that it was the first nation ever created solely for Islam.

JINNAH, PARTITION, AND CIVIL WAR

The idea of Pakistan was born on the banks of the River Cam in East Anglia in the 1930s. A student at Cambridge University, Chaudhary Rahmat Ali, envisioned a Muslim state created from the union of several British-controlled territories and princely states in the northwestern part of the subcontinent. He referred to this new state as "Pakistan" in a pamphlet he wrote in 1933 titled *Now or Never, Are We to Live or Perish Forever?* The name *Pakistan* is basically an acronym compiled from the names of the areas of Punjab, Afghania, Kashmir, Sindh, and Baluchistan.[1] In Persian and Urdu, *Pakistan* also translates as "the land of the pure." Notably absent from Ali's vision was the eastern province of Bengal, which in those years was home to more Muslims than any other province of the British Raj. Its omission would be a signal of much trouble to come.

Although Ali was a strong force in the Pakistan movement in the United Kingdom, the prime mover back in South Asia was Muhammad Ali Jinnah, also known as Baba-e-Quam (the father of the country) or Quaid-e-Azam (the great leader). Jinnah and his Muslim League Party spearheaded the drive to independence. Indeed, it is fair to say that Jinnah changed the map of South Asia and that without him there would be no Pakistan. Not surprisingly, a portrait of this towering figure can be seen in every government office in the country.

Unfortunately, the partition of South Asia in 1947 led to the deaths of at least 1 million people and one of the largest refugee transfers in human history as millions of Hindus and Sikhs struggled to find new homes on the subcontinent.[2] The region and the world are still reeling from the aftershocks of that division.

In many ways, Jinnah seemed an odd candidate for the role he played in the creation of the world's first state intended for Muslims. He was not a practicing Muslim, he drank alcohol, smoked fifty cigarettes a day, and dressed like the English-educated lawyer that he was. According to his preeminent biographer, Stanley Wolpert, Jinnah never wore the same silk tie twice, which he would have ordered from an expensive tailor in London to go with his more than 200 Savile Row suits.[3] He was, reported the *New York Times,* one of 1946's best-dressed men in the British Empire. At one point, he owned seven flats in London's posh district of Mayfair. In 1930 Jinnah sought to win a seat in Britain's Parliament but was unable to break the race barrier in English politics. Had the British accepted Jinnah as an equal, he might well have lived out the rest of his life in London. As his Indian biographer, Jaswant Singh, put it: "Jinnah was committed to his three-piece suits, his lorgnette, his cigarette holder and the King's English."[4]

Clearly, Jinnah's vision of Pakistan was not rooted in religious piety. Although he was a Shia Muslim—a minority sect of Islam (almost 90 percent of Muslims are Sunni, including most of those living in Pakistan today)—he apparently spent little time in mosques or in studying the Quran. Extremism had no place in his views either. The subcontinent did have an established jihadist tradition, dating back to the so-called Indian mutiny of 1857 (increasingly referred to in India as the first war for independence) and the subsequent founding of the jihad-espousing Deobandi movement. Though sparked by a military revolt, the mutiny attracted large numbers of jihadists fighting to reestablish Muslim rule in the Indian subcontinent. When the British resumed control, some of these militants created a madrassa near the town of Deoband to advocate Islamic fundamental views. Jinnah was never a Deobandi.[5]

Rather, Jinnah's great concern was that a united India would treat its Muslims as second-class citizens, persecuted by the Hindu majority. Muslims, he once remarked in 1937, "do not want to be reduced to the position of the Negroes of America."[6] He saw a separate Pakistan as a haven where they could practice their religion to whatever degree of piety they desired. Founded for Muslims, it would not be a secular state but would in many ways act like one in advocating tolerance and diversity.

Despite a substantial following, Jinnah met with some strong opposition in the Islamic camp. Mawlana Sayyid Abu A'ala Mawdudi and the political party he founded in 1941 to represent South Asia's Muslims were unenthusiastic about the Pakistan idea at first, preferring to keep the entire subcontinent united, but under Muslim domination in a form reminiscent of the Mughal Empire. Ironically, noted one observer, "the pious among the Muslims of the subcontinent did not create Pakistan."[7] Indeed, Mawdudi was deeply distrustful of Jinnah because of both his political ambitions and lack of religious piety. Even Jinnah's Muslim League was not Muslim enough. However, Mawdudi's Jamaat-i-Islam Party was unable to garner mass support in the new Pakistan, although it did become the flag bearer for those wanting a more Islamic Pakistan and succeeded in developing independent but related branches in the rest of South Asia.[8]

One of the many tragedies of Pakistan's history is that after helping Pakistan gain independence, Jinnah did not live long enough to make his vision of the state a reality. A victim of tuberculosis and lung cancer, he died on September 11, 1948, little more than a year after Pakistan's birth. He had so dominated the independence movement that he left no potential leaders in the wings with the stature to take on the difficult job of shaping the kind of state he had in mind.

To add to the nation's distress, Jinnah's chief lieutenant and successor, Liaquat Ali Khan, was assassinated in 1951, in the first in a series of violent deaths that have scarred Pakistan's history and continue today. With the loss of its founding fathers, the new nation seemed destined for turmoil. One can easily imagine what would have happened in America if Washington, Adams, Jefferson, and Madison had not lived long enough to become president.

During Pakistan's first quarter century, the legacy of partition, with its division of the country into East and West Pakistan, only confounded the region's politics. At the time, the majority (56 percent) of Pakistanis lived in East Pakistan, in a part of the divided province of Bengal, the first headquarters of the British Raj in South Asia. As already mentioned, Bengal had been overlooked in the naming of Pakistan, reflecting its secondary importance from the beginning, although Rahmat Ali had dreamed of a united Bengal dominated by its Muslim population and expanded to include Azzam and the rest of northeast India as a separate state called Bang-i-Islam.[9]

Jinnah saw Bengal in somewhat the same light, as a separate state with Muslims and Hindus united, one that could thus further weaken India. The British and Indians refused to consider that option and instead divided Bengal along religious lines. The predominantly Muslim part became East Pakistan, which in the process was cut off from its traditional political, intellectual, and economic capital, Calcutta.

From the beginning, West Pakistan was dominated by the province of Punjab, which was better endowed than Sindh, Baluchistan, the North-West Frontier Province, and the rump of Kashmir that had joined Pakistan. Punjab not only had the largest population and the richest farmland, but it also provided the overwhelming majority of the officer corps for the Pakistani army. Many Punjabis, especially members of that corps, believed Pakistan was created to serve their interests first and foremost; many also regarded Bengalis as second-class citizens, even as inferior humans lacking the alleged martial skills of Punjabis.

This issue boiled up immediately after partition and independence in relation to language. Should Bengali be an official language of the new Pakistan? West Pakistan's establishment, including Jinnah, said no, opting solely for Urdu. Within a few months of independence, demonstrations broke out in Dhaka protesting the lack of Bengali on official papers of the new Pakistani state. Despite his failing health, Jinnah was forced to come to Dhaka in 1948 to try to calm the situation.

But Jinnah only intensified the discontent by insisting "the state language of Pakistan is going to be Urdu and no other language. Any one who tries to mislead you is an enemy of Pakistan."[10] Though Bengalis were allowed to speak and write in their language in East Pakistan, they were shocked to hear Jinnah imply they were not only inferior citizens but could even be considered enemies of Pakistan because they wished to retain a mark of their culture.

When Pakistan eventually drew up its first constitution in 1956, it recognized Bengali as a national language but still gave primacy to Urdu. By then, however, language was but one of many issues dividing East and West Pakistan. The country's Punjabi-dominated government in Karachi (the capital until 1958) emphasized development in the West; the army and bureaucracy were overrun by West Pakistanis, especially Punjabis; and the East was treated almost like a colony separated from its motherland by India.

The contradictions between Pakistan's majority population in the East and the ruling establishment in the West proved fatal for Pakistani democracy—which was already facing monumental challenges. Pakistan's economy was still very weak, it had little experience with democratic institutions, its tribal regions along the Afghan border were a bed of chaos, and the conflict with India had not let up. With the East and West so divided, it became almost impossible to sustain a democratic form of government.

In October 1958 Pakistan's government was toppled in its first military coup, with the chief of army staff, Major General Ayub Khan, at the helm abrogating the constitution, banning political parties, and naming himself president. Ayub Khan had been army chief for eight years, succeeding a British officer from the Raj. He was a graduate of Sandhurst Royal Military Academy, Britain's prestigious officer training school, and had fought in World War II with the British Indian army in Burma. Like Jinnah, he was almost as much English as Pakistani. Among the several reasons for his coup, a primary one was the fear that a truly democratic election would tilt the balance of power toward East Pakistan at the expense of the army-dominated West.

In preparation for the construction of a new capital in Islamabad, Khan moved the government from Karachi to Rawalpindi. Under his rule, the Pakistani intelligence services, especially the army's Inter-Services Intelligence Directorate (ISI) grew in size and importance. Founded by British Major General William Cawthorne at independence to conduct military intelligence, the ISI now took on the role of spying on Ayub's enemies inside Pakistan.[11] It would be the beginning of the ISI's rise to power.[12]

Khan also staged the first of Pakistan's many rigged elections. In 1965 he was officially elected president by the country's electoral college but was suspected of using patronage and intimidation to influence the vote. His opponent in this election was Jinnah's sister Fatima, who ran on a platform for restoring civilian government. This suppression of democracy further alienated the East.

Khan had an ambitious plan to oust India from the disputed territory of Kashmir and gain control of the entire province for Pakistan. Kashmir was the only Muslim-majority province of India that was not awarded to Pakistan at partition. In 1947 it was a princely state under the rule of a Hindu maharaja who dithered over which country to join, hoping Kashmir could actually become independent. Jinnah ordered a tribal army to invade the province and join it to Pakistan; India responded by sending in its army. India's first prime minister, Jawaharlal Nehru, did not want to see his favorite territory wrenched from India. This clash of 1947 was the First Indo-Pakistani War.

The war ended with the partition of Kashmir. India took the bulk of the province, including the capital Srinagar and the surrounding Vale of Kashmir. Pakistan held on to a smaller part, which it named Azad Kashmir, meaning "free Kashmir." Determined to get it all for Pakistan, Khan devised a plot code-named Operation Gibraltar to infiltrate Indian-held Kashmir with teams of Pakistanis who would foment an uprising that would then require Pakistani intervention. In a second maneuver, Operation Grand Slam, a Pakistani-armored column would strike into India to cut off Kashmir and win the war. This plan was closely guarded within a small circle around Khan so was never properly vetted for its possible weaknesses—a pattern common throughout future Pakistani army operations. The plan misfired completely. There was no insurgency but a Second Indo-Pakistani War. In 1965 India and Pakistan fought an enormous tank battle on the Punjabi plain outside of Lahore.

This war ended in a stalemate but made clear that East Pakistan was very vulnerable to an Indian attack. Surrounded on three sides by India, it was virtually indefensible. Ayub Khan said as much both during and after the war, much to the chagrin of Bengalis, awakened to the fact that their leader was prepared to lose their country in order to gain Kashmir.

Thus an unintended side effect of the second war was the East's further estrangement from the West. Feeling more and more like an occupied territory and a reluctant partner in the nation of Pakistan, citizens in the East launched a Bangladeshi independence movement. Initially focused on obtaining redress of grievances and greater autonomy, its mission gradually evolved into demands for de facto independence.

By 1968 Ayub Khan's popularity was waning as the public had grown discontented with the corruption in government. Many complained that Ayub's family had enriched itself during his rule, allegedly having stolen as much as $20 million from the state.[13] Faced with growing unrest, in 1969 Ayub Khan relinquished power to General Yahya Khan, another product of the British Indian army. He, too, had fought in World War II, serving in North Africa and Italy with the British Eighth Army. The Pakistan he inherited from Ayub was dissatisfied with army rule, especially in the East. Less skilled in politics than Ayub, Yahya proved a disaster for Pakistan.

At the outset, Yahya tried to appease Bengali anger by promising to bring more Bengalis into the army and the bureaucracy. In 1970 there were only 300 Bengalis in the army's 6,000-man officer corps.[14] Yahya also agreed to hold free elections, but when voters came out in December 1970, the Awami League, the independence-leaning Bengali party, swept the East, winning 160 of the 162 seats there and thus gained a majority of seats in Pakistan's National Assembly. Punjabi concerns about Bengali domination pushed the country into civil war. Yahya Khan dissolved his cabinet and postponed indefinitely a meeting of the National Assembly, whereupon East Pakistan broke out in strikes, demonstrations, and open revolt.

In response, in late March 1971 Yahya Khan ordered a brutal crackdown on the East that virtually guaranteed the end of the union with the West. His next move, Operation Searchlight, was a deliberate attempt to decapitate the intellectual elite of East Pakistan. Close to 3 million people were reputedly killed and 400,000 Bangladeshi women raped by the Pakistani army. Even at half that number of deaths, it would have been an appalling slaughter, bordering on genocide.[15]

Faced with massive refugee flows into Calcutta and elsewhere, India intervened in the fighting in support of Bangladeshi resistance. Sensing that a full-scale invasion was coming, Yahya ordered a preemptive strike on India, dubbed Operation Genghis Khan, bringing into full swing the Third Indo-Pakistani War. Summarily routed in the East, 90,000 Pakistani soldiers surrendered to India on December 16, 1971, one of the darkest days in Pakistan's history.

Yahya was not only a poor leader but also one who enjoyed his liquor. The day after the war began, his aides found him "sloshed."[16] His behavior during the crisis was erratic, leaving his commanders in the East humiliated and defeated.

In the wake of the debacle, the army was disgraced, and violent demonstrations broke out against the military government. Yahya had little alternative but to turn power over to the civilians. The new head of state, Zulfikar Ali Bhutto, was a former foreign minister and leader of the Pakistan Peoples Party, a left-of-center party that he had founded and that has remained under the direction of a Bhutto family member ever since.

In less than a quarter century, the idea of a single state for all the Muslims of South Asia had died. Pakistan's identity crisis, perhaps not unusual for a new state emerging from a colonial past, only deepened. It could no longer claim to be the home of the subcontinent's Muslims. It could no longer claim to be their defender, especially after its army had killed hundreds of thousands of its countrymen in a horrific repression.

Ironically, the original vision of Pakistan formulated on the banks of the Cam in England had pertained to only one part of Muslim South Asia. Under Bhutto, the new nation would briefly flirt with democracy again, but the seeds of military dictatorship had been planted deeply and would germinate again and again in the soil of Pakistan's politics.

WASHINGTON AND PAKISTAN'S EARLY YEARS

During World War II, the British-controlled territories of the subcontinent found a strong advocate of independence in President Franklin Delano Roosevelt. He pressed Prime Minister Winston Churchill to promise them postwar independence, both because it was consistent with American belief in self-determination and because it would ensure greater Indian support for the war effort. By the end of the war, the Indian army had more than two and a half million men engaged in fighting Germany and Japan.[17]

No other issue at the time so divided FDR and Churchill; it even drove the prime minister to seriously consider resigning from office.[18] In the end FDR backed down since Churchill was adamantly opposed to the idea of Indian independence, a position he persisted in for the rest of his life. Had Churchill not been defeated in the 1945 elections, India would have faced a much harder time securing its freedom. As it was, he worked quietly behind the scenes to promote partition and thereby help Pakistan and Jinnah, hoping to at least humiliate Mahatma Gandhi and his new state. His backroom support in this regard was so important, writes one historian, that "if Jinnah is regarded as the father of Pakistan, Churchill must qualify as its uncle; and, therefore, as a pivotal figure in the resurgence of political Islam."[19]

Churchill's Labor Party successors, on the other hand, were eager to get out of India so as to better focus on Britain's enormous domestic problems in the aftermath of the war. They would see partition as the means to quit.

After FDR, President Harry Truman had less to do with securing the freedom of the subcontinent, being more tied up in issues such as the emerging cold war with the Soviet Union. Although most Americans favored a unified India and were sympathetic to Gandhi, they did not feel strongly about Pakistan one way or the other. Truman recognized the new state at its birth but offered it no significant American assistance. Given its enormous challenges after independence, Pakistan was eager for American help, hoping in particular to secure a half billion dollars' worth of arms aid. But Washington had its hands full elsewhere and turned these requests aside, even when Prime Minister Liaquat Ali Khan made a point of visiting Washington in May 1950, the first senior Pakistani official to do so.

With the onset of the Korean War, however, the Truman administration began showing more interest in helping Pakistan, thinking it might be willing to send troops to fight with the United Nations forces in Korea. Pakistan declined.

Dwight D. Eisenhower, Truman's Republican successor, believed an arms relationship with Pakistan—even an alliance—would be beneficial. In its eight years, the Eisenhower administration focused on making Pakistan a bulwark against communism in South Asia. Ike decided to move forward with arms aid and established a relationship between Pakistan and the CIA that endures even today.

Eisenhower's secretary of state, John Foster Dulles, had a connection with South Asia. His grandfather, John Welsh Dulles, had been a Presbyterian missionary in British India and had written a book titled *Life in India* that praised the Raj for its colonial rule. But it was John Foster Dulles's fierce anti-communism that drew a cold reception on a visit in May 1953, the first to South Asia by a U.S. secretary of state. New Delhi was also opposed to his ideas for setting up regional alliances in the Middle East and South Asia akin to NATO, to contain Russia and China.

By contrast, Karachi welcomed Dulles with enthusiasm, eager for American military aid and for an alliance that would strengthen its hand against India. Pakistan was quite happy to join the anti-communist chorus—as an Islamic state, it was opposed to atheistic Marxism anyway—but its eyes were mainly on its own agenda. India, not China or Russia, was its strategic concern. The Eisenhower team was prepared to overlook Pakistan's agenda if it would play ball on the U.S. side in the cold war. Thus was born an alliance.

Dulles returned to Washington praising the Pakistanis and criticizing India. He told the Senate Foreign Relations Committee that Pakistan would fight communists with its "bare hands"—that its "lancers were 6 feet 2 inches" tall and sat on "great big horses and were out of this world."[20] Of course, what Pakistan wanted was to equip its antiquated lancers with American tanks.

In the fall of 1953 Chief of Army Staff Ayub Khan arrived in Washington with a shopping list and an engaging personality. The Eisenhower team became enraptured with the Sandhurst-trained general. After his visit to South Asia in December 1953, Vice President Richard Nixon came back a convert, a true believer in the U.S.-Pakistan relationship. As he informed the National Security Council, "Pakistan is a country I would like to do everything for. The people have less complexes than the Indians."[21] Arms aid began in 1954. The Pakistanis consistently pressed for more than the Pentagon was prepared to sell or give, but the White House, especially the Office of the Vice President, pushed to give more.

In 1955 Pakistan joined two of the U.S. administration's new alliance systems: the Southeast Asia Treaty Organization (SEATO) and the Central Treaty Organization (CENTO). With its membership in these organizations, Pakistan officially became America's "most allied ally" and its full partner in waging the global cold war.

Thereafter intelligence cooperation expanded rapidly. Dulles's brother, CIA director Allen Dulles, worked to develop a strong liaison with the ISI. The CIA even helped Karachi draft a constitution, sending over American expert Charles Burton Marshall as an adviser.[22]

The centerpiece of the new clandestine intelligence relationship was an airbase outside of Peshawar, constructed in 1958. This top-secret base housed U.S. Air Force 6937 Communications Group, which included two important facilities: a listening post for the National Security Agency to monitor communications in the Soviet Union and China, and a base for the secret photo reconnaissance aircraft, the U2, to be flown over Russia. Both facilities were crucial to collecting intelligence on communism in the late 1950s and early 1960s and put Pakistan on the front line of the cold war. The United States was indebted to Pakistan for the use of these facilities.[23]

When a U2 was shot down by Soviet observers in May 1960, the secret airbase was exposed to the world. Nonetheless it remained in operation until 1968 and would be far from the last manifestation of the intelligence relationship between Pakistan and the United States.

That relationship had the support of Ayub Khan, who had seized power in the coup of October 1958. Ayub Khan was not only well known and liked in Washington but helped offset the recent loss of another critical partner in America's alliance systems when Iraq's Hashemite government was toppled by a leftist coup in July 1958. Eisenhower's America was happy to have a strongman in Pakistan to ensure the alliance lasted and in December 1959 sent Ike on a first-ever presidential visit to the subcontinent, with stops in India and Afghanistan, as well as Pakistan, which gave him a warm welcome. (The trip was also the maiden voyage for Air Force One, the president's special executive airplane.)

Following the coup, however, parts of the American intelligence community forecast—accurately, as it turned out—that a military dictatorship would only further exacerbate Pakistan's underlying weaknesses, especially the East-West division. The State Department's Bureau of Intelligence Research believed that a prolonged period of military rule would increase "discontent in East Pakistan and jeopardize the unity of the two wings of the country."[24]

Strong ties with Pakistan continued into the new Democratic administration of John F. Kennedy, which sought better relations with both Pakistan and India. JFK welcomed Ayub Khan to the White House in July 1961, hosted a state dinner for him at Mount Vernon—the only such event ever held at the home of the nation's first president—and welcomed him back to Washington in September 1962, with side visits to Kennedy's farm in Middlesex, Virginia, and the summer White House in Newport, Rhode Island.

The relationship survived despite growing U.S. ties with India, particularly after the brief Indo-Chinese border war in late 1962. Pakistan was nervous about U.S. arms aid to India but was assured by Kennedy that no harm would come to U.S.-Pakistani relations.

In 1965, however, the tide turned when India and Pakistan went to war. Kennedy's successor, Lyndon B. Johnson, cut off aid to both countries in a bid to put a quick stop to the fighting. This came as a great blow to Pakistan, which had a longer and deeper arms relationship with the United States than India did. Pakistanis felt betrayed. After all, they were a treaty ally of America and hosted the U2 base, while India was a nonaligned nation that often tilted toward Moscow.

One consequence of the rift was that Pakistan now approached India's nemesis of 1962, China, for help. In just a few years, it built a strong relationship with Beijing and moved from a putatively arch anti-communist ally, a SEATO and CENTO member, to one of China's closest partners. China would supplant the United States as Pakistan's chief source of arms and in time would become its nuclear partner as well.

The rift with Washington was short lived, however, and arms ties resumed with the election of Richard Nixon in 1968. Nixon was now an even more enthusiastic Pakistan supporter than he had been as vice president. Pakistan became the key to Nixon's secret diplomacy as president, the means to opening the door to Beijing. During a visit to South Asia in August 1969, Nixon approached Yahya Khan with the idea of Pakistan serving as an intermediary to establish direct American-Chinese contacts. For the next two years, Pakistan passed messages back and forth between Nixon and Mao.

On July 9, 1971, Nixon's national security adviser, Henry Kissinger, visited Pakistan. After a day of talks, the press was told Kissinger had become ill and would rest for a short time in the hills outside Islamabad. In fact, he secretly flew to Beijing to consummate the budding rapprochement with China. On July 15, 1971, Nixon divulged the secret talks to the nation and the world, announcing that he would fly to China himself.

Nixon felt indebted to Yahya Khan for brokering the most important diplomatic achievement of his presidency. So it was no surprise that he "tilted" toward Pakistan in the crisis over Bangladeshi independence later that year. Nixon ordered the CIA to tell Jordan and Iran it was their duty to send arms to help Pakistan, including American arms, even though this violated the arms ban still in place from the 1965 war. Despite the horrific brutality of Khan's Operation Searchlight and protests within the State Department about supporting it, Pakistan was not condemned by Washington and, when the Indo-Pakistani war began, Nixon sent an American carrier battle group into the Bay of Bengal to try to intimidate India's prime minister, Indira Gandhi, whom Nixon loathed. But she was not in the least frightened by American gunboat diplomacy.

Pakistan's defeat in the 1971 conflict proved to be another setback for American-Pakistani relations. As in 1965, Pakistanis felt the United States had let them down. What was the purpose of a strong military and intelligence connection with Washington if it abandoned them in a conflict with their greatest enemy, India? The triangle Washington had entered with New Delhi and Islamabad now seemed heavily tilted toward India. Pakistan's generals had governed their country badly and grossly misread their American friends. Their relations with the United States had become enveloped in distrust. Witnessing his country's defeat on television, a young Pakistani student at the University of Louvain in Belgium, A. Q. Khan, summed up the nation's mood: "I was in Belgium in 1971, when the Pakistani army surrendered in the then East Pakistan and faced utmost humiliation. Hindus and Sikhs were beating them with shoes, and their heads were being shaved in the concentration camps. I saw those scenes with horror."[25]

CHAPTER TWO
―――――――――――――

ZIA'S JIHAD

THE DIRECTOR'S CONFERENCE ROOM on the seventh floor of Central Intelligence Agency (CIA) headquarters in Langley, Virginia, was well known to me. Over the course of a decade, I had spent hours in this richly paneled windowless room, seated in one of two dozen chairs surrounding the large table that dominated it, or in one of many more placed along the walls for backbenchers. On this day in 1983, I was a backbencher watching the National Foreign Intelligence Board (NFIB) review a new National Intelligence Estimate on Afghanistan, which I had helped draft and coordinate as the deputy national intelligence officer for the Near East and South Asia. NFIB had to approve every NIE before it was sent to the president and other senior officials. All the heads of America's various intelligence organizations were members of the NFIB. This was a meeting of the nation's top spymasters to discuss the war in Afghanistan.

Chairing the meeting was CIA director William Casey. Handpicked by President Ronald Reagan, Casey had the president's ear more than any other man in Washington. He had managed Reagan's election victory in 1980 and shared his tough anti-communist views. Earlier in life Casey had been a member of the Office of Strategic Services (the CIA's predecessor, formed during World War II) and supported underground resistance movements in Nazi-occupied Europe. Casey was a genuine expert in the art of covert warfare. As CIA director, he supervised America's clandestine war aimed at wearing down the Soviet Union and bleeding it to death. Afghanistan was at the center of that battle.

Casey opened the discussion by recounting his latest trip to Islamabad. Pakistan's new dictator, Muhammad Zia ul-Haq, had shown him a map of Afghanistan bearing a red triangle with one vertex pointing to the Indian Ocean, just 300 miles from the Afghan-Pakistani border. Zia was determined to prevent Moscow from acquiring a warm-water port on the Indian Ocean, but he needed to be careful not to provoke the Soviet regime too much, too soon. Pakistan was willing to help the *mujahedin* (Afghan resistance), but it could not to let the pot boil too fast. As Casey's deputy for operations in Afghanistan would later recount, "Zia was a believer. Without Zia, there would have been no Afghan war, and no Afghan victory."[1]

One issue not seriously discussed in the NIE but gaining the attention of the ranks of analysts and operators watching Afghanistan was the start of what would become a growing number of Arabs and other Muslims who were flocking to Pakistan to join the war effort. Militants from around the Islamic world—from Syria, Iraq, Algeria, and elsewhere—were migrating to Pakistan, mainly to Peshawar, to help the mujahedin fight in the "holy war" against Soviet forces. According to Robert Gates, then Casey's deputy director for intelligence and the man responsible for all intelligence analysis,

Most fought with the Islamic fundamentalist Muj groups, particularly that headed by Abdul Rasul Sayyaf. We examined ways to increase their participation, perhaps in the form of some sort of "international brigade," but nothing came of it. Years later, these fundamentalist fighters trained by the Mujahedin in Afghanistan would begin to show up around the world, from the Middle East to New York City, still fighting their Holy War—only now including the United States among their enemies. Our mission was to push the Soviets out of Afghanistan. We expected post-Soviet Afghanistan to be ugly, but never considered that it would become a haven for terrorists operating worldwide.[2]

Gates wrote these words in 1996, five years before those so-called holy warriors struck on 9/11, in the first foreign attack on the United States since 1814, and changed the course of world history. He was remarking on the birth of global Islamic jihad in Pakistan in the 1980s. Ironically, American and Pakistani policies would nurture its growth and development. Pakistan's dictator, Zia, was most influential in this regard, through his use of the Inter-Services Intelligence Directorate (ISI) to secure Pakistan's foreign policy goals and to make Pakistan an Islamic state.

ZIA'S JIHAD AND THE ISI

Zulfikar Ali Bhutto, the civilian successor to Yahya Khan's disastrous dictatorship in 1971, inherited a country torn in two following the military defeat by its hated Indian enemy and attempted suppression of its fellow Muslims in Bangladesh. A populist leader from one of the grand families of Sindh, Bhutto embarked on a crash program to equip Pakistan with a nuclear weapon to make the state secure and give it an edge on India. On January 24, 1972, in a secret meeting with the nation's scientific elite in the city of Multan, Bhutto ordered them to begin a frantic effort to build a bomb.[3] Pakistan, he commanded, must get a bomb even if it meant Pakistanis had to starve and "eat grass."

Bhutto quickly sought and obtained crucial assistance from China, including the design of one its own first nuclear weapons. An unsolicited letter then arrived from a young Pakistani offering equally vital help: A. Q. Khan, who had studied at Belgium's University of Louvain and was now working at a physical dynamics research laboratory in Holland, said he had access to the centrifuge technology needed to make fissile material for a bomb. Upon hearing that India had tested a "peaceful nuclear device" in 1974, Bhutto stepped up his program and instructed the ISI to give A. Q. Khan all the help he needed to steal the technology.[4] A refugee from India who had fled the massacres following partition, Khan was more than eager to be of assistance, as one might have gathered from a large painting in his office of the last train that left New Delhi in 1947, engulfed in flames as it rushed to Pakistan.

Bhutto's most enduring legacy to his country would be the nuclear program. As a national leader, he fared less well, making his biggest mistake in choosing Zia for the sensitive job of chief of army staff, apparently without the slightest doubts about Zia's loyalty.

Less than a year later, on July 5, 1977, Zia ousted and arrested Bhutto in a coup. The day before, at the American embassy's annual July Fourth party, its political counselor had asked Zia if he would be available for a meeting the next day. Zia declined, saying he would be very busy.[5] The coup was code-named Operation Fair Play.

With the overthrow, Zia transformed Pakistan and altered the course of its future more than anyone since Jinnah. He can also rightly be called the grandfather of global Islamic jihad.

Born on August 12, 1924, to a father who worked in army general headquarters in Delhi, Zia had military ties from the outset. In 1944 he joined the British army in India and fought with its Indian forces in Italy against the Nazis. Between 1962 and 1964 he received training at Fort Leavenworth, Kansas, then returned home to fight in the 1965 war with India as a tank commander.

In 1967 Zia was posted to Amman as part of Pakistan's military advisory group helping Jordan recover from its defeat in the Six-Day War with Israel. Over the next three years, he would distinguish himself in the Hashemite government's fight with Palestinian guerillas led by Yasir Arafat, helping King Hussein plan battles against the *fedayeen*. He even commanded some of the Jordanian forces fighting the Palestinians in the civil war that engulfed Jordan in the notorious Black September of 1970, when Hussein defeated and drove the Palestinians out of the kingdom. According to Hussein's brother, Prince Hassan, Zia became the king's "friend and confidant": "He was a well-respected figure, a professional soldier, and as the soldiers' General, he not only advised on military tactics he also earned the respect and trust of the Jundis [soldiers]."[6] He probably exceeded his orders and was almost court martialed for his role in the war, which exceeded what attachés normally do, but he built a very strong relationship with the Hashemites. His exploits in Jordan soon made Zia famous at home.[7]

Zia next became an armored division commander in Pakistan. To gain favor with the leadership, he fawned on Bhutto, promising him loyalty. Since Zia was a refugee from India with no tribal connections in the Punjab, he was thought to be more or less isolated from army politics. But when Bhutto massively rigged the elections in 1977 and the opposition took to the streets in protest, Zia turned on his mentor. To guard against any threat of a comeback, Zia had Bhutto arrested on trumped-up charges of murder, for which he was hanged in April 1979.[8]

Unlike the earlier generation of Pakistani military dictators, Zia was an Islamist. He aligned himself with the country's Islamic Jamaat-i-Islam Party, depicted himself as a pious Muslim, and took steps to Islamize the army. For example, army officers were encouraged to join communal prayers with their troops and for the first time were required to have promotion boards review their moral and religious behavior as well as their normal military duties. He also sought and received the endorsement of party leader Mawlana Sayyid Abu A'ala Mawdudi, who enthusiastically praised the new regime. In the view of today's foremost expert on the Pakistani army, Shuja Nawaz, "Islamization was the legacy [Zia] left Pakistan."[9]

One measure of this transformation was the enormous growth of Islamic schools, or madrassas. Between 1971 and 1988 their numbers multiplied from 900 to 8,000 official religious schools and another 25,000 unregistered ones.[10] Under Zia, diplomas granted by the madrassas became equivalent to university degrees. Their influence throughout the country increased proportionately.

The army's social status also rose. Following up on Ayub Khan's decision to grant retiring army officers state land in rural areas to improve their retirement pensions and to encourage rural development, Zia expanded the program, giving favored officers prime pieces of property in Pakistan's growing urban areas. As a result, by 1999 the armed forces as a group owned the largest share of urban real estate in Pakistan.[11]

Zia devoted special attention to the ISI, beginning in 1979 by handpicking its new director, a Pashtun who knew the Afghan world well: Akhtar Abdur Rahman, better known as General Akhtar. "A cold, reserved personality, almost inscrutable, always secretive," according to his subordinates, Akhtar hated publicity and the press, avoided being photographed, and was difficult to fathom even among his most senior lieutenants—but he was a gifted intelligence officer.[12] He developed close working ties to many of the Afghan mujahedin leaders, especially fellow Pashtuns, and organized them into political parties to give more legitimacy to their struggle. Akhtar also built strong ISI links to the CIA and Saudis. He was the first ISI director I met with.

At Zia's direction, Akhtar vastly expanded the size and strength of the service. By one estimate, its staff jumped from 2,000 in 1978 to 40,000 in 1988 with a billion-dollar budget.[13] It came to be seen as omnipotent, taping every phone call with informants in every village, city block, and public space. Politicians were on its payroll, and its enemies simply disappeared. Much of its growth was directed at keeping Zia in power, but much also at waging jihad. As one of Akhtar's deputies would later remark, "The ISI was and still is probably the most powerful and influential organization in the country," with Akhtar the object of either "envy or fear" among his fellow officers.[14] In short, Zia gave Pakistan "the incendiary mix of despotism and Islamization."[15]

Events outside of Pakistan only served to create more opportunities for Zia to Islamize at home. First came the Shia revolution of 1978 in Pakistan's western neighbor, Iran, a revolution that surprised the world and had ripples next door. Unrest among Pakistan's large Shia minority—perhaps as many as a quarter of Pakistanis are Shia (Jinnah was one)—awakened sectarian tensions inside Pakistan, which only intensified when its Shia dissidents began receiving support from Iran. Zia tried to appease their demands and bargain with Tehran, but when that failed he used force. With the support of Zia and the ISI, militant anti-Shia Sunni groups like the Sipah-e-Sohaba Pakistan (the Army of the Prophet's Companions) blossomed and carried out attacks on Shia mosques and religious festivities to intimidate the Shia community into quiescence.[16]

In toppling the shah, the Iranian revolution also removed a key American ally in the region. It seemed to many cold war warriors that Moscow must have had a hand in the overthrow, although in fact it was as surprised as everyone else. The sudden demise of Iran made events in Pakistan's eastern neighbor, Afghanistan, immediately seem more important.

Since 1947 Afghanistan had been in a very uneasy relationship with Pakistan, mainly because of a border dispute that actually dated back to the British Raj. In 1893 the Raj had unilaterally drawn the 2,640-kilometer border between Afghanistan and British India in a way that placed the region's dominant ethnic group, the Pashtuns, into separate territories. The so-called Durand Line—named after its architect, then foreign secretary for India Henry Mortimer Durand—remained in place following partition, with the Pashtuns in Afghanistan now separated from their fellow tribesmen in Pakistan. No Afghan government has ever recognized the legitimacy of the Durand Line.

As the British prepared to leave India, Afghanistan pressed for a revision of the border. When its request was refused, Afghanistan voted against Pakistan getting a seat in the United Nations and called for an independent Pashtunistan to be carved out of Pakistan. Such a move would have expanded Afghanistan all the way to the Indus River, and even to the Indian Ocean if Baluchistan were gobbled up as well.

Events took a new turn in 1978, when Marxist officers in the Afghan army overthrew the country's neutralist government and began to import communist ideology and politics. The rural countryside rose in rebellion, large parts of which had long-standing contacts with the ISI and with Pakistan's religious parties, especially the Jamaat-i-Islam. Openly favorable to the rebels, Zia asked Akhtar's ISI to arm and help them. In response, the Afghan communist government appealed to Moscow for arms and advisers, then for troops.

At first, Moscow was reluctant to get into what appeared to be a budding civil war and a possible quagmire. But as the situation deteriorated, the Soviet leadership felt compelled to intervene to save a client state. On the eve of December 25, 1979, 85,000 Soviet troops entered the country, and the borders of the Soviet bloc advanced to Pakistan's western frontier. Still ambivalent toward the invasion, Moscow kept the size of its invasion force down, though it had plenty more troops to put into the fight if it chose to do so—in 1968 it had invaded Czechoslovakia with a 250,000-man army—and even though it was now fighting on a much larger and more challenging terrain.

Zia immediately turned to Saudi Arabia for help, with which Pakistan had a long history of cooperation. Pakistan had received much aid from Riyadh, and many Pakistani émigré workers were employed in the kingdom, including in the Saudi army and air force. The Saudis had been worried about a Marxist threat in Afghanistan even before the officer coup. The year before, their intelligence chief, Prince Turki bin Faysal, had warned Afghan's president, Mohammed Daoud Khan, of a communist officer threat during his visit to Riyadh.

As soon as he heard Soviet troops had entered Afghanistan, Zia dispatched General Akhtar Rahman to Riyadh with an urgent message to the king requesting assistance to strengthen the anti-communist rebels in Afghanistan, the mujahedin. According to Prince Turki, King Fahd agreed immediately, putting Turki's General Intelligence Directorate (GID) in immediate touch with the ISI and providing funds in support of the mujahedin. The Saudi authorities also encouraged citizens to lend private financial support to the Afghan freedom fighters and to join in their jihad. The Saudis and Pakistanis would soon acquire another partner, the CIA, but it is well to remember that the ISI-GID alliance predated the expanded partnership.[17]

In part grateful for the Saudi response, Zia dispatched a Pakistani expeditionary force of brigade strength to the kingdom to help keep its regional enemies at bay. The Twelfth Khalid bin Waleed Independent Armored Brigade would be stationed in Tabuk, Saudi Arabia, near Israel for more than six years, from 1982 to 1988. At its peak, it had 20,000 men under its command, and the Saudis paid all of its costs.[18]

With the money from the Saudis and later the CIA, the ISI was able to train Afghans to fight the Soviet invaders more effectively. The ISI set up training camps along the Durand Line where Afghans learned more sophisticated tactics and skills for waging jihad. The ISI included instructors from Pakistan's own special fighting forces, the army's elite Special Services Group (SSG).

By the end of the war against the Soviet invaders, the ISI camps had trained at least 80,000 to 90,000 Afghans in ten-day or three-month courses.[19] Among the trainees in 1985 was a young Afghan from Kandahar named Muhammad Omar who would later found the Taliban. Omar was selected for the longer course, and the ISI trainer would remember Omar as one of his best students.[20]

Pakistan's support for the Afghans did not come without costs. First, there were the refugees. Entire cities in Afghanistan were depopulated, with about 4 million of its people crossing into Pakistan to escape the war and the communists. The population of Kandahar alone plummeted from 250,000 to 25,000, especially after it was subjected to Soviet carpet-bombing instigated to break a mujahedin rebellion. The refugees poured into the poorest parts of Pakistan: the Pashtun-dominated North-West Frontier Province, the Federally Administered Tribal Areas (FATA), and Baluchistan. The burden of caring for them put enormous strain on Pakistan.

With the refugees came a Kalashnikov culture. The violence and tribal lifestyles of the displaced refugees bred lawlessness in the border regions, undermining the traditional tribal authorities and Pakistani government alike. To add to this volatile mix, the opium trade from Afghanistan's large poppy fields made corruption and gangsterism part of everyday life.

Meanwhile the Soviet Union and its Afghan communist allies sought to destabilize Pakistan. The Soviet intelligence service, the Committee for State Security (KGB), and its Afghan client, the Government Information Agency (KHAD), paid agents to plant bombs in the refugee camps, assassinate mujahedin leaders, and attack the ISI training facilities. These infiltrators also tried to blow up arsenals of weapons and ammunition before the ISI could put them in mujahedin hands. An explosion from the most successful of these attacks, near the end of the war, rocked the entire city of Islamabad.

Soviet aircraft also intentionally strayed into Pakistani air space to intimidate Zia and the ISI. As the Pakistani air force retaliated, dogfights became common along the border. Some of these verged on escalating into a mini air war between the respective air forces.[21]

Emboldened to take the war into the Soviet Union itself, Pakistanis at times accompanied trained mujahedin units crossing the northern border of Afghanistan to conduct sabotage in Soviet Central Asia. Experts from the SSG were present on some of these missions.[22]

Initially Zia was very cautious about taking such enormous risks in fighting a superpower having the world's largest army. He could not be assured that Moscow would not invade Pakistan as well or work with its ally, India, to carve up the Muslim state. Consequently his early orders to the ISI were to heat up the situation in Afghanistan, but not to let it boil over.[23] Maintaining control of the arms and money going to the mujahedin was the key to keeping the pot simmering just right.

The ISI thus took great pains to oversee the flow of outside help, money, and arms to the various mujahedin factions. This also meant it could favor some factions, notably the Pashtun and Islamic groups, at the expense of non-Pashtun and more modern elements.[24] The man who ran the operation for much of the 1980s was Mohammad Yousaf, the chief of the ISI's Afghan bureau. His two accounts, *Silent Soldier: The Man behind the Afghan Jehad* and (with Mark Adkin) *The Bear Trap: Afghanistan's Untold Story*, are the best pieces on the war from the Pakistani perspective. *The Bear Trap* describes the "pipeline" for U.S. aid as follows: "As soon as the arms arrived in Pakistan, the CIA's responsibility ended. From then on it was our pipeline, our organization that moved, allocated and distributed every bullet that the CIA procured."[25]

From the earliest days of the Afghan war, Zia had already begun planning for the next stage of jihad, to be waged in India and Kashmir. He first approached the Jamaat-i-Islam Party, with which he and the army had long-standing ties. Jamat's founder, Islamist writer Mawlana Sayyid Abul A'ala Mawdudi, had advocated the use of force to establish a Muslim state in India and had no sympathy for the secular Jinnah and his independence movement. Later the party was an enthusiastic ally of the army in the war against Bengali freedom in 1971, which helped solidify its ties with army jihadists like Zia.

In early 1980 Zia met secretly with Maulana Abdul Bari, a Jamaat leader and veteran jihadist who had fought in Operation Gibraltar in 1965, and proposed that the party begin preparations for jihad in Kashmir. Zia promised that he would use the war against the Soviet invaders to help build a support base for a Kashmiri insurgency. In other words, the Afghan war would also train cadres for another jihad, this time against India. Zia also promised that some of the American assistance earmarked for the Afghan jihad would be diverted to the Kashmiri project and that the ISI would help with both.[26]

Jamaat-i-Islam found, however, that many Kashmiris doubted Zia's promises of support. Having been let down by Pakistan in 1947 and 1965, they were reluctant to trust the ISI. As a result, the new jihad took time to develop, largely through clandestine meetings between the ISI and Kashmiri militants from Indian-controlled Kashmir. For security reasons, many of these meetings were held in Saudi Arabia, a country that an Indian militant leader could easily enter, often under the cover of performing the hajj, whereas a visit to Pakistan would have immediately aroused the scrutiny of Indian intelligence. Zia and General Akhtar were directly involved in the effort. Finally, in 1983 some Kashmiris began to receive training in the ISI's Afghan camps.[27]

Zia, Akhtar, and the ISI also reached out to other groups in Kashmir, including the Jammu and Kashmir Liberation Front (JKLF), which had been founded in 1977 by Kashmiris living in the United Kingdom. The JKLF was much more sympathetic to Kashmiri independence than to union with Pakistan. It was also reluctant at first to accept ISI help, but Akhtar opened talks with its members in 1984, and by 1987 JKLF militants were also present in the ISI training camps.

THE AMERICAN CONNECTION

Relations between Pakistan and the United States had cooled considerably during the 1970s, after the debacle of Nixon's tilt toward Yahya Khan. Feeling America had let Pakistan down in the 1971 war, Bhutto moved the country closer to China and, as mentioned earlier, began seeking a nuclear deterrent. Washington strongly opposed further proliferation of nuclear weapons in the world and urged Pakistan not to seek the bomb.

The new American president in 1977, Jimmy Carter, sought to rejuvenate the nonproliferation regime begun by John F. Kennedy but got nowhere with Islamabad. The relationship soured further when Zia overthrew Bhutto. Carter rightly saw the coup as a serious setback for democracy in Pakistan and was particularly anxious that Zia not compound the problem by executing Bhutto. He appealed to Zia repeatedly not to go forward with the trumped-up charges and the trial. When Zia did go through with the execution, his relationship with the United States hit bottom. Carter, traveling to South Asia in 1977, visited India but flew over Pakistan to Iran. The message was clear: Pakistan and America were no longer allies.

That began to change with the pro-Soviet coup in Kabul. Shaken by the fall of Iran's shah and by the Marxist coup in Kabul, Washington wondered if Southwest Asia was crumbling into enemy hands. In July 1979—six months before the Soviet invasion—Carter ordered the CIA to provide low-level assistance to the rebellion against the communist government in Kabul. The aid consisted mainly of propaganda support and very modest amounts of money.[28]

With the Soviet invasion, Washington renewed its cold war love affair with the Pakistani army and the ISI. Carter's national security adviser, Zbigniew Brzezinski, traveled to Pakistan and offered more assistance for the mujahedin and for Pakistan. Zia turned down the first offer as "peanuts," a gratuitous insult to the peanut farmer from Georgia. But in time Zia came around, and the bilateral ISI-GID relationship became a trilateral one between the CIA, ISI, and GID in which Washington and Riyadh provided matching grants of money and purchased arms, while Islamabad handled distribution and training.

The size of the program grew steadily. By 1984 CIA funding was approaching $250 million annually and peaked in 1987 and 1988 at close to $400 million.[29] Since the program was largely about fund-raising and arms procurement, it had very little staff. No more than a hundred people were involved in the Afghan effort, slightly less than half of them at CIA headquarters in Langley, the others in Islamabad or Riyadh.[30]

Given the operation's enormous consequences, it has to be one of the most cost-effective programs ever run by the U.S. government.

It was also backed by one of the most colorful figures in modern American history. Representative Charlie Wilson from Texas was an early and enthusiastic supporter of the war effort, the Afghans, and especially Zia. He sat on key House committees that funded covert operations and literally gave the CIA more money than it asked for. He also pushed to equip the mujahedin with the Stinger surface-to-air missile system that denied the Russians air control and ensured the Afghans victory. Charlie made close to three dozen trips to the region, stopping in Cairo, Jerusalem, Riyadh, and Islamabad each time to get backing from America's key allies.

Usually accompanied by a beautiful woman, Charlie flattered the allies, and they flattered him, even to the point of making him a secret field marshal in the Pakistani army. When Zia died in August 1988, Wilson wept, telling Akhtar's successor, Hamid Gul, "I have lost my father on this day."[31] Charlie had even planned to get married in Pakistan and persuaded Zia to hold an elaborate ceremony for the event in the Khyber Pass, with lancers and cavalry in attendance. Guests were to come from around the world, even from Israel. But the wedding never came off.[32]

Wilson, the CIA, and the other Americans involved in the Afghan operation had no contact with another contingent of Zia's jihad: the volunteers flocking to Pakistan to help the mujahedin. The agency paid only limited attention to them—most were not fighters. Washington's mind was on Moscow, not on another jihad that Zia was nurturing.

THE OTHER JIHADI: ABDALLAH AZZAM

While William Casey and Charlie Wilson were meeting their agenda, which was to defeat the Fortieth Red Army, some very different agendas were also being implemented in the Afghan war. They were the brainchild of a Palestinian, Abdallah Yusuf Mustafa Azzam, rightly named the father of modern global Islamic jihad by a former head of Israel's Secret Intelligence Service, the Mossad.[33]

Azzam was born in 1941 into a modest family living near the city of Jenin in the British mandate of Palestine.[34] Though known for their piety, family members were not regarded as extremists. Raised in what is now the West Bank, Azzam would have suffered through the Palestinian defeat in the first Arab-Israeli war of 1947–48, which Palestinians refer to as the Naqba, or catastrophe. At its conclusion, Israel achieved independence, while Palestine was divided between Gaza, which came under Egypt's control, and the West Bank, which was annexed to the Hashemite Kingdom of Jordan. As a result, hundreds of thousands of Palestinians lost their homes and became refugees.

In 1963 Azzam moved to Syria to attend Damascus University, where in 1966 he obtained a degree in Islamic law. Here he was greatly influenced by faculty belonging to the Muslim Brotherhood, the oldest Islamist party in the Arab world, though he probably was already a member from his youth in Jordan.[35] After graduation he returned to the West Bank, just before the June 1967 Arab-Israeli war. Israel's swift conquest of the West Bank led to another flow of Palestinian refugees fleeing Israeli rule; Azzam's family joined the exodus to Jordan's East Bank.

They settled in a refugee camp outside the city of Zarqa, which would become a hotbed of Islamism over the next half century. Azzam joined the Palestinian fedayeen resistance movement and participated in their attempts to attack Israelis across the Jordan. Though an active fighter in the fedayeen forces, he wanted to continue his studies so moved to Cairo, Egypt, in late 1968, where he obtained a master's degree with honors at the Islamic world's premier institution of higher learning, Al Azhar University. He then took up a teaching position at Jordan University but apparently sat out Jordan's civil war in 1970, not fighting on either the fedayeen or the government side.

In 1971 he returned to Al Azhar for his doctorate, awarded in 1973. In Cairo he became further embedded in the underground world of the Muslim Brotherhood and the Islamist movement. Upon graduation, he went back to teaching at the university in Amman, also becoming well known in Jordan as an Islamic leader and speaker. King Hussein's government tolerated the Muslim Brotherhood and the Islamists in order to keep the more radical nationalist Palestinian movements in check, but it also watched their activists closely to ensure they did not get out of control and pose a threat to the Hashemites.

Azzam's impressive credentials as an Islamic scholar and his increasingly radical views attracted the attention of Jordan's intelligence service, which, like the Saudi service, was called the General Intelligence

Directorate (GID). When it pressured Azzam to tone down his statements, he refused and in 1980 left Amman for a new teaching position at King Abdul Ibn Saud University in Jidda, a stronghold of the Muslim Brotherhood and other radicals evicted from their native Arab states but welcomed in the kingdom. In Jidda, Azzam met and befriended a young Saudi studying at the university, Osama bin Laden, and lived in one of the bin Ladens' homes there.[36]

Azzam did not stay long in Saudi Arabia. Within a year he obtained a new position at the Islamic University of Islamabad in Pakistan. There he came under the influence of Zia's jihad in Afghanistan—and his life changed profoundly.

Azzam became increasingly involved in the mujahedin cause, spending time with them in their camps along the border and writing pamphlets urging Muslims from all over the Islamic world, especially his fellow Arabs, to come to Pakistan to join the jihad. In 1984 he wrote a book crucial to the expansion of jihad, *The Defense of Muslim Territories,* in which he argued that every Muslim had an obligation to join the Afghan struggle, the most important jihadist cause of the time. This was the place to defeat the unbeliever and enemies of Islam, Azzam emphasized, not only because the invaders posed the greatest threat to the Islamic community, the ummah, but also because the payoff in defeating a superpower would be vastly increased stature for Muslims throughout the world. Backed by Azzam's impressive credentials as a serious scholar with degrees from prestigious Islamic schools, the book became a major influence in the entire ummah.

Also significant, the book's foreword was written by Saudi Arabia's leading scholar and religious figure, Sheikh Abdul Aziz bin Baz, who was very close to the royal family and whose Wahhabi faith favored an extremist interpretation of Islam.[37] He believed the earth was flat, for example, and opposed high heels for women because they were too provocative. The blind sheik was both a colorful and influential person in the kingdom, and his endorsement of Azzam was strong support.

Azzam's book became as important to the Afghan jihad as Thomas Paine's *Common Sense* was to the American Revolution. Azzam would follow it with dozens of articles and other books urging support for the jihad. Soon he broke with the Muslim Brotherhood, declaring it too timid, and began spending all his time in Peshawar with the mujahedin or traveling around the ummah urging Muslims to join the jihad in South Asia.

To assist jihadis arriving from all points of the ummah, Azzam created the Maktab al Khadamat (Service Bureau) in Peshawar to provide them with housing and food while they joined the Afghan war. Its cofounder was the fabulously rich young Saudi, Osama bin Laden, whom Azzam had met in Jidda. A scion of the kingdom's wealthiest construction magnate, bin Laden had come to Pakistan to join the jihad and brought with him financial support for an army of jihadi volunteers. Initially Azzam and bin Laden set up hostels for jihadists in Peshawar, then graduated to training camps where Arabs and others could "learn jihad" and go off to fight the Soviet troops in Afghanistan.

Azzam traveled widely to promote the war, even to the United States and Europe. In 1988 he was the featured speaker at the annual conference of the Islamic Association for Palestine (IAP) in Oklahoma City, where he helped raise funds for both the Afghan jihad and Palestine's Hamas. After Azzam's assassination in 1989, the IAP dedicated that year's conference in Kansas City to his memory.[38] His lectures were video-recorded and replayed to dozens of audiences. His trips produced sizable contributions of cash for the jihad.

In prodigious works on his views of jihad, Azzam emphasized that it should be a pan-Islamic struggle, not just an Afghan or Pakistani war. Therefore the entire ummah should unite in the endeavor. Nationalist identity only served to divide the ummah, whereas it needed to form a solid base, or *qaeda sulba,* to fight its enemies and prevent them from stealing Muslim lands, whether in Afghanistan or in Palestine. The jihad, he reiterated, was a global cause.

Moreover, wrote Azzam, jihadists who died fighting to repel the outsiders, or "the far enemy," would be glorified as martyrs and assured a special place in heaven. Azzam's works espoused the seminal ideas that would propel the new jihad into a cult of martyrdom and bring him recognition for turning it into a global struggle. For him, "the mountains of the Hindu Kush [were] the theater of battles without precedent in the history of the Muslim world."[39] And through the title of one work, he urged all Muslims to "Join the Caravan."

Thousands from across the ummah, from Morocco to Indonesia, responded to the call. Some were trained in the ISI camps, some joined various mujahedin factions, and some worked with bin Laden in forming an Arab commando force. As bin Laden later noted, "Volunteers from all over the Arab and Muslim countries . . . were trained by the Pakistanis, the weapons were supplied by the Americans, the money by the Saudis."[40] Although their military contribution to the mujahedin war was actually marginal, the political implications of their actions and the legitimacy they gained in the eyes of other jihadis were enormous. They would become the leaders and role models for global Islamic jihad and eventually for al Qaeda, named for Azzam's proposed solid base for jihad.

In addition to creating the Service Bureau with bin Laden, Azzam was instrumental in setting up another organization to assist jihad in nearby Kashmir, the Markaz-ud-Dawa-wal-Irshad (MDI), or Center for Proselytization and Preaching. Here he had the help of Hafez Saeed, a prominent Pakistani Sunni scholar who, like Azzam, had studied in Saudi Arabia in the 1980s. The mission of the MDI was to apply the lessons of the Afghan war—which was winding down in 1987 as the Soviet forces prepared to leave—to Kashmir and India. The center's first priority was to train Kashmiris to fight alongside the mujahedin in order to gain combat experience. Camps were set up in Afghanistan's Konar Province for this purpose. The ISI helped get the new group set up and trained MDI operatives in its camps as well. A military wing of MDI named Lashkar-e-Tayyiba, or the Army of the Pure, would become the most violent and effective terrorist group fighting India.[41]

Azzam played an inspirational role in the creation of an important organization back in Palestine as well: Harakat al-Muqawamat al-Islamiyyah (Hamas), meaning Islamic Resistance Movement. Founded in 1987, the group to this day regards Azzam as one of its key ideological influences. He was also directly involved in writing its constitution or covenant, which calls for a jihad to destroy Israel.[42] In addition, Azzam trained Palestinians in Pakistan and sent them back to Gaza and the West Bank with their new skills.[43] Even now, Hamas leader Khalid Mishal speaks movingly of Azzam as "a great man" to whom Hamas owes "a lot"[44]

Of the thousands who came to "join the caravan," the most famous was Osama bin Laden (his contribution is discussed in chapter 3), but they also included the mastermind of 9/11, Khalid Sheikh Muhammad, a Pakistani who worked briefly as an aide to Azzam in Peshawar, and Abu Musaib al Zarqawi, who later would lead the al Qaeda war against the U.S. occupation of Iraq.[45] One who arrived in 1987 from Indonesia was Riduan Isamuddin, better known as Hambali, who helped create Jamaah Islamiyah and carried out a wave of terror attacks in Southeast Asia, including the night club bombings of October 12, 2002, in Bali, Indonesia, which left more than 200 dead, including 88 Australians and 24 Britons.[46]

According to one estimate, some 35,000 Muslims from forty-three countries received their baptism-of-fire training with the mujahedin, and tens of thousands more were educated in the madrassas in Pakistan associated with the war.[47] Among the less well-known figures who responded to Azzam's call is Abu Mus'ad al-Suri, a Syrian who would train in the ISI and mujahedin camps and then author some of the most important ideological books of the modern Islamic jihad. His 1,600-page *Global Islamic Resistance Call* expounds the strategy of al Qaeda and the jihad. In it Suri also argues that jihad needs to be decentralized and pan-Islamic. The work became a jihadi best-seller and has been widely read and distributed in the jihadist underground.[48]

Born in Aleppo in 1958, Suri was active in the Syrian Islamist movement crushed by the Asad government in 1981. In 1987 he came to Peshawar and met with Azzam, who convinced him that the struggle in Afghanistan warranted the utmost attention of Islamists and should be transformed into a pan-Islamic struggle. Suri became a trainer in one of the ISI-built camps for the mujahedin but after several years turned to writing and became a major ideological influence in the new jihadist movement stirring in the wake of the Soviet defeat. He moved to London in the mid-1990s and served as bin Laden's spokesman in Europe, arranging interviews for him and publicizing his works.

'Abd al-'Aziz al-Muqrin, a Saudi born in Riyadh in 1973, also joined the caravan in Pakistan, arriving just after Azzam's death but already heavily influenced by his works. Like Suri, he became a disciple of bin Laden. He would later return to the Saudi kingdom and write a manual for waging a terror campaign titled *A Practical Course for Guerrilla War*.[49] Under his leadership, the Saudi branch of al Qaeda would follow the guide's principles in waging war against the House of Saud in 2004.

Nine days after the Soviet forces left Afghanistan in February 1989, Azzam delivered a sermon in Islamabad laying out his vision of a jihadist future: "We will fight, defeat our enemies and establish an Islamic state on some sliver of land, such as Afghanistan. Afghanistan will expand, jihad will spread, Islam will fight in other places, Islam will fight the Jew in Palestine and establish Islamic states in Palestine and other places. Later these states will unite to form one Islamic state."[50]

Less than a year later, on November 24, 1989, Azzam was mysteriously assassinated when a powerful bomb destroyed the car carrying him and his two eldest sons, Muhammad and Ibrahim, through the streets of Peshawar. The assassins were never identified. Some speculate that Ayman al Zawahiri, an Egyptian jihadist seeking bin Laden's support, may have been involved, or that bin Laden himself was responsible, supposedly because he and Azzam had secretly quarreled. This seems unlikely, however, as bin Laden and Zawahiri continue to publicly extol Azzam as a martyr for jihad. Others point to the ISI, always a target for conspiracy theories. Most jihadists blame the CIA and Mossad.[51] On December 27, 1989, Hamas declared a general strike in Gaza and the West Bank in protest of the assassination.[52]

The mystery may actually have been solved by al Qaeda. On December 30, 2009, a Jordanian al Qaeda operative, Abu Dujannah al Khorasani, blew himself up at the CIA's forward operating base in Khost, Afghanistan, killing seven CIA officers and a member of the Jordanian GID. Khorasani had earlier taped an interview for al Qaeda to broadcast in which he described in detail how he had successfully fooled the GID into believing he was their agent and would help them find Ayman Zawahiri and Osama bin Laden. He said the Jordanian intelligence service had bragged to him that it was behind Abdallah Azzam's demise and even identified the assassin as the current head of GID's counterterrorism branch, Ali Burjaq. It is very possible that Khorasani was told the truth by his Jordanian case officer, Sharif Ali bin Zaid, but since both died in the attack, one may never be sure.[53]

Ironically, those who hosted Azzam and his colleagues in Pakistan in the 1980s, Zia and Akhtar, also died as the war was coming to an end. On August 17, 1988, Zia and Akhtar, who had then been promoted to chairman of the Joint Chiefs of Staff, along with several other senior Pakistani generals and the U.S. ambassador to Pakistan, Arnold Raphel, were killed when their C130 aircraft crashed shortly after takeoff. Suspicions of foul play surfaced immediately. No one ever claimed responsibility, and there are dozens of conspiracy theories about what happened and why.

A thorough and credible investigation has never been held. Akhtar's ISI biographer, Mohammad Yousaf, suspected that "the KGB or KHAD [its Afghan counterpart] had been involved," but that the Americans were eager to see Zia killed now that the jihad was almost over.[54] The U.S. ambassador to India at the time, John Gunther Dean, accused Israel's Mossad of targeting Zia, possibly with a view to halting Pakistan's bomb program.[55] In the most recent, thorough study based on interviews with many of the Pakistani air force officers who investigated the crash, Shuja Nawaz concludes that "many questions still remain" about why the plane crashed and why the investigation of the crash was so incomplete.[56] Like much else in Pakistan's history, its cause remains a mystery.

CHAPTER THREE

OMAR'S JIHAD

THE WILLARD HOTEL IS one of Washington's finest and most historic lodgings. General Ulysses S. Grant stayed there when he took command of the Union armies in 1864. At first, the desk clerk did not recognize him, but on learning his error announced to the lobby the presence of the Union's greatest warrior, whereupon Grant was mobbed by well-wishers. Since then the Willard has hosted dozens of prominent leaders, including many foreign heads of state.

In April 1995 I was calling on one of them, Pakistani prime minister Benazir Bhutto, the first woman to be a head of government in the Muslim world. Bright, attractive, and articulate, she was widely admired. She had served years in prison after the Zia coup. The daughter of executed Zulfikar Ali Bhutto, Benazir was in her second term as prime minister and visiting Washington to try to mend Islamabad's badly fractured ties with America. The happy days of the 1980s had long soured and relations were in a deep hole.

My job as national intelligence officer for the Near East and South Asia included regularly meeting with foreign leaders to brief them on the U.S. intelligence community's assessment of international developments. So I spent over an hour with Benazir, reviewing issues in the region. She listened carefully to the analysis in her suite at the Willard. I had wondered how she would receive me. In her autobiography, she had expressed her suspicions that the U.S. Central Intelligence Agency (CIA) had been behind General Zia's coup, which had toppled her father's government and led to his execution.[1] She also suspected the CIA of killing her brother.[2] Would she raise these concerns with me?

Instead she poured out her views on U.S. relations with Pakistan and Afghanistan. America had encouraged Zia to take on the Soviet army in the 1980s and then, once victory was achieved, abandoned both Afghanistan and Pakistan, leaving them to deal with the bitter aftermath: millions of refugees, hundreds of thousands of casualties, and a Kalashnikov culture that spread violence and extremism in both countries. Equally upsetting, it had looked away during Zia's brutal treatment of her family and democracy in her country,

Sanctions, she further complained, were imposed on Pakistan for its nuclear weapons program when Washington had known for years it was the Zia administration that had developed them—under Bill Casey's protection. It was unfair to have sold Zia F16 fighter jets, then invoke sanctions after he was dead and refuse to deliver them or return the money Pakistan had paid for them. America had betrayed democracy in Pakistan, undermined the efforts to restore it, and treated her country unfairly. All in all, the United States was an unreliable ally.

I had heard this argument many times before and have heard it many times since. Most Pakistanis, left and right, believe it to be true. Much of it is true. Benazir warned that dark forces had been released in Pakistan in the 1980s. She all but said the Inter-Services Intelligence Directorate (ISI) was plotting to throw her out of office for a second time and that radical extremists were planning to murder her, as they would eventually.

I was the test case for Prime Minister Bhutto's argument. In the next couple of days she would make the same arguments with President Bill Clinton and others. Clinton would say after meeting Bhutto that she was right; the United States was dealing unfairly with Pakistan. Ironically, while she was making these points in Washington, she was also overseeing the rise of the next generation of jihadis in Afghanistan. It is one of the many paradoxes of Pakistan's history that the most liberal and enlightened of its leaders, Benazir Bhutto, would be the one to help midwife the Taliban, an action that would ultimately lead to her assassination.

Troubled Democracy with Two Jihads

With the death of Abdallah Azzam, General Akhtar, and especially Muhammad Zia ul-Haq, one chapter in the rise of the modern global jihad came to an end and another began. For Pakistan, the Zia years had been relatively stable at the top, despite its citizens' growing anger at the lack of a voice in the country's future. For the jihad, these years were filled with friendly ISI support. Over the next decade, Pakistan would become much messier and more unstable under a frequently changing leadership. The prime minister's job would rotate between two remarkable politicians, Benazir Bhutto and Nawaz Sharif, until the army took over again in a coup that brought Pervez Musharraf to power. The ISI, which had known only one director general for a decade, would see more leadership changes as well. It would also find itself the target of attack and criticism.

On April 10, 1988, the largest supply depot for the ISI's war in Afghanistan, located just outside Rawalpindi at the Ojhri ammunition storage facility, was racked by a massive series of explosions. Ten thousand tons of arms and ammunition were destroyed in the blast.[3] While most of the arms were for the Afghan mujahedin, some equipment at the site was being stored for the Kashmiri jihad. More than a hundred people died in the disaster, including five ISI officers. The KGB may have been responsible.

In Srinagar, the capital of Indian Kashmir, Muslim crowds blamed India, and riots broke out, the opening salvo of a rapidly building insurgency against the Indian occupation.[4] It was a harbinger of how Zia's jihad would spread east, as he had always envisioned. In 1988, among his last acts, Zia ordered the ISI to step up support for the Kashmiri insurgency.

Following Zia's death, army leaders were reluctant to try to take his place, while Pakistanis yearned for a civilian government again after a decade of military rule. The global political climate in 1988 also favored a return to democratic politics. Changes under way in the Soviet Union seemed to foreshadow a springtime of global reform.

On November 16, 1988, Benazir Bhutto won Pakistan's first relatively fair and free elections and became prime minister at the age of thirty-five. From Zia she inherited two jihads along with an army and ISI that were deeply suspicious of her. Benazir was just as suspicious of the ISI and the army, however, despising them for her years of repeated house arrest, imprisonment, and exile after her father's execution. She also felt that the

ISI, Jamaat-i-Islam, and Osama bin Laden had made a concerted effort to defeat her and back her opponent Nawaz Sharif.[5]

Once in office, Benazir learned from the ISI that the mujahedin expected to sweep to total military victory quickly after the last Soviet soldier left Afghanistan in 1989; the CIA gave President George H. W. Bush the same estimate.[6] It would not turn out that way. The communist government in Kabul actually outlived the Union of Soviet Socialist Republics and did not fall from power until 1992.

This turn of events was due in part to a strategic miscalculation by the new ISI director, Hamid Gul. Now that the Soviet forces were gone, Gul decided the mujahedin should move from guerrilla tactics to conventional warfare. The first target would be the city of Jalalabad, on the road from the Khyber Pass to Kabul. The siege that followed would be a terrible mistake. The Afghan communist army held off the mujahedin, and the stalemate led to bitter recriminations within the mujahedin factions. After the debacle, Bhutto engineered Gul's removal from the ISI leadership, whereupon he became a public advocate for the Taliban, the Kashmiri insurgency, and Osama bin Laden, later blaming 9/11 on Israel's Mossad and calling it an excuse for U.S. intervention in Afghanistan.[7] Just before her assassination in 2007, Benazir claimed he was plotting her murder.[8]

While the Afghan insurgency stalled, indigenous anger in Kashmir was blossoming. After years of heavy-handed oppression by India, the Muslim population's fury exploded into riots and violence throughout Kashmir. Incidents of violence jumped from 390 in 1988 to 2,100 in 1989 and almost 4,000 in 1990.[9] Hafez Saeed's Lashkar-e-Tayyiba began setting up its infrastructure inside Kashmir, while its camps in Afghanistan and Pakistan trained hundreds of militants.[10] In the next two decades, an estimated 200,000 militants went through these camps.[11]

The ISI had to play catch-up to gain control over the movement. At that point, it was largely in the hands of the dangerously independent Jammu and Kashmir Liberation Front (JKLF), whereas Zia's clients, the Jamaat-i-Islam and Lashkar-e-Tayyiba, were still relatively small players. The great concern for the ISI, "what [it] wanted to prevent, above all else, was the creation of a separate state in Kashmir that would include both the Pakistani and Indian-controlled sections of Kashmir, which was precisely the JKLF's goal."[12]

It did not take long for the ISI to gain the upper hand as the Kashmiri insurgents were split into unruly factions the JKLF found very difficult to control. As many as 180 groups had sprouted up to fight the Indians. By setting up an umbrella group, Hizbul Mujahedeen, to unite the pro-Pakistan elements, the ISI gradually isolated the JKLF, cut off its aid, and took control. When the JKLF tried to appeal directly to Benazir to overrule the stoppage of support, the ISI blocked all communications between the insurgents and the prime minister. Engulfed in increasingly violent infighting as well as the struggle against India, the factions eventually yielded to ISI supervision, although the agency was never able to fully control all elements of the insurgency.[13]

Some of the more illustrious insurgents already had connections with the ISI. Perhaps the best example is Muhammad Ilyas Kashmiri, who was born in Kashmir on February 10, 1964. Trained in the ISI border camps in North Waziristan, possibly with the Pakistan army's Special Services Group (SSG), Kashmiri spent several years of combat in the Afghan war, which cost him an eye and a finger. After the Soviet defeat, Kashmiri returned to his homeland, where, with ISI assistance, he formed a militant group known as the 313 Brigade. This unit made itself famous harassing and attacking the Indian army. In 1991 he was captured and spent two years in an Indian prison but then escaped.

In 1994 Kashmiri took the war into India proper. A team of his men kidnapped several Western tourists and held them for ransom in a safe house near New Delhi. They demanded the release of a senior Kashmiri militant, Maulana Masood Azhar, who had been arrested in Kashmir early in the year. The Indian army tracked down the band and raided the house, but Kashmiri escaped. His campaigns in Kashmir made him an ISI hero, especially in 2000, when he arrived at ISI headquarters in Islamabad with the severed head of an Indian soldier. He was personally thanked for his accomplishments in the jihad by General Pervez Musharraf, the dictator of Pakistan at the time, and Lieutenant General Mahmud Ahmad, then head of ISI.[14]

The tension in Kashmir of the late 1980s had put intense strain on Indo-Pakistani relations. To suppress the unrest, in August 1989 India reinforced its already large troop presence in the province, using a very heavy hand and accusing Islamabad of helping the insurgents. In December Pakistan responded with a massive military exercise, deploying

200,000 ground troops and virtually the entire Pakistani air force in a display of its might and determination.[15]

The rhetoric on both sides heated up as well. On March 13, 1990, Benazir declared Pakistan would fight for a "thousand years" to free Kashmir. To calm the two countries, now seemingly headed toward war, President Bush dispatched deputy national security adviser Robert Gates and senior director for Near East and South Asia Affairs in the National Security Council (NSC) Richard Haass to the region. Their trip ended in May, by which time the tensions had begun to abate. It would not be the first or the last time that Pakistan-based terrorism seemed to be driving the two countries to the brink of war.[16]

As soon as the crisis eased, the army and Pakistan's president, Ghulam Ishaq Khan, moved to oust Benazir Bhutto on allegations of corruption. In advance of new elections, the ISI worked hard in support of Nawaz Sharif, a prominent Punjabi politician. Its former chief, Hamid Gul, reputedly ran the anti-Bhutto campaign for the army, which included charges that Bhutto had "strong Zionist links" and was too pro-American.[17] Benazir's suspicions of what the ISI and the army had planned for her proved all too accurate.

Before Sharif took office, U.S.-Pakistan relations also hit a new low. In October 1990 President Bush told Congress he could not certify that Pakistan was agreeing not to cross the nuclear threshold and believed that it in effect had a bomb, a suspicion made stronger by the spring 1990 crisis and observations of the Gates/Haass mission. After all, why would Bush be worried about a possible nuclear exchange in South Asia if Pakistan did not have the capability? Invoking the Pressler Amendment of 1985, which mandated that U.S. aid to Pakistan was not to be used to further its nuclear ambitions, Washington decided to halt all assistance to Pakistan immediately. Even paid-for equipment, such as Pakistan's order of F16 fighter jets, was not to be delivered.

Pakistanis saw the situation differently, arguing that the United States had been aware of Pakistan's nuclear ambitions even under Zia but pretended that Islamabad had not stepped over the threshold. The nuclear card was played just as an excuse, they said, so Washington could dispense with its ally, no longer needed now that the Soviet forces were in retreat. Some pointed out, however, that the Afghan war had provided Zia with the crucial cover Pakistan needed to build the bomb without

American sanctions. A. Q. Khan, for example, has said he urged Zia to test a bomb in 1984 but was told to wait while the war continued. Testing was too public; it would remove any cover the war provided. In Khan's opinion, "Had the Afghan war not taken place, we would not have been able to make the bomb as early as we did given the U.S. and European pressure on our program."[18]

Prime Minster Nawaz Sharif thus found himself with a legacy of two jihads on his hands, but without the U.S. support Zia and Benazir had enjoyed. Under the circumstances, his position greatly depended on the ISI and the army, as well as the religious parties. By then Sharif had a new ISI commander, Lieutenant General Javid Nasir, a self-proclaimed Islamist who was very eager to prosecute the wars in both Afghanistan and Kashmir. According to some former ISI officers, Sharif also reached out to Osama bin Laden in early 1990 for assistance and secretly met with him in Saudi Arabia, where bin Laden had returned after the withdrawal of the Soviet troops.[19] But these accusations have not been proved and probably are part of a later smear campaign, launched in 1999 when the army broke with Sharif.

The Afghan war came to a head in April 1992 when a key commander in the communist army, Abdul Rashid Dostam, broke ranks and defected to the mujahedin. The communist government quickly collapsed from within, and the jihad finally took Kabul. At last, after twelve hard years, Zia's jihad had triumphed—but it was a hollow victory. The mujahedin fell to fighting among themselves. The brutal and bloody civil war that followed is still being waged today.

In this new conflict, Pakistan found itself backing its major clients in the mujahedin, especially Gulbudin Hekmatayar's Pashtun group, and working against other factions, notably the Tajik group led by Ahmad Shah Massoud. The civil war grew incredibly complex, with players switching sides and much violence directed against civilians. Afghanistan was descending into anarchy, not the vision of a Pakistani ally that could provide strategic depth for Islamabad against India. The Kashmir war was also at a stalemate now. India had a half million men in the province, and despite having peaked, violence levels remained high.

On January 8, 1993, in another mysterious turn of the nation's history, the chief of army staff, General Asif Nawaz, died suddenly. His wife intimated that he had been poisoned and that the plotters may have included Prime Minister Sharif. Asif Nawaz had taken command with the determination to get the army out of politics. In his first order of the day, he stated the army must allow the democratic process to work and return to the business of being a professional military. Another of his goals was to try to persuade Nawaz Sharif and Benazir Bhutto to reconcile for the good of the nation.[20] Also high on his agenda was the deteriorating security in the country's only port, Karachi, where sectarian violence was boiling out of control. In addition, he was said to be increasingly concerned about the prime minister's job performance. Nawaz's death has never been fully explained, but it would usher in yet another significant change at the top.[21] Charged with corruption (and with failing to investigate Nawaz's death adequately), Sharif was removed from office just as Benazir had been.

The new elections held in 1993 returned Benazir to office for a second term as prime minister. A new ISI chief was appointed to replace the jihadi Nasir: General Javad Ashraf Qazi, whose goal was to reduce ISI's profile in Pakistani politics and "to make [it] invisible again."[22] As the two jihads raged on, Kashmir saw more Westerners being kidnapped and held hostage, and tension heightening in its relations with India.

Meanwhile a new phenomenon was emerging in Afghanistan that would change the direction of its history and, in turn, deeply affect Pakistan's own course. The years of anarchy following the fall of Kabul to the mujahedin fomented what came to be known as the Taliban, or students' movement—the most extreme Islamist movement ever to govern a country. The details are discussed later in the chapter, but for now suffice it to note that, ironically, its rise was presided over by the most liberal and secular ruler in Pakistan's history, Benazir Bhutto. Although Pakistan did not create the Taliban, soon after the movement's founding, Islamabad, including the ISI and the Ministry of the Interior, began to give it significant support. Pakistan under Bhutto would be the Taliban's champion in the international arena, arguing that it was the only hope for stability and ultimately peace in Afghanistan. One of only three countries to recognize the Taliban government and open an embassy in Kabul, Pakistan provided critical oil supplies for the economy and crucial military advice and assistance. When the Taliban's Islamic Emirate of Afghanistan was sanctioned by the United Nations, Pakistan continued its strong moral and economic support.

This is not to say that Pakistan controlled the Taliban. To the contrary, Islamabad, beginning with Benazir, found the Taliban a very difficult client to work with. Some Taliban resented Pakistani help and ignored its advice, even from the ISI. A few Taliban leaders look back disparagingly at the ISI, as does Abdul Salam Zaeef, former Taliban ambassador to Pakistan who was turned over to the United States by the ISI after 9/11 and sent to Guantánamo prison:

> The ISI acts at will, abusing and overruling the elected government whenever they deem it necessary. It shackles, detains and releases, and at times it assassinates. Its reach is far and it has roots inside and outside its own country. The wolf and the sheep may drink water from the same stream, but since the start of the jihad the ISI extended its roots deep into Afghanistan like a cancer puts down roots in the human body; every ruler of Afghanistan complained about it, but none could get rid of it.[23]

Zaeef recalled his arrest and detention in an ISI headquarters as being confined in the "devil's workshop."[24]

Benazir Bhutto's second term as prime minister ended shortly after the mysterious murder of another prominent person—her brother, Murtaza Bhutto. Like Benazir, he had been a student at Harvard and Oxford but after his father's death cut short his education to form a leftist opposition group, al Zulfikar, with the idea of avenging his father's execution at the hands of Pakistan's military government. Al Zulfikar received support from the communist government in Afghanistan and other pro-Soviet states like Syria and Libya. In March 1981 some of its members hijacked a Pakistani airliner to Kabul and forced Zia to trade jailed members of the Pakistan Peoples Party (PPP) for the hostages. Labeled a terrorist in many quarters, Murtaza stayed out of Pakistan during Benazir's first tour as prime minister.

In Benazir's second term, Murtaza returned and quarreled with her husband, Asif Ali Zardari, who saw his brother-in-law as a threat to the PPP's leadership. As the male heir of his father, Murtaza was demanding the right to run the party. In one of their fights, Murtaza famously cut off Zardari's mustache. On September 20, 1996, Murtaza was killed in a shootout with the police in Karachi, with suspicion pointing to Zardari. Within two months Benazir was out again, and new elections were scheduled.

In 1997 Nawaz Sharif was back in as prime minister. This time he had the constitution amended so the president could no longer sack the prime minister and took other steps to consolidate power. Critics saw his moves as an attempt to become a civilian dictator. Nawaz continued the policy of backing the Taliban and, like Benazir, tried to persuade the United States that they were the best of a bad lot.

In early 1998 Sharif's government arranged for a visit to Kabul by the U.S. ambassador to the United Nations, Bill Richardson. This would be the only high-level, face-to-face American exchange with the Taliban before 9/11. Sharif hoped the exchange would lead to U.S. recognition of the Taliban government in Kabul. As explained later in the chapter, the talks completely failed to put to rest American concerns about Osama bin Laden.

The defining events in Sharif's second term involved India. On May 11, 1998, India tested several nuclear weapons. Sharif faced enormous domestic pressure to test Pakistan's weapons in turn, even though this would lead to international sanctions. He decided to appease his audience within Pakistan and tested. While bin Laden publicly congratulated Pakistan for doing so, others moved to isolate it more than ever.

Despite the tensions created by multiple nuclear tests in the subcontinent, Sharif hosted a historic visit to Lahore by India's prime minister Atal Vajpayee in 1999. The two signed the Lahore Declaration pledging to seek to resolve their long-standing differences. One Pakistani official conspicuously absent from the events was Sharif's new chief of army staff, General Pervez Musharraf, handpicked over more senior officers after his predecessor was fired for criticizing the leadership and arguing that the military should have only a constitutional role in governing the country. A thoughtful and competent man, General Jehangir Karamat accepted his dismissal, but many in the officer corps were angered and felt humiliated by Sharif's move. As mentioned earlier, the choice of Musharraf was based on his apparent loyalty and lack of connection with the Punjab establishment but would prove to be as bad as Zulfikar Ali Bhutto's choice of Zia ul-Haq.

After being promoted, Musharraf turned his attention to an ambitious plan for a showdown with India, which was put in motion just as the prime minister was hosting the Lahore Summit. For years, the Pakistani army had contemplated a limited military offensive in Kashmir that might break the stalemate over the future of the state in favor of Islamabad. At the northern tip of Indian-controlled Jammu and Kashmir in Kargil District, a major highway, Route One, passes close to mountain peaks so that if it were severed much of northeastern Kashmir would be isolated from the rest of the state. These peaks were occupied by India in 1948, but owing to the extreme weather conditions in winter, it would pull back from its forward position during the cold and return in the spring. Pakistan's generals had long considered jumping the gun and moving into the Indian trenches before their occupants came back at the thaw. By gaining the upper hand logistically, they could then force open the political process.

Of course, the problem was that India might not cry uncle. Indeed, New Delhi might well cry foul, fight back, and possibly escalate the battle by expanding the conflict zone to other parts of Kashmir where geography favored its forces, perhaps even around Lahore. When General Zia was briefed on the plan in 1987, for example, he asked the director general of military operations who was proposing the idea if the Indians might escalate. The answer was yes, to which Zia responded: "So in other words, you have prepared a plan to lead us into a full-scale war with India!"[25] Though no dove on Kashmir, Zia rejected the idea.

Benazir Bhutto was also briefed on the plan, she claimed years later, but what she heard had a new twist: the attack was to be led by Kashmiri insurgents with only limited Pakistani army support. She, too, rejected it because while "it's doable militarily, it is not doable politically."[26]

Musharraf decided to launch the Kargil offensive in the winter of 1998–99 using the charade that the attack force consisted only of Kashmiri jihadists. In fact, the army did the real fighting. He claims he briefed Sharif thoroughly on the plan. Sharif claims not. Whatever the truth, the operation was a sheer disaster for Pakistan. Interestingly, preparations for the operation were not divulged beyond a small circle in the army, a pattern seen in 1965 and 1971. Pakistan's diplomats, air force, navy, and most of the high command were not brought in on the secret. And no one seemed to consider how India or America might react.

Even the ISI was not apprised of the operation, largely because Musharraf and ISI director General Ziauddin Butt, a Sharif appointee, were rivals. As a result, no preparation took place in Kashmir to support the incursion with increased insurgent operations. And no one asked the intelligence experts how the operation would be viewed externally.[27]

World reaction, led by the United States, was swift: Pakistan had committed an act of aggression and must withdraw its forces back behind the Line of Control (the military line between Indian- and Pakistani-controlled parts of Jammu and Kashmir). After a last-ditch summit with President Clinton on July 4, 1999, at Blair House, Pakistan had to cave in and was humiliated again by India.[28] The Lahore peace process was dead, Sharif and Musharraf were on a collision path, and in October Musharraf seized power after Sharif tried to fire him while he was out of the country. Another episode in Pakistan's quest for democracy had ended, and another military officer and jihad advocate was in power.

AMERICA AND THE WITCHES' BREW

American policy toward Pakistan in the 1990s was dominated by one man, Larry Lee Pressler, a Republican senator from South Dakota. Pressler was the sponsor of a 1985 amendment to the Foreign Assistance Act of 1961 that banned all aid to Pakistan, military and economic, unless the president could certify that Pakistan was not building nuclear weapons. When George H. W. Bush was unable to do so in 1990, all aid to Pakistan ended abruptly. As mentioned earlier, even the twenty-eight F16 jets already paid for would not be delivered, nor would the money ($658 million) be returned, as that was considered a form of aid.[29]

It would take five years and another amendment, named for Senator Hank Brown from Colorado (also a Republican), to remove economic assistance from the clutches of the Pressler Amendment and allow some limited development assistance to go forward to the Pakistani people. The Brown Amendment also allowed a one-time provision of some of the military equipment frozen in 1990, but not the F16s. The United States returned the money for those aircraft only in 1999, when the Department of Justice concluded that Washington would lose a court case brought by Pakistan's lawyers in America demanding the money or the planes. By then the United States had imposed other sanctions on Pakistan for testing nuclear weapons in 1998, effectively cutting off all military and economic assistance to Pakistan again.

The Pressler Amendment had a devastating decade-long impact on American diplomacy toward Pakistan, severely limiting what two presidents—George H. W. Bush and Bill Clinton—could do to engage Pakistan. Their hands were tied by Congress in many significant ways, and they lacked the votes on Capitol Hill to change the ground rules. As Bob Gates has accurately observed, "Washington cut off military-to-military exchanges and training programs with Pakistan, for well-intentioned but ultimately short-sighted and strategically damaging reasons."[30]

Hoping to rebuild U.S. relations with Pakistan when he came into office, George H. W. Bush invited Benazir Bhutto to the first state dinner of his administration. He only reluctantly invoked the Pressler Amendment in 1990 after intelligence overwhelmingly indicated that Pakistan was building a nuclear arsenal. Indeed, the Gates mission in early 1990 made certification all but impossible. When the president dispatched Bob Gates and Richard Haass to South Asia to calm the crisis created by Pakistan's support for jihad in Kashmir, the administration gave the press background information about its worries that the crisis could go nuclear. America found itself in a catch-22: if it were worried about a nuclear crisis, then Pakistan must have a nuclear weapons program.

Yet South Asia was not a high priority for most of the Bush administration. The president and his national security adviser Brent Scowcroft hardly mention it in their White House memoirs. Washington's attention was on other crises, such as the Iraqi invasion of Kuwait, the collapse of the Berlin Wall, and the dissolution of the Soviet Union. The collapse of the Najibullah government in Kabul did not even warrant a meeting of the NSC Deputies Committee. America had lost interest in Afghanistan following the Soviet departure, although it continued pouring arms into mujahedin camps for another couple of years, including many captured from the Iraqis. Again Bob Gates put it well: "In the decade before 9/11 the United States essentially abandoned Afghanistan to its fate."[31] Pakistan's backwater status in the Bush I era was also due to declining interest in both Afghanistan and the Pressler Amendment. Bush never traveled to Pakistan as president.

William Jefferson Clinton came to office in 1993 with an ambitious domestic agenda but with little experience in foreign affairs. From early in his term, however, he wanted to undo the damage of the Pressler Amendment but found himself constrained by concerns about nuclear proliferation. His first secretary of defense, William Perry, was also convinced that the Pressler Amendment was impeding efforts to support democracy in Pakistan, curb its nuclear ambitions, discourage its ties to terrorism, and ease Indo-Pakistani tensions. He traveled to Islamabad to try to open a dialogue on strategic issues and pressed Congress to amend Pressler. His efforts produced the Brown Amendment of 1995.

I traveled with Secretary Perry to Honolulu in 1995 for a meeting with his Pakistani counterparts that was intended to encourage more dialogue. We met on August 15, the anniversary of Japan's surrender in World War II. The Pakistani delegation listened to Perry's argument that a larger nuclear program would not make Pakistan safer; it would only spark an arms race with India. The Pakistani generals replied with a long critique of the Pressler Amendment.

At that time, the Clinton team was also keeping a watchful eye on the rise of the Taliban, while Benazir lobbied the administration to support the movement as the only way to end the murderous inter-mujahedin civil war. The Union Oil Company of California (UNOCAL) joined in the call, urging Washington to work with the Taliban to stabilize the country so that Central Asian oil could be exported to the Indian Ocean via a pipeline through Afghanistan and Pakistan. But Benazir backed a rival company, which added further strain to U.S.-Pakistan relations. When the Taliban captured Kabul in September 1996, U.S. officials initially hoped that they would be a force for law and order and considered opening an embassy in Kabul. On hearing criticism of the Taliban filtering in from human and women's rights groups, they backed down.[32] The future of U.S.-Afghan ties was then put off to the next Clinton administration.

Clinton's second term would be far more focused on the South Asian agenda. As senior White House adviser for South Asia issues from early 1997, I was given a seat at the table deciding policy. But the second Clinton administration was still hamstrung in that region by the Pressler Amendment's sanctions.

In July 1997 Deputy Secretary of State Strobe Talbott laid out the administration's view that it was time to move beyond the legacy of the Afghan war of the 1980s and to end regional competition in the civil war between the Taliban, backed by Pakistan, and the Northern Alliance, backed by Russia, Iran, India, and others:

It has been fashionable to predict a replay of the Great Game in Central Asia. The implication is that the driving dynamic of the region, fueled and lubricated by oil, will be competition of the great powers. Our goal is to avoid and actively to discourage that atavistic outcome. Let's leave Rudyard Kipling and George McDonald Fraser where they belong—on the shelves of history. The Great Game which starred Kipling's Kim and Fraser's Flashman was very much of zero-sum variety.[33]

This desire to find a solution to the Afghan war would, in 1998, lead to the only senior American effort to deal with the Taliban face-to-face.

Nawaz Sharif, by then back as prime minister, would facilitate the American mission to Kabul in April 1998 led by the U.S. ambassador to the United Nations, Bill Richardson. On April 17 he and I flew into Kabul, described in Bill's memoirs as "stark and desolate, with no building seemingly untouched by the two decades of conflict."[34] He pressed for a meeting with Taliban leader Mullah Muhammad Omar to discuss handing Osama bin Laden over to the Saudis before he could carry out his threats to attack Americans. The Taliban refused either to arrange a meeting with Omar or to turn over bin Laden, whom they called their "guest." They appeared slightly more accommodating in the matter of a cease-fire with the Northern Alliance, suggesting they would wait until the winter's snow melted before starting their annual spring offensive, thus perhaps opening a chance for UN mediators to talk to both sides. But they made no such attempt.

The meeting ended with a banquet lunch. We had brought one female staff member with us to the talks, Mona Sutphen, who joined the lunch. The Taliban were horrified but accepted her presence glumly. Our only senior-level dialogue with the Taliban had underscored the differences between us on policy and on human rights. Richardson went on to visit the opposition Northern Alliance in Sherbergan, in the Uzbek north, but its leader, Ahmad Shah Massoud, did not turn up at the meeting as promised. The trip was a failure.

Richardson also pressed Sharif to cut Pakistan's ties to supporters of terror, especially bin Laden, and to use Islamabad's influence in Kabul to persuade the Taliban to turn him over to the Saudis. Sharif was not helpful, arguing that the Taliban were out-of-control fanatics, that Pakistan was only reluctantly supporting them as the only means to stabilize the country. As for bin Laden, Sharif said the Pakistanis had no contacts in that regard—even though bin Laden himself had mentioned contacts with the ISI to a journalist, noting that Pakistan had "some governmental departments which, by the grace of God, respond to the Islamic sentiments of the masses in Pakistan. This is reflected in sympathy and cooperation."[35] By this time, bin Laden was an active supporter of both Pakistan's jihads, in Afghanistan and Kashmir.

The May 1998 Indian and Pakistani nuclear tests brought further sanctions down on Pakistan, as required under the Glenn Amendment of 1977. Despite an intense effort by Clinton and Talbott, Sharif had moved ahead with them in response to the Indian tests, further souring U.S.-Pakistani relations and creating a legal minefield of sanctions on top of sanctions. Talbott would try hard for the next year to persuade Sharif to take action that would break the cycle, such as signing the Comprehensive Test Ban Treaty, but this strategy had little effect in Islamabad.

Strains only intensified after al Qaeda attacked the American embassies in Tanzania and Kenya in August 1998, and Clinton responded with a cruise missile strike intended for bin Laden, reported by the CIA to be visiting the camp that was hit. Instead, a team of ISI officers was killed along with several Kashmiri fighters they were training. For Washington, the fact that bin Laden was visiting a camp with ISI officers present dramatically underlined the close ties between al Qaeda's top leader and Pakistan's army and intelligence service.[36]

A subsequent Defense Intelligence Agency assessment would put the pieces together succinctly: "Consider the location of bin Laden's camp targeted by U.S. cruise missiles. Positioned on the border between Afghanistan and Pakistan it was built by Pakistani contractors, and funded by the Pakistani Inter Services Intelligence Directorate . . . the real hosts in that facility [were] the Pakistani ISI, [so] then serious questions are raised by the early relationship between bin Laden and ISI."[37] To me and others in the White House, the connections were already clear in 1998.

Musharraf's Kargil adventure put yet a further barrier in the way of U.S. relations with Islamabad. The Clinton administration held Pakistan solely responsible for the 1999 crisis and from the beginning pushed for a complete withdrawal from occupied territory in Indian-held Kashmir. I have described in detail elsewhere the dramatic meeting between Clinton and Sharif on July 4, 1999, at Blair House in which Clinton persuaded Sharif to pull back Pakistan's army.[38]

Sharif opened the meeting with a long and rambling account of his efforts to defuse the crisis by working directly with India and indirectly with China. Clinton listened and then told Sharif that Pakistan was flirting dangerously with full-scale war. He said the United States blamed Pakistan entirely for starting the crisis and would hold it responsible for any escalation. Noting that the CIA believed Pakistan was preparing its nuclear arsenal, Clinton added that Sharif had a simple choice: escalate to disaster or back down. If Sharif agreed to back down and withdraw behind the Line of Control, Clinton would try his best to ease tensions over Kashmir.

Sharif accepted the president's help, and we announced Pakistan would withdraw with no conditions. He had bravely done the right thing, saving Pakistan, India, and the world from a potential disaster. Needless to say, the Pakistani army did not see it that way. It was humiliated and angry.

Under growing international pressure because of Pakistan's ties to the Taliban, Sharif made a late effort to persuade the Afghans to recognize why they were being isolated and take some steps to accept the UN demands regarding al Qaeda. He met with the Taliban's number two leader, Mullah Rabbani, the same person Bill Richardson had talked to in Kabul. The two met alone in Islamabad for almost an hour with a notetaker in attendance, and Sharif laid out the dangers facing the Taliban and Pakistan. Rabbani's answer was simply that the Taliban listened only to Allah, not to the United Nations. He told Sharif he should do the same.[39]

By now frustrated with the Taliban, Sharif traveled to Abu Dhabi with the message that he was prepared to take tougher measures against the Afghans if he had the support of the United Arab Emirates and Saudi Arabia, the only other two countries that recognized the Taliban government as legitimate.[40] Upon returning to Islamabad, however, Sharif first tried to move against Musharraf, taking advantage of the fact that he was traveling abroad. Sharif dismissed Musharraf and replaced him with the director general of ISI, Musharraf's rival Ziauddin.

Refusing to step down, Musharraf flew home, orchestrating a coup from the air that made him Pakistan's fourth military dictator. The overthrow also led to more American sanctions. Another piece of U.S. legislation mandated that a coup in a democratic country required Washington to sever all American assistance. At this point there was little left to sever, and little of a U.S.-Pakistani relationship to speak of. Meanwhile, the jihad was gathering force.

MULLAH OMAR, OSAMA BIN LADEN, AND THE ROAD TO 9/11

Mullah Omar is an unusual man by any standard. He has met with only a handful of non-Muslims in his life. He has no record of any major written work or memoir. He has been a soldier almost all his life, with scars from his combat wounds. Since late 2001 he has been in hiding and virtually unseen. Most striking of all, he has led his supporters to two major military victories, first in taking over most of Afghanistan in the 1990s and then in staging a spectacular comeback after being routed from Afghanistan in 2001 by the American-led coalition and the Northern Alliance. Nor can one overlook the remarkable alliance, even friendship, he developed with Osama bin Laden, which seems to have remained intact to this day. Throughout his career, he has worked with Pakistan, not always easily but certainly strategically.

According to his official Taliban biography released in 2009, Muhammad Omar was born in 1960 in Kandahar Province to a family of religious scholars. Orphaned at three, he was brought up by an uncle and received religious training. In 1979 he joined the mujahedin and for a time fought in neighboring Orzugan Province. He was wounded three times in the war against the Soviet invaders, losing his right eye on the third occasion.

This injury took him to Quetta in Pakistan for hospital care. The official biography emphasizes that this was his only visit to Pakistan and that, unlike most other mujahedin leaders, he did not reside in Pakistan during the war or send his family there for safety. All stayed in Afghanistan to fight the "Red Soviet Bear," as the official story puts it. The implication is that Mullah Omar was an individualist and did not succumb to the temptations of the more cultured life across the Durand Line. Preferring an austere lifestyle, apparently he even refuses to eat cream or soft bread in favor of soup and stale bread.[41]

Also significant, as noted earlier, Mullah Omar received ISI training in Pakistan during the war.[42] His rise to power in Afghanistan in the 1990s was greatly facilitated by Pakistan once it concluded that his new party, the Taliban, was the most effective means of advancing Islamabad's ambitions in its neighbor country. The rise of the Taliban has been extensively researched and documented by several authors, most notably by Ahmed Rashid, a brilliant Pakistani journalist. He says that by 1997 the Pakistanis were providing the Taliban with $30 million in aid annually as well as free oil to run the country's war machine.[43] By 1999 one-third of the Taliban's fighters were either Pakistani fundamentalists or foreign volunteers who arrived via Pakistan.[44]

Since the early 1990s Afghanistan has been mired in a civil war. In its essence, it is a struggle with ethnic and sectarian roots, pitting Pashtuns against the rest of the country. The Taliban emerged in Kandahar in 1994 as the Pashtun champions, swept into western Afghanistan in 1995, and seized control of Kabul in 1996. They were successful in the Pashtun south and east because they represented both a Pashtun and an Islamic movement. They met with considerable difficulty, however, when they tried to expand into non-Pashtun areas of the country dominated by Tajiks, Uzbeks, and Shia Hazaras. Holding non-Pashtun areas was often a challenge.

The Tajiks, Uzbeks, and Hazari Shia communities fought back under the leadership of the Northern Alliance and with the assistance of several neighbors, including India, the Soviet Union, and especially Iran. The Iranians almost came to blows with the Taliban in 1997 when the latter captured the northern city of Mazar-e-Sharif and massacred several Iranian diplomats, spies, and journalists. Pakistan had to intervene to persuade Mullah Omar to apologize and give back the bodies.

Pakistan would also play a critical role in bringing Mullah Omar and Osama bin Laden together in Afghanistan. After participating in the jihad against the Soviet forces, bin Laden left for Saudi Arabia, returning to his home like many other foreigners who had come to Peshawar to join the caravan. Once there, however, bin Laden became increasingly disenchanted with the Saudi establishment because of its close relationship with the United States and especially its support for the American-led Oslo peace process with Israel. He moved to Sudan to escape Saudi efforts to control him, setting up his nascent al Qaeda movement in Khartoum.

On May 18, 1996, bin Laden and his entourage, including three wives and thirteen children, flew from Sudan to Afghanistan. The Sudanese government had concluded he was more of a liability than an asset and made it clear he needed to move on. When his former comrades in Afghanistan offered him refuge from Khartoum's intrigues, bin Laden moved in with his former friends from the mujahedin in Jalalabad. By this point the mujahedin were either at war with the Taliban, as was Massoud's group, or had been forced to make their peace with the Taliban. Which mujahedin leader protected him upon his arrival in Jalalabad is unclear. Accounts differ as to whether it was Yunis Khalis, Gulbudin Hekmatayar, or others. It was probably a collective action of the Jalalabad shura council.[45] At first, however, the Taliban saw bin Laden as a potential friend of their foes. When Jalalabad fell to an advancing Taliban column in September and shortly afterward entered Kabul, bin Laden was de facto under Taliban control, or was at least on their turf.

According to *The 9/11 Commission Report,* the ISI set up the first meeting between the Taliban and bin Laden in the hope that the two would work together, especially to help train Kashmiri militants.[46] The Taliban in Jalalabad told Mullah Omar that "bin Laden is a good man and has taken part in the Afghan jihad against the Soviets."[47] At their first face-to-face meeting, Omar introduced bin Laden to a crowd at the Kandahar mosque as "a friend, a brother, and a holy warrior." Then the two led the Friday prayers together.[48] It was an auspicious beginning for an important partnership.

Although there would be strains in the relationship at times, the bonds would be stronger than the irritants. Bin Laden's frequent public comments promising to bring the jihad to America and to others of the Crusader Zionist alliance caused some friction because they exposed the Taliban as allowing a terrorist to operate in their midst. The Taliban promised Pakistan and Saudi Arabia to "control" their "guest," but he continued to issue statements, and no real effort was made to rein him in. Bin Laden moved to Kandahar to be close to Mullah Omar, proclaimed his loyalty to the "commander of the faithful" (Omar's self-proclaimed title), and married one of Omar's daughters to further cement their bond.[49] Perhaps the most striking aspect of this partnership was its strength in the face of growing pressures.

That strength may have rested in part on the exchange of assets. The Taliban gave bin Laden protection and room to operate. Under Pashtun tribal custom, it was incumbent on a Pashtun to offer protection if asked for by a visitor, a guest. According to Abdallah Azzam's son, Hutaifa, bin

Laden requested asylum soon after arriving in Jalalabad, urging the Taliban to "never surrender me." Omar replied, "We will never give you up to anyone who wants you"—and stood by his promise.[50] When pressed after the two African bombings in 1998 to turn him over, Omar refused: "Even if all the countries of the world unite, we would defend Osama with our own blood."[51] In March 2001, after the United Nations had passed a half dozen resolutions demanding that Omar turn over Osama, he again refused: "Half of my country has been destroyed by two decades of war. If the remaining half is also destroyed in trying to protect Mr. bin Laden, I am willing for this sacrifice."[52]

In effect, this meant refuge not only for Osama but also for his al Qaeda followers and the thousands who would flock to train with him in the next few years. Al Qaeda was even allowed to import vehicles and equipment for their camps. The Taliban Ministry of Defense provided license plates. The national airliner, Ariana, helped bring in volunteers, guns, and money. In short, al Qaeda operated as a state within the state.[53]

In return, bin Laden and al Qaeda provided money and soldiers to help the Taliban fight their war against the Northern Alliance. Their contribution began with a few million dollars for the campaign to take and hold Kabul.[54] In time it became an annual subsidy of more than $10 million.[55] Most of this did not come from bin Laden himself because by now his access to the family fortune was limited by the Saudi authorities. But as a hero of the jihad, he retained many contacts with rich Saudis and others in the Gulf States, and he tapped this source on behalf of the Taliban.

Volunteers eager to fight with the Taliban and Pakistanis came as well. Al Qaeda formed its own unit in the Taliban army, the 55 Brigade, which by 2000 had several thousand Arabs and other Muslims under arms and was known for its ferocity on the battlefield.[56] According to French records, between 1994 and 2001, more than 1,100 French converts to Islam or young Frenchmen of North African descent alone trained in al Qaeda's camps.[57]

But the chemistry between Omar and Osama went beyond a trade of assets. Omar found in Osama and al Qaeda an ideology that transcended Afghanistan, played to his ego, and validated his role as commander of the faithful. Mullah Omar's ambitions reached far beyond wanting to be just another Pashtun warlord. With al Qaeda's support, he did indeed become far more. At the same time, his Islamic emirate became increasingly radical. It went so far as to recognize the breakaway Chechen Islamists as an independent country of like-minded jihadists, a move no other country in the world even considered (an embarrassed Pakistan arrested the Chechen ambassador when he arrived to take up this post via Islamabad).[58] Finding himself isolated for the barbarity of his Islamic emirate—which stoned adulteresses to death in public, banned kite flying, destroyed ancient Buddhist statues, and almost started a war with Iran—Mullah Omar needed allies, and bin Laden proved a very good ally, as became evident in the plot to assassinate Ahmad Shah Massoud. By the end of the 1990s, the complex web of ties among Pakistan, Mullah Omar, and Osama bin Laden had created a new jihad, one that now had a global agenda inspired by Azzam and was ready to take action on the international stage.

THE MILLENNIUM PLOT: TERROR ACROSS THE GLOBE

In early December 1999, Samih Batikhi, the brilliant head of Jordan's General Intelligence Department (GID), unraveled an amazing plot. The first whiff of it came on November 30, when the GID intercepted a phone call between an al Qaeda cell in Amman and Abu Zubaydah, a senior al Qaeda operative in Pakistan. It heard Abu Zubaydah tell the Jordanian team, "The time for training is over." The GID rightly saw this as the sign of an imminent attack. It discovered the cell was planning multiple simultaneous attacks on a large hotel in Amman (the SAS Radisson), a border crossing between Israel and Jordan, and two Christian holy sites, Mount Nebo and the site of John the Baptist's baptism of Jesus on the Jordan River. The terrorists had accumulated hundreds of pounds of chemicals to make their bombs and promised that "bodies will pile up in stacks."[59]

The mastermind of the plot was Jordanian Abu Musaib al Zarqawi, who had gone to Afghanistan in 1989 to join the jihad. According to Benazir Bhutto, Zarqawi was working for the ISI then. By 1999 Zarqawi had spent several years in the GID's prisons for plotting against King Hussein but had been released in a general amnesty in February, after the king's death. He had gone back to Afghanistan and offered his services to bin Laden and Mullah Omar, who set him up with his own training camp in Herat in western Afghanistan, near the Iranian border.[60]

Jordan was only one part of the larger plot bin Laden was orchestrating from Kandahar. The GID reported the news to the CIA immediately, noting the links to Pakistan. Sandy Berger, Clinton's national security adviser, put the U.S. national security system on alert. For the rest of December, the NSC principals focused round the clock on the al Qaeda threat. Berger and CIA director George Tenet were convinced bin Laden was planning a spectacular series of attacks to coincide with the end of the twentieth century. They were right.

The next act unfolded inside North America. On December 14, 1999, a twenty-three-year-old Algerian, Ahmed Ressam, was arrested in Port Angeles, Washington, when he was found in a car loaded with explosives. Ressam had immigrated to Canada illegally in 1994 and lived in Montreal. In 1998 he traveled to Afghanistan and Pakistan and joined al Qaeda, which trained him in building car bombs. In collusion with several other Algerians living in Montreal, he devised a plan to attack Los Angeles International Airport on New Year's Day 2000, in order to bring al Qaeda's jihad into the United States for the first time.[61]

The third act of bin Laden's global plan was to take place in Aden Harbor in southern Yemen. An al Qaeda team planned to load a small boat with explosives and then ram it into an American destroyer in the harbor, the USS *Sullivan*. They miscalculated the weight of the load and their boat sank. A year later they would try again and successfully attack the USS *Cole*.

The final plot also succeeded. On Christmas Eve 1999, five terrorists hijacked Air India flight 814 in Katmandu, Nepal. The terrorists were Pakistanis from the group Harakat ul Mujahedin (HuM), long supported by bin Laden (it was a HuM camp bin Laden was visiting in Afghanistan when Clinton's cruise missiles failed to kill him). The plane refueled in Amritsar, India, then in Lahore, Pakistan, and Dubai in the United Arab Emirates before finally settling in at Kandahar on December 25 for negotiations with India on the terms for the hostages' release. The hijackers told the flight's captain, "Fly slowly, fly carefully, there is no hurry. We have to give India a millennium gift."[62] In fact, there was a bomb in 814's cargo hold that had been smuggled on in Nepal and was timed to go off at midnight on December 31, 1999.[63] The terrorists murdered one passenger, a young bridegroom. His bride was widowed on her honeymoon.

With the Kandahar airport under Taliban control, al Qaeda was able to set up an office there, as the 9/11 Commission later reported, with Osama bin Laden behind the scenes directing the negotiations and the plot.[64] According to the Indian government, the ISI, which had helped the hijackers procure weapons in Nepal, was in constant contact with them by satellite phone from its headquarters in Rawalpindi.[65] The cabal demanded the release of three Kashmiri terrorist leaders held in India: Maulana Masood Azhar (Ilyas Kashmiri's partner in the Delhi kidnappings), Sheikh Amer Omar Saeed, and Mushtaq Ahmed Zargar. India's foreign minister, Jaswant Singh, flew to Kandahar and arranged the deal.[66] After the exchange, the ISI took the three freed terrorists to Pakistan, where they participated in a fund-raising tour for a new terrorist group founded by Azhar, Jaish-e-Muhammad. Saeed would later be implicated in the murder of American journalist Daniel Pearl.

The millennium plots were history's most ambitious effort at simultaneous terror around the world: in India, Jordan, Yemen, and the United States. All the attempts proved a failure except for the hijacking in South Asia, where Pakistan's ISI played a central role. Indeed, the ISI chief at the time, Lieutenant General Mahmud Ahmad, would later be forced from office because of his close connections to the Taliban. If Osama's ambitious jihad for the end of the twentieth century was less than a resounding success, it would become a truly global endeavor in the next. Pakistan would be the epicenter yet again.

CHAPTER FOUR

OSAMA'S JIHAD

WE WERE MEETING IN a large conference room in President Pervez Musharraf's office in Islamabad. Chief Executive (as he called himself) Musharraf and his team sat on one side of the long conference table, and President Bill Clinton and his team on the other. A large picture of Jinnah hung on the wall. Every office in Pakistan has one. Clinton had just arrived from India, where he had spent March 19–25, 2000, enjoying a very warm welcome. The streets of New Delhi, Mumbai, and other cities had been crowded with millions of adoring Indians. The same had been true in Dhaka, Bangladesh. The contrast in Pakistan was striking. Security was so intense, at the insistence of the U.S. Secret Service, that the streets of the capital were completely empty. While Clinton was in India, there had been a major terrorist attack in Kashmir, a stark reminder that the threat from al Qaeda and its allies was real and serious. The Secret Service had taken extraordinary steps during the trip to protect the president.

Clinton had a huge agenda for his meeting with Musharraf, the first by a foreign head of state with the new dictator since his coup. Human rights, democracy, the future of Nawaz Sharif, nonproliferation, tensions with India, the nuclear test ban, fissile material cutoff talks, World Bank loans, and a host of other issues were vying for the top tier. But Clinton focused on one: Osama bin Laden, al Qaeda, and terrorism. It was less than a hundred days since the millennium plot had been uncovered. He pressed Musharraf to use Pakistan's influence with Kandahar on bin Laden—clearly an international outlaw, branded as such by the United Nations. Musharraf promised to cooperate with covert and secret intelligence operations but said he could not afford to alienate the Pashtuns next door; he was in a precarious position, with so many threats to Pakistan that it was impossible to press this issue now. His plate was very full. And America had little to offer him, other than the blessing of a presidential visit, which he now had in his pocket.

By March 2000 Pakistan was under virtually every type of sanction the United States could impose. No military or economic aid was flowing. Many other countries had joined in sanctions in the wake of Pakistan's nuclear tests, and some had added more after the coup. The United Nations had also imposed sanctions on the Taliban regime next door, cutting off arms sales, freezing what few assets the Taliban had, suspending flights by the national airline, Ariana, and urging all states to press Mullah Omar to hand over bin Laden. In short, the levers of sanctions had been pushed to the limit yet had failed utterly to influence either Pakistan or its ally, the Taliban. Pakistan had the bomb, sold it to others, and harbored terrorists at home and in its client Taliban state.

Clinton used all the formidable skills he had developed over the years in politics and diplomacy to persuade Musharraf to do more to destroy al Qaeda. But his hands were tied by the reality that he had nothing to offer Pakistan, thanks to Congress's reaction to Pakistan's policies of more than two decades. Musharraf replied that he could not influence Omar, noting that the Taliban leader had refused requests to come to Islamabad more than once. Clinton pressed again, knowing how much aid the ISI gave the Taliban, but to no avail. The roller-coaster U.S.-Pakistani relations were, perhaps, in their darkest moment yet. Much worse was soon to come. Clinton could only warn Musharraf that "terrorism would eventually destroy Pakistan from within if he didn't move against it."[1]

During his four hours on the ground in Islamabad, Clinton also wanted to speak directly to the Pakistani people. Intense negotiations surrounded this and every other part of the visit. The Americans did not want to turn the visit into a legitimization of an army coup and a military dictator, while Musharraf wanted to do just that. Our very capable ambassador, Bill Milam, handled the discussions with great skill, and Clinton got his chance to deliver a speech on Pakistani television.

In it the president focused on his vision for Pakistan's future. He urged the army to return to their barracks soon and allow free and early elections. Despite Pakistan's many problems and the many obstacles it faced, he strongly believed that "Pakistan can make its way through the trouble, and build a future worthy of the visions of its founders: a stable, prosperous, democratic Pakistan, secure in its borders, friendly with its neighbors, confident in its future." This was, he stressed, "as Jinnah promised, a Pakistan at peace within and at peace without."[2]

It was an extraordinary moment, indeed a unique one, in the history of America's relations with Pakistan. An American president was in Islamabad urging the generals to relinquish power and restore democracy. Since Congress had tied his hands and he made little effort to persuade it to amend the Pressler and other sanctions, Clinton's appeal to the Pakistani people was eloquent but lacked a mechanism to bring change. Its message would also prove to be short-lived. America was about to again fall in love with a man in uniform.

Pervez Musharraf would dazzle Clinton's successor, George W. Bush, and the two would return U.S.-Pakistani relations to a close partnership, now built around counterterrorism. At the same time, Musharraf took the minimal steps necessary to keep America happy: fighting al Qaeda somewhat, yet maintaining strong ties to a host of terror groups like Lashkar-e-Tayyiba (LeT) and the Afghan Taliban. He did help capture several key al Qaeda figures, often just before important meetings with American officials, but he never delivered Osama bin Laden. Furthermore, the Afghan Taliban thrived on his watch and that of his ISI director general, Ashfaq Parvez Kayani, after being driven from Afghanistan. According to former Afghan foreign minister Abdallah Abdallah, Musharraf skillfully played the American administration, throwing "dust in Bush's eyes."[3] Beneath the dust, the jihad would flourish.

MUSHARRAF'S PAKISTAN

Pervez Musharraf and I are alumni of the same prestigious staff college, the Royal College of Defence Studies, in Belgravia in the heart of London. He attended before I did, and I still recall the magnificent model of a Pakistani tank that he gave the college after his coup as a token of his fondness for the institution and its fine home, Seaford House. Schooled in the Western tradition, Musharraf was no Islamic fanatic. He enjoyed his whiskey from time to time. He even named a pet dog Whiskey. He sends out Christmas cards to friends and acquaintances (I have been a recipient). Not demonstrating any proclivity for Islamic extremism, he would become the target of the jihad, escaping assassination more than once. Moreover, under him Pakistan would see a further growth in the strength of the global Islamic jihad, of al Qaeda, and of a jidahist threat to the survival of Jinnah's Pakistan.

Musharraf was a refugee, a *mohajir*, from New Delhi. His family had fled the capital during partition. His memoirs, *In the Line of Fire*, begin with a description of the train ride from Delhi to Karachi in August 1947, when he was only four years old (the same train is depicted in A. Q. Khan's office). He writes, "It was the dawn of hope; it was the twilight of empire. There was the light of freedom: there was the darkness of genocide."[4] This refugee status made him somewhat of an outsider in the Punjabi-dominated army and, as mentioned earlier, was one of the reasons Sharif picked him for chief of army staff.

Although his father was a graduate of a prestigious Islamic center, Aligarh Muslim University, Musharraf attended elite Catholic missionary schools before entering the military academy. When his father was posted to Ankara, Turkey, as a junior diplomat, Musharraf became an admirer of the Turkish strongman, Mustafa Kemal Ataturk, who secularized the country after World War I.[5]

The all-consuming passion of Musharraf's life has been the struggle with India. He fought in the 1965 and 1971 wars. He said later he wept when Pakistan's army surrendered in Dhaka in 1971.[6] As president he would visit his old neighborhood in New Delhi.

After the venture into Kargil, the relationship between Prime Minister Sharif and his army chief turned explosive, each blaming the other for its disastrous outcome. Sharif complained that Musharraf had committed the country to a military operation with no political strategy, while Musharraf accused Sharif of pulling the rug on the operation at the behest of the United States. Sharif would subsequently chastise Musharraf for almost taking the country to the brink of nuclear Armageddon.

Late in the summer of 1999 Sharif sent his brother, Shahbaz, to Washington to discuss Kashmir as a follow-up to the Blair House summit. Shahbaz met with Assistant Secretary of State for South Asia Karl (Rick) Inderfurth and myself at the Willard Hotel. Shahbaz came with a message: Sharif was convinced Musharraf would sooner or later try to overthrow the government and take power. He was looking for the United States to make clear it opposed a return to military rule. Washington was very much opposed to a renewal of military government, as was clear from legislation requiring all U.S. assistance to end in the event of a coup. It was Sharif who took the first step, however, dismissing Musharraf from office just as he was returning from a trip to Sri Lanka aboard a Pakistani International Airways flight. Sharif ordered the plane to return to Sri Lanka and not land in Karachi. In a quick turn of the tables, Musharraf's allies in the army seized power and imprisoned Sharif. The key general in the coup was the Tenth Corps commander in Islamabad and Rawalpindi, Lieutenant General Mahmud Ahmad, who was named director general of ISI in reward for his loyalty.

The first substantive issue on Musharraf's agenda after the coup was what to do about the perpetrators of the millennium plot, especially Abu Zubaydah. The first American delegation to visit Islamabad under the new administration, led by Assistant Secretary of State Inderfurth, pressed General Mahmud Ahmad and the ISI to track down Zubaydah for his role in the plot and arrest him. The CIA believed Zubaydah was in Peshawar and operating openly for al Qaeda. According to William Milam, U.S. ambassador to Pakistan at the time, Mahmud turned Inderfurth down, claiming the ISI did not know where Zubaydah was. Instead, as Milam put it, "The ISI just turned a blind eye to his activities, even though everyone knew where he was." Zubaydah was even helping ISI recruit and vet Kashmiri militants and sending them to al Qaeda training camps in Afghanistan.[7] Milam and the CIA station chief then went to Musharraf directly, warning him that if Zubaydah was not apprehended and al Qaeda struck again, the consequences for U.S. relations with Pakistan could be devastating. Musharraf paid no heed.[8]

Back in Washington, the first six months of the Bush administration failed to produce any real changes in the bilateral relationship. The new team reviewed policy toward Islamabad and began thinking about how to get out of the Pressler sanctions trap, but nothing significant developed. All eyes were on the risk of nuclear proliferation in Pakistan rather than al Qaeda. In mid-2001 the president's national security principals met to discuss Pakistan's nuclear activities, but without coming to any decisions.[9] Meanwhile, efforts to convene a principals' meeting on the al Qaeda threat fell on deaf ears. Richard Clarke, the holdover special assistant to the president for counterterrorism issues, and I urged that a meeting be held immediately after the president's inauguration.[10] To press the case, Clarke sent National Security Adviser Condoleezza Rice a memo arguing, "We urgently need a Principals' level review of the al Qida network. We would make a major error if we underestimated the challenge al Qida poses."[11] No such meeting was held until months later, and there, too, no decisions were made.

In September 2001 Musharraf dispatched General Mahmud to Washington to try to soften the relationship by convincing his CIA counterparts and the administration that the Taliban were misunderstood. They were, he argued, simple Pashtuns and Afghan nationalists who could deliver law and order. Their extreme views on women's rights and other issues were part of their tribal culture. The United States should stop trying to isolate them and engage with them instead.

On September 9 Mahmud had lunch with the director of the CIA, George Tenet, who later wrote, "The guy was immovable when it came to the Taliban and al Qaeda. And bloodless, too." His inflexibility should have come as no surprise. When al Qaeda blew up the USS *Cole* in Aden, Yemen, on October 12, 2000, Mahmud sent a message of condolence for the loss of life but failed to offer any help to catch bin Laden.[12] Mahmud, said Tenet, reflected Musharraf's "mistrust and resentment," as well as that of the Pakistani army and elite, caused by years of sanctions and betrayals that had bedeviled their country's relationship with the United States.

On September 11, 2001, I was in the White House Situation Room when the Pentagon and the World Trade Center were attacked. We prepared an urgent message for Pakistan. The next day Mahmud was summoned to the State Department to see Deputy Secretary of State Richard Armitage. According to Musharraf's account of the meeting, Mahmud was told either Pakistan cooperated with the United States against al Qaeda or the Taliban, or it would be bombed mercilessly back into the Stone Age. Both Mahmud and Armitage deny referring to the Stone Age, although Mahmud later complained bitterly to Ambassador Wendy Chamberlin in Islamabad that Armitage had been very rude in the meeting.

Ambassador Chamberlin then met directly with Musharraf. After being pressed for an hour, he agreed to support the United States. Pakistan would allow U.S. aircraft to fly over its territory to strike targets in Afghanistan, as long as they did not fly from India; the United States could also use Pakistani airbases for emergency landings and station a few personnel at one or another base to deconflict flight operations. On the other hand, Musharraf insisted, India must have no role in the Afghan war or in the government that would follow the Taliban, and while Pakistan would assist in capturing al Qaeda operatives who fled into Pakistan, Pakistani citizens, meaning LeT and other Punjabi groups, would be off limits in any move to counter terrorism.[13]

Next Mahmud was sent to Kandahar to convince Mullah Omar that the world had changed and bin Laden was a liability. The two met alone; Mahmud ordered the rest of the Pakistani delegation to stay outside. What they said remains unknown. Mahmud later told Shuja Nawaz that he felt he could not press Omar to hand over a fellow Muslim. Even if Mahmud did try to convince Omar to do so, perhaps he failed because his heart was not in the mission. He may have actually told him to hang tough and fight.[14] Mahmud told the CIA station chief, Bob Grenier, that he found it distasteful to betray the Taliban to America when Washington had betrayed Pakistan and adhered to the Pressler Amendment.[15] Mahmud may well have proposed that the Taliban make a half-hearted show of appeasing America's anger because he did not want to abandon the course the army and ISI had been following in Afghanistan for more than a decade.

Later, some would suggest an even closer link between the ISI and the 9/11 terrorists, alleging that General Mahmud had personally facilitated the flow of funds to them in the United States before the attacks.[16] Grenier says these accusations had no basis in fact, and neither he nor anyone else raised them with Musharraf.[17] I have found no evidence to back them up.

In any event, Musharraf fired Mahmud. It was a brave decision since Mahmud had been responsible for helping Musharraf seize power in the coup. Yet Mahmud was clearly not willing to do what Musharraf felt essential: move toward the Americans. Otherwise Pakistan would be isolated as the terrorists' friend. In his memoirs, Musharraf relates that he "war-gamed" what would happen if Pakistan stayed with the Taliban, only to conclude that India would be the major beneficiary and Pakistan's nuclear arsenal would be at risk: "Our military forces would be destroyed . . . and the security of our strategic assets would be jeopardized. We did not want to lose or damage the military parity that we had achieved with India by becoming a nuclear weapons state."[18]

Musharraf put it succinctly—Pakistan's policy derived from its concerns about India. There would be no role for India in the Afghan war. Pakistan would temporarily sacrifice its terror pawns if necessary to save its nuclear arsenal: "The ultimate question that confronted me was whether it was in our national interest to destroy ourselves for the Taliban. Were they worth committing suicide over? The answer was a resounding no."[19] Years later Musharraf told me that it was an agonizing decision for him, especially as he knew many of his fellow officers would not like it.[20]

Musharraf immediately evacuated the Pakistani advisers among the Taliban in Afghanistan and cut off supplies to the Taliban army. The impact on the cohesion of the Taliban forces was devastating: they collapsed rapidly under the weight of American air power and a Northern Alliance revitalized with CIA support and money. After taking six years to build, the Islamic Emirate of Afghanistan collapsed in less than three months. The United States had intervened in the Afghan civil war and tilted the balance decisively against the Pashtuns.

Mullah Omar ordered the defeated Taliban fighters to scatter and avoid further direct confrontation with the enemy while they regrouped. Many just went home. The leadership and the hard core fled south from Kandahar into Pakistan. Most relocated in Baluchistan around the city of Quetta, where Omar himself seems to have settled. Though in exile, he began rebuilding his Taliban.[21]

Osama bin Laden and the al Qaeda core went into the Federally Administered Tribal Areas of Pakistan (FATA), a fairly lawless land, beyond the control of the central government. This was the area they knew from the mujahedin war in the 1980s and where their old connections were strongest. Meanwhile some of the Taliban connected to Pashtun warlords like Gulbudin Hekmatayar and the Haqqani family moved back into their old home turf in the eastern Afghan provinces and near the FATA. Some al Qaeda operatives like Abu Zubaydah sought refuge among allies and friends like Lashkar-e-Tayyiba in Pakistan's major urban areas, such as Karachi, Faisalabad, and even Rawalpindi.

The Pakistanis arrested a handful of Taliban officials, most notably their ambassador in Islamabad, who was turned over to the United States and sent to Guantánamo prison camp in Cuba. The substantial contingent in Quetta along the Baluchi border remained at large. Instead of rounding them up, the ISI gradually resumed relations with them. By

2003, after the United States had turned its attention to Iraq, they were being allowed to recover and rebuild. Soon the Taliban were again raising funds for operations against the U.S. and allied forces in Afghanistan.

Despite frequent protests by the new Afghan government and its pleas for U.S. pressure to get Pakistan to act, Islamabad considered it better strategy to retool the Taliban to maintain an asset in the Afghan game. To keep the Afghani officials at bay, Musharraf simply denied the Taliban had any presence in Quetta or anywhere else in Pakistan. For its part, the CIA failed to press the Pakistani security services to do more because its was focusing on al Qaeda.[22]

However, the security services did assist the CIA in attacking the al Qaeda presence in the country's major cities. First to be captured was Abu Zubaydah, found on March 28, 2002, in a safe house belonging to Lashkar-e-Tayyiba in Faisalabad.[23] The following year, on March 1, 2003, the so-called mastermind of the 9/11 attacks, Khalid Sheikh Muhammad, was caught in Rawalpindi, the home of Pakistan's army high command. By 2006, according to Musharraf's account, the Pakistanis had helped capture 670 al Qaeda operatives.[24]

All the same, the Pakistanis did not go into the al Qaeda safe havens in the FATA and other tribal areas. Those areas had never been policed by the central government, and the ISI had only limited capability to do so. In any case, such a move would only have stirred up Pashtun animosity against Musharraf's government and could provoke a tribal revolt (as it ultimately did). Yet the Bush team pressed for more. Only belatedly, in 2004, did the army make an attempt—but a half-hearted one—to move into the FATA. It suffered very high casualties, and several hundred were captured. After a desultory offensive, it arranged a peace deal with local tribal leaders.

Much earlier, on December 13, 2001, Pakistan's attention was abruptly diverted from Afghanistan by a dramatic terrorist attack in New Delhi. I was on the National Security Council staff at the White House when the news came in that five terrorists had attacked the Indian parliament. They apparently planned to murder as many of India's senior political leaders and officials as possible. Fortunately, their timing was off; both houses had just adjourned and the top leaders had left. The guards reacted promptly, killing all five of the terrorists.

It was immediately clear to me that even by the standards of modern terrorism this was an extraordinary attack. By targeting the legislature of the world's largest democracy, the terrorists were deliberately seeking to provoke India to strike back. Had they succeeded in killing, say, Prime Minister Atal Vajpayee or Congress Party leader Sonia Gandhi, the terrorists would have left India with few options but to use force against the terrorists' sponsors.

India was quick to allege connections between the ISI and the five, all Pakistani citizens and members of the ISI-supported, if not created, Jaish-e-Muhammad (JeM) terror organization. JeM was founded by Maulana Masood Azhar, the long-time terrorist freed in exchange for the release of the hostages captured by the hijackers of Indian Airlines flight 814. The money raised from Azhar's victory tour through Pakistan following his release was used to create JeM.

Indian Foreign Minister Jaswant Singh and others have made a convincing case linking JeM and ISI to the New Delhi attack.[25] A former head of ISI, Javad Ashraf Qazi, later admitted JeM was responsible, although at the time, a Pakistani spokesman suggested it was all a put-up job by India.[26]

Interestingly, Musharraf fails to mention the attack and barely touches on the ensuing crisis in his otherwise very chatty autobiography. It is as if it never happened. Musharraf privately told our ambassador in Pakistan at the time that it was a very "dirty" business but never clarified what he meant.[27] He seemed to suggest that both the ISI and its Indian counterpart, the Research and Analysis Wing (RAW), engaged in supporting terror routinely. But this begs the question. Did the ISI not inform him of the plan to attack the parliament? Or did ISI's client operate outside its control on behalf of someone else?

I asked myself then and still do: who benefited from this attack? The answer is JeM's friend and ally, Osama bin Laden's al Qaeda. In December 2001 al Qaeda was on the run, even on the ropes. U.S. and allied forces had overthrown the Taliban Islamic Emirate of Afghanistan in a lightning operation. Musharraf had switched sides, at least for the time being, reversing a decade of Pakistani support for the Taliban and promising to help Washington catch bin Laden and the rest of the fleeing al Qaeda gang. By diverting Pakistan's army to the east, to the border with

India for the next year, the parliament attack helped save al Qaeda. Was that the purpose of the attack, or only an unintended consequence?

Perhaps it was all payback for earlier cooperation between JeM and al Qaeda. Jaswant Singh argues in his memoirs that the close contacts between the hijackers, ISI, al Qaeda, and the Taliban strongly suggest the IA 814 hijacking was a "dress rehearsal" for al Qaeda's 9/11 attacks.[28] Behind the scenes, says Ahmed Rashid, bin Laden was masterminding the hijack and the plot to secure the release of JeM's founder.[29] Did JeM pay bin Laden back for his help in 1999 by diverting the Pakistani posse away from the chase in 2001? Did al Qaeda play a hand in the attack plan itself?

For the next year, until late October 2002, India and Pakistan were on the verge of war. Both mobilized and prepared for conflict. I spent three weeks with the Indian army in the summer of 2002 and can say they were ready and eager. But New Delhi held back and, with intense American and British diplomacy, war was averted. In January 2002 Musharraf gave a major speech promising an end to support for terror and banning JeM and LeT as part of the cooling-off process. But the ban was only a formality; neither organization was seriously disrupted or dismantled. Hardly touched by the crackdown, LeT was spared the most.

Musharraf's policy of selective counterterrorism, fighting only an arm of the jihadist Frankenstein when he had to and tolerating the greater parts, did not save him from the ire of the extremists. They repeatedly tried to kill him and came close on several occasions. In at least two episodes, in December 2003, it was clear the plot had included elements of his own security detail and ISI members who knew his travel plans. He has described these two attacks as very near misses.[30]

Concerned about the constant threats, Musharraf installed a new ISI director in November 2004 to replace General Ehsan ul Haq, who had succeeded General Mahmud. He gave the job to his most loyal corps commander, Ashfaq Parvez Kayani, head of the crucial Tenth Corps, which controls Rawalpindi and is an essential tool to any coup-plotter (Tenth Corps was the position General Mahmud had held in 1999 when Musharraf ousted Sharif). Kayani had been director of operations during the 2002 crisis with India. At the ISI, he led the investigation into the two most serious coup plots against Musharraf and urged some house-cleaning in the agency. On Kayani's watch, the Taliban comeback in

Afghanistan would accelerate rapidly, spurred perhaps by Kayani's decision to direct the Taliban's energy outward into Afghanistan. The ISI would encourage the resurgence by providing training, a safe haven, and even some advisers.

By then relations with India were gradually improving. Musharraf belatedly took up the dialogue with India that Sharif had started in Lahore before the Kargil conflict. In time, a back channel of discussions developed between Musharraf and India's new prime minister, Manmohan Singh. Meeting in great secrecy, their representatives hammered out ideas on how to resolve all the key issues dividing India and Pakistan, including the most important and difficult: Kashmir. By early 2007 Musharraf felt close enough to a deal to summon his corps commanders and other key generals to Rawalpindi for their endorsement of the draft package.[31]

The most anti-Indian leader since Zia was now trying to find a diplomatic solution to Pakistan's sixty-year-old dispute with its neighbor. Arguably, Musharraf had already tried other options: a limited war at Kargil, asymmetric warfare waged by backing terrorists, and nuclear blackmail. Nevertheless, he did ultimately try to find a peaceful end to the conflict. I have spoken to him about this since he left office, and he remains clear in his resolve. It is the most graphic example of the man's fundamental pragmatism.

At this point, Musharraf's domestic political position went into a tragic spiral. After a positive start, years of rigged elections, interference in the judicial process, ISI's heavy-handed repression of all dissent, and his refusal to let Benazir and Nawaz return from exile gradually undermined his popularity. Ironically, his decision to allow the operation of a free and open press hurt him. Pakistanis heard a wealth of opinion about everything he did on a growing number of twenty-four-hour television news stations (more than eighty are in operation today, some from abroad). Clashes with Islamic militants who took over the largest mosque in Islamabad in 2007 were broadcast live on television and further fed the dissatisfaction. When Musharraf ousted the chief justice of the Supreme Court in early 2007, he awoke an angry movement among the country's lawyers, which gradually strengthened and became the active face of opposition.

On November 3, 2007, Musharraf imposed martial law, in effect staging a coup against his own government. It was too late; domestic and international support for his rule was eroding rapidly. Before the end of the month, Musrarraf had no choice but to give up his uniform, as he put it, and resign from the army if he was to remain president. Kayani, his ISI chief, became the new chief of army staff. Kayani was supposed to keep Musharraf in power. Both Benazir and Nawaz were allowed to return to Pakistan. New elections in March 2008 produced one of the fairest electoral outcomes in Pakistani history, with a new government dominated by Bhutto's Pakistan Peoples Party (PPP) and her husband, Asif Ali Zardari, as president. By early August 2008 the parliament was moving to impeach Musharraf, and he resigned on August 18, 2008. Kayani had abandoned his mentor.

BUSH AND MUSH

During the 2000 U.S. presidential campaign, a reporter asked George W. Bush who the president of Pakistan was. Bush stumbled and could not recall the name—an odd beginning to what became a close relationship. Better prepared, his national security team understood the Pressler sanctions had trapped America into a losing relationship with Pakistan, which they hoped to change. The events of 9/11 gave them that opportunity.

After Musharraf resolved to help the United States against al Qaeda in mid-September 2001, the administration approached Congress to obtain sanctions relief. Probably only a catastrophe as enormous as 9/11 could have created the necessary political opening, and the Bush team was wise to grab it quickly. Sanctions were ended and aid relations reopened. Musharraf became a frequent visitor to the Bush White House and Pakistan a major recipient of American military aid. The military assistance would exceed $10 billion by 2008, when Musharraf left office. Much of it was payment for the use of facilities in Pakistan or compensation to the Pakistani army for counterterror operations. There was very little oversight of the process.

The one thing the Bush administration did not give Pakistan was what it wanted most, tariff concessions that would have allowed more Pakistani textile exports into the U.S. market. Such rights would have created thousands of jobs. Musharraf's ambassadors in Washington consistently pushed for tariff relief, but domestic politics trumped them. As one observer put it, "In this case the Carolina congressional delegation representing the U.S. textile industry overruled even alliance politics."[32]

In turn, Musharraf provided limited but crucial aid in the president's "war on terror." More senior al Qaeda operatives were arrested in Pakistan than anywhere else in the world. The Pakistani security services became the CIA's most important partner in the battle against al Qaeda. But it was also the most difficult: even as it worked against al Qaeda, the ISI continued its problematic ties to the Taliban, Lashkar-e-Tayyiba, Jaish-e-Muhammad, and other jihadi groups. Moreover, the cooperation on al Qaeda soon diminished: by 2005–06 the Pakistanis were doing far less to detain al Qaeda operatives than in their zealous efforts of 2002–03. Because of Pakistan's continued tolerance of LeT, JeM, and other anti-Indian terrorists, crises like the 2001 attack on India's parliament strained bilateral relations with Washington. Meanwhile the Bush team was eager from the outset to build a strategic partnership with India, the world's largest democracy with a rapidly growing economy and a potential balance to China's expanding role in the world, especially in Asia. The 2001–02 crises forced the Bush administration to engage in intensive diplomacy to try to prevent war in the subcontinent.

Secretary of State Colin Powell and his deputy Richard Armitage led the effort. Working closely with their British and French counterparts, they persuaded India to hold back from war and Musharraf to at least take some cosmetic steps to ban terror groups and promise to exert more control over their activities. The American and allied interventions were critical to keeping the crisis from exploding out of control. The United States stayed away from any suggestion of brokering a resolution of underlying issues such as Kashmir, calculating that those were too difficult to handle. When Musharraf and Singh began their back-channel talks, Washington was an observer, not a participant.

U.S. relations with Pakistan took another serious turn with the proliferation of Pakistani nuclear technology to countries like North Korea, Iran, and Libya and the activities of the father of the Pakistani bomb, A. Q. Khan. Khan had been an irritant since the 1980s, but as the CIA learned more and more about his behavior, U.S. concerns multiplied.

In a one-on-one meeting in New York on September 24, 2003, CIA director Tenet confronted Musharraf with evidence of planned proliferation to Libya (including the design for a bomb) via A. Q. Khan. Tenet said Khan "is betraying your country and has stolen some of your nation's most sensitive secrets."[33] It was a way out for Musharraf and the army. Decades of Pakistani help to North Korea and Iran for their nuclear programs and now for a Libyan one could all be blamed on one man.

Seizing the opening, Musharraf had Khan put under house arrest and forced to confess on Pakistani television that he had operated beyond the authority of his job. Pakistan ceased providing help to Libya, which dismantled its nuclear program. But no one was given access to Khan. Neither the CIA nor the International Atomic Energy Agency (IAEA) was allowed to question Khan about his decades of business with North Korea and Iran (and Saudi Arabia). After Musharraf resigned in 2008, Khan reappeared and began putting out his story.

Khan claims he was authorized to carry out all the nuclear technology transfers by the highest levels of the Pakistani state, starting with Zia and continuing up to and including Musharraf. He was, he averred, no rogue operation but a bureaucrat working for the government and trading nuclear secrets for technology from other states. For example, in return for nuclear help to North Korea, Pakistan gained access to Korea's medium-range missiles, which it has copied and now produces as the Ghauri missile.

The truth is that Khan was probably both: he did act under the orders of the army and the state, and he probably did operate as a loner as well. The details may never be known because the Pakistani military does not want them exposed to outside scrutiny. For the Bush administration, the fiction of a nuclear pirate helped resolve a troubling problem that might have derailed the budding rapprochement between Bush and Mush, a nickname increasingly heard in Pakistan.

An ultimately fatal threat to their romance was a dispute over democracy—which the Bush team would bring on themselves. In the wake of 9/11, the Bush administration began making the argument that the global Islamic jihad was a product of repressive authoritarian societies in the Islamic world, especially the Arab world. The police states of the Islamic world, it said, had repressed all dissent and thus pushed their critics toward extremism. These *muhkabarat* states (named after the Arab word for secret police) had been propped up for decades by American foreign policy during and after the cold war in order to maintain stability throughout this critical region, from Morocco to Indonesia.

The president first presented this analysis at West Point in June 2002, in a commencement speech calling for "the rule of law, limits on the power of the state, free speech and equal justice . . . across the Islamic world." Seven months later, on the eve of the invasion of Iraq, Bush argued that "stable and free nations do not breed the ideologies of murder." In his second inaugural address in 2005 he returned to the theme of promoting democracy and "the expansion of freedom in all the world" to curb al Qaeda and other terrorists. The new doctrine became the Freedom Agenda, and the State Department was tasked to aggressively promote it. In the Middle East that task went to the vice president's own daughter, Liz Cheney.[34]

There was much truth in the Bush analysis. Repression and dictatorship are important factors in the rise of global Islamic jihad—but they are not the sole reasons, or the leading ones. Equally significant, American administrations, both Democrat and Republican, had emphasized stability over freedom in the Islamic world so were willing to assist its mukhbarat states. As events make plain, that was certainly the case in Pakistan, where support for military dictators was remarkably bipartisan until Bill Clinton. At the same time, American support for such states certainly helped fuel intense anti-Americanism in the Islamic world.

The problem with the analysis was that Bush had little intention of pushing his friend Musharraf to endorse a freedom agenda. And Pakistanis, already profoundly mistrustful of America, saw his call for freedom as sheer hypocrisy: the Bush administration had done little to press Musharraf to allow a return to democracy after his coup. It had complained merely half-heartedly when Musharraf rigged elections in 2002 that endorsed his rule, even when those elections produced the first provincial governments dominated by Islamist parties in Pakistani history. The key provinces bordering on Afghanistan, Baluchistan, and the North-West Frontier Province both elected officials very sympathetic to the Taliban largely because of ISI help, intended to weaken the major secular political parties backing Benazir and Nawaz.

The supporters of Benazir and Nawaz pressed the United States to push Musharraf to allow their leaders to come home and compete in the political process. Musharraf would then have been forced to promise they would not be arrested for alleged past corruption, or in Sharif's case, for trying to eliminate Musharraf by forcing his plane to land outside of Pakistan. Musharraf had no intention of letting his sworn political foes back into Pakistan and received no pressure from Bush to do so. Since Benazir's PPP and Sharif's Pakistan Muslim League (PML) still dominated the political process at the grass roots level and would certainly do very well in any reasonably open elections, Musharraf could not afford to let them come home.

So, in the eyes of a growing number of Pakistanis, Bush was all for democracy except in the second largest Muslim country in the world, their homeland. There, Bush wanted to keep a military dictator in office indefinitely. Bush's ambassador in Islamabad, Ryan Crocker, told the press that "there is no dictatorship in Pakistan" and that the country was fast heading forward to "true democracy" under Musharraf.[35] The hypocrisy drove all the more Pakistanis to hate America and some to support the jihad.

When Musharraf's regime began to unravel in 2007, Bush stood by his man. Instead of calling for the rule of law and an independent judiciary, the U.S. administration urged patience and compromise. It did criticize the coup of November 2007 and the imposition of martial law, but only reluctantly. Then it came up with another idea: to try to soften the face of military rule in Pakistan through a shotgun marriage between Musharraf and Benazir.

This marriage of hated foes would bring Benazir Bhutto back to Pakistan to serve as prime minister and run domestic issues while Musharraf would remain president and control national security issues. Encouraged by the White House, Musharraf met secretly with Benazir in Dubai to see if they could reach a deal, and the two found they might be able to do so. Benazir saw a chance to return home, have the corruption charges against her and her husband lifted, and compete for power. Still, Musharraf was very reluctant and also increasingly desperate to hold onto power.

It was a foolish idea. The two could not really share power, and the issues could not be so easily separated. Musharraf was especially opposed to giving up his uniform—that is, to stop being the chief of army staff—since that was the real source of his power, while Benazir recognized she could not really run the country if he still headed the military. I said so at the time, telling the *New York Times* in October 2007, "This backroom deal is going to explode in our face. . . . Ms. Bhutto and Mr. Musharraf detest each other, and the concept that they can somehow work collaboratively is a real stretch."[36]

Nawaz Sharif opposed the deal for obvious reasons; it left him on the outside. He demanded fair treatment. If Benazir came home, so should he. The Bush team did not like that idea at all because Sharif was certain to push for Musharraf's impeachment for the 1999 coup. So the deal to broker a little democracy was actually a barrier to real democratic reform.

Benazir returned to Karachi on October 18, 2007, and that very evening was almost killed in an assassination attempt while traveling to her home amid throngs of adoring PPP followers. The assassins persisted, striking her down on December 27, 2007, while she was attending a political rally in Rawalpindi—in the same square where Liaquat Ali Khan was murdered in 1951. The elections that followed in 2008 were relatively free and fair and brought her husband, Asif Ali Zardari, to power. At his request, the United Nations was asked to launch an inquiry into the "facts and circumstances of the assassination" of Benazir Bhutto. The result is a fascinating document and analysis of Pakistan's political system and the links between the army and the jihad.

The UN investigators concluded that Benazir was probably killed by al Qaeda and its Pakistani Taliban allies, who recruited the fifteen-year-old suicide bomber. Claiming credit for the murder, an al Qaeda spokesman boasted, "We have terminated the most precious American asset" in Pakistan.[37] The UN report singles out the notorious al Qaeda operative, Ilyas Kashmiri, discussed earlier, as a possible mastermind.[38] It also notes that Benazir Bhutto represented everything the jihad hated: a woman in politics who was educated in the anti-extremist West, and who advocated a harsh crackdown on the jihadist movement in Pakistan. Furthermore, many were opposed to her because of her Shia connections, through her mother and husband.[39]

The more damaging finding of the UN inquiry, however, is that the Musharraf government did far too little to protect Benazir despite her repeated requests, then deliberately and effectively made a thorough investigation of the crime impossible. With adequate protection, the UN investigators say, "Ms. Bhutto's assassination could have been prevented." Instead, the Musharraf government denied her the normal security arrangements for any prominent person in Pakistan, even after the first attack in Karachi. The cover-up was even worse. The crime scene was immediately washed down by fire hoses to remove forensic evidence, a proper autopsy was not conducted, and "high-ranking Pakistani government authorities obstructed access to military and intelligence sources" to impede the inquiry.[40]

The investigators also concluded that the ISI played a key role in the cover-up and intimidated the Pakistani police to keep them from doing their job. The ISI may even have been quietly encouraging the assassins through former officials who had well-known contacts with the extremists. Benazir herself had alleged that former ISI officials, including former director General Hamid Gul, were plotting her demise in collusion with al Qaeda.[41] Musharraf's hand-picked ISI director, General Kayani, had just left the job in October 2007, and his successor, Nadeem Taj, would last only a year in office. If he came to be an embarrassment to the new regime, Taj may have been expendable.

Within a year, Musharraf was out of office. But according to a Transparency International report on global corruption, by then he had converted an investment of about $690,000 in army-granted farmland in Islamabad into more than $10 million in assets and has now moved into self-imposed exile in London.[42]

In sum, the United States tried to arrange a political deal to save the Musharraf regime and saw that deal blow up in its face. After eight years of dealing with Musharraf, the United States did not have Osama bin Laden or Mullah Omar captured or dead, had not slowed Pakistan's nuclear arsenal's growth, and had lost the faith of the Pakistani people by staying with a dictator for too long.

AL QAEDA ON THE RAMPAGE

The twenty-first century has opened with a global terror rampage, the handiwork of the first-ever worldwide terrorist group, al Qaeda. Within a short span of time, the group has built a large and effective network of terror cells, consisting of its own and those of its allies. For a relatively small number of fanatics with modest funding, it is a remarkable achievement. The cells have wreaked carnage from New York to Bali. Thousands have been wounded or killed, the vast majority of them Muslims. The epicenter is Pakistan. The global Islamic jihad came to maturity in Musharraf's Pakistan, where it has threatened the survival of the state itself.

This century's wave of terror dates back perhaps to a series of explosions in the cliffs facing Bamyan City, the capital of Bamyan Province in the Shia heartland of central Afghanistan. In March 2001 the Taliban systematically and deliberately destroyed two sixth-century statues of Buddha carved into the cliffs, each more than 100 feet high. The United Nations Educational, Scientific and Cultural Organization (UNESCO) had designated them world heritage sites. Osama bin Laden called them idols and had urged Mullah Omar to destroy them as a sign of Islamic piety, with a view to further radicalizing the Taliban.[43] Bin Laden visited the site to oversee their collapse personally.[44]

In April bin Laden wrote to Omar congratulating him for "success in destroying the dead, deaf and mute false gods" and urging him to now turn to "destroying the living false gods," meaning the United States. The letter was retrieved from a laptop found in Kabul after the city's liberation.[45]

By the spring of 2001 plans for the Manhattan Raid, as al Qaeda refers to 9/11, were well advanced. The key terrorists, the four pilots who would fly the hijacked jets into the targets, were in the United States. Bin Laden had even hinted to the press a year earlier that an attack in the United States was coming. When Bill Clinton visited Islamabad in March 2000, bin Laden said in an interview the jihad against—and within— America was already under way.[46]

How much bin Laden told Mullah Omar about the 9/11 plot in advance is uncertain. In his memoirs, Musharraf says Omar knew an attack was coming.[47] Omar was clearly aware of a simultaneous plot to murder Ahmad Shah Massoud, the last enemy of the Taliban still fighting in Afghanistan. Bin Laden had been personally orchestrating that plot for months, handpicking the assassins and helping them gain access to the Northern Alliance leader. On September 10, 2001, the day after Massoud was assassinated, the Taliban launched a major attack on the alliance's last stronghold in the Panjsher Valley. According to an eyewitness in the al Qaeda camp at the time, an Australian convert to Islam, Osama had told his closest advisers and Omar in August 2001 an attack on America was imminent, but many of his aides objected to the idea as too dangerous. Osama decided to go forward anyway.[48] The Taliban failed to stop him or hand him over to the United States after the attack.

The 9/11 attacks forced the United States to intervene directly in Afghanistan's civil war on the side of the Northern Alliance. This is precisely what bin Laden wanted: to re-create the struggle he had fought against the Soviet Union in the same place and with the same result, the enemy ground down in a quagmire, but now with the United States as the adversary. This was, bin Laden's son later confirmed, "my father's dream . . . to bring the Americans to Afghanistan. He would do the same thing he did to the Russians."[49] Bin Laden and Ayman Zawahiri have often gloated over their success in tricking the Americans into Afghanistan.

At first, however, the plotters were the ones off balance. The attack on Massoud did not destroy the Northern Alliance. He was replaced and the alliance rallied quickly with an influx of cash from the CIA. The story has been well told by the CIA officer first on the ground, Gary Schroen, who agreed to the assignment even though he was due to retire on September 11, 2001.[50] Backed by American and allied air power, the Taliban were no match for the coalition of Afghans and Western forces. Pakistan's defection made the fight even more one-sided.

It was probably too easy. The Bush team considered the Afghanistan mission completed and al Qaeda and the Taliban all but destroyed. Richard Haass, the Bush official who was appointed the U.S. government's coordinator for Afghanistan in October 2001, urged the administration to increase the American military presence on the ground to 30,000 men to stabilize the country and ask the North Atlantic Treaty Organization (NATO) to provide an additional 30,000. The international force would maintain order and train Afghans to take over in a few years. Bush and his national security team rejected Haass's suggestion, as well as proposals from key allies such as the United Kingdom and Turkey for the creation of a robust international security force.[51] Hence American troop strength in Afghanistan remained below 10,000 men until 2004. To make matters worse, key resources were diverted from the search for bin Laden and his gang to the war coming in Iraq. Furthermore, Pakistani attention was shifting to the December crisis with India.

By 2003 al Qaeda was en route to a comeback in the badlands of Pakistan along the Afghan border and in the large urban slums of Karachi. At the same time, bin Laden ordered his followers in Saudi Arabia to organize an insurrection against the House of Saud and rallied other jihadists to fight the American invasion in Iraq. Within a year, both Saudi

Arabia and Iraq were in flames, thanks largely to al Qaeda. It would take two years for the tide to turn against al Qaeda in both countries, thereby unleashing the longest sustained violence in the kingdom's history since its founding in the early 1900s and taking Iraq to the brink of civil war.

From Pakistan, al Qaeda launched operations against the NATO forces in Afghanistan. Most were small hit-and-run raids that caused few casualties but kept the pot boiling. Al Qaeda videotaped many of these attacks and then released them as propaganda films through a new media organization, As Sahab Foundation for Islamic Media Publication (As Sahab means "from the clouds" over the Hindu Kush). Between 2004 and 2009, it put out eighty-nine such videos about al Qaeda operations in Afghanistan. Most were taken in the eastern provinces, close to the Waziristan base of the Haqqani family across the border in Pakistan. More than half of all the videos depict attacks in Paktiya Province, long the Haqqani and bin Laden stronghold.[52]

Al Qaeda also assisted the Taliban as it regrouped in Pakistan. In conversations with journalists, Taliban fighters have remarked that scores of al Qaeda "Arabs" helped them learn the techniques of insurgency in the years between 2003 and 2008. They were especially important in teaching the Taliban how to make bombs, including the improvised explosive devices that would be their most effective means of killing NATO soldiers.

Among the al Qaeda members recruited to train the Taliban was Muhammad Ilyas Kashmiri, the Pakistani trained by the ISI in the 1990s to fight India and decorated by Musharraf himself for his valor in Kashmir. Kashmiri broke with the ISI in 2002 over the decision to help America in the "war on terror" and brought his considerable skills into the al Qaeda camp. He was probably involved in the attempts to assassinate Musharraf in 2004.[53]

However, al Qaeda's help to the Afghan Taliban was secondary to that of Pakistan. Interviews in 2010 with former and active Taliban commanders indicate that in 2004–06 the ISI was actively encouraging a Taliban revival and assisting their war effort after two years of training Taliban on a large scale in Quetta and other locations.[54] This was when Kayani took over the ISI. Some ISI camps had 2,000–4,000 recruits at a time, and one commander estimated that 80 percent of his fighters had attended such a camp. Several said ISI officers were members of the

Quetta shura and even participated in Taliban attacks inside Pakistan. In 2008 British Special Air Service commandos identified a dead Taliban leader as a Pakistani officer.[55]

Afghanistan's Karzai government complained to Washington and London about the ISI, but without success. Hamid Karzai told Bush that a Taliban spokesman captured in Afghanistan in January 2007 said Mullah Omar was living openly in Quetta.[56] It was an extraordinary act of duplicity by Pakistan, but Washington did not call Musharraf on it.

The turmoil in Afghanistan then spread into Pakistan itself as a bewildering number of Pakistani Pashtun and Punjabi groups began proclaiming themselves jihadist freedom fighters in sympathy with the Afghan Taliban, and sometimes with al Qaeda. At first, these groups showed little cooperation, and the Pakistani army tried to manipulate and control them. This proved harder and harder to do—much to Musharraf's embarrassment when extremists took over the so-called Red Mosque, or Lal Masjid, in Islamabad in 2007 and used it to arrest "prostitutes" from the streets of the capital. Several women who were picked up and held hostage were from China, which created a diplomatic problem with Pakistan's critical ally.

After weeks of delay, the army finally stormed Lal Masjid in July 2007, killing hundreds and wounding thousands more. A symbol of jihadist Pakistan, the mosque had been a prime recruiting post during the war against the Soviet Union and for the Taliban in the 1990s. Thousands of male and female students attended its madrassas. Al Qaeda lauded its resistance to Musharraf, and after it was stormed by the army, Zawahiri used the occasion to declare jihad against Musharraf, calling for his murder and bidding the army to rise up.

By the end of Musharraf's era, the various new Pakistani jihadist groups had coalesced into what was being called the Pakistani Taliban. Though they lacked a single leader or a single hierarchy, they were increasingly supportive of al Qaeda. In effect, al Qaeda now had a Pakistani partner in which to embed itself, a force multiplier with which to threaten the survival of Jinnah's vision of a moderate Pakistan. In December 2007 this alliance would kill Benazir Bhutto.

Al Qaeda also continued to build ties to Lashkar-e-Tayyiba and other anti-Indian terror groups, which had nominally been banned in 2002 but in fact functioned openly. LeT was renamed Jamaat ud Dawa (JuD).

Hafez Saeed remained in charge, now building camps and training facilities all over the country. The largest, outside Lahore at Muridke, covers several hundred acres, with schools and dormitories for thousands of students, a garment factory, an iron foundry, and a massive mosque. By 2008 a Pakistani intelligence source told the *New York Times* that JuD/ LeT has an active membership of 150,000 in Pakistan.[57]

Unlike the Pakistani Taliban, who recruit primarily from Pashtuns (although increasingly from Punjabis as well), LeT is primarily a Punjabi group. Thus it recruits from the same families and neighborhoods as the Pakistani army and ISI. As one Pakistani general told me: it is a family affair. Therefore it is hard to distinguish official ISI support for LeT from informal connections. A good number of LeT camps lie adjacent to army bases. Retired army officers, especially from elite units like the Special Services Group (SSG), help train LeT fighters. Some elements of LeT would turn against the Musharraf government and may well have assisted in at least one plot against his life. But in the Musharraf days on the whole, LeT and the ISI remained partners under General Kayani's watch.

These complex syndicates of terror are not under al Qaeda's control or direction, nor are all of its parts committed to bin Laden's jihadist vision of a global struggle. The Afghan Taliban, for example, are much more focused on freeing Afghanistan of foreign forces, and LeT on re-creating a Mughal empire in South Asia. But they are working together on the operational level more and more. Individuals like Kashmiri can go from one group to another and cooperate on specific missions. However, all share the same target lists—Crusaders, Jews, and Hindus—also the same list as that of the global Islamic jihad.

During the Musharraf era, al Qaeda used Pakistan to mount its most important raids into the West, a highly successful one being the London bombings of July 7, 2005. Four British citizens, three of whom were of Pakistani descent, blew themselves up on British mass-transit vehicles. Three blasts occurred in underground trains within fifty seconds of each other, shortly before nine in the morning, just at rush hour. A fourth hit a two-decker bus an hour later. Fifty-eight people were killed and more than seven hundred wounded. Two weeks later, four more terrorists tried to repeat the attack, but their bombs failed to go off.

Al Qaeda claimed credit for the London attack, described by Zawahiri as a "slap in the face of the arrogant British Crusaders." A videotape to the authorities contained a martyrdom message from one of the four terrorists, Mohammad Siddiq Khan. In a later message, Zawahiri reiterated the raid was payback for "more than 100 years of Crusader British aggression against the Islamic nation." Al Qaeda also issued a second martyr video by another one of the terrorists.[58]

The two terrorists who appeared in the videos broadcast by As Sahab, Siddiq and Shehzad Tanweer, had trained in LeT camps before carrying out their deadly attacks.[59] It was graphic evidence of the multiple connections between terror groups that al Qaeda was developing. The British security services successfully prevented more than a dozen other al Qaeda plots, all of which tried to use the 800,000 British citizens of Pakistani origin as foot soldiers in the global jihad. Although the vast majority of these citizens are loyal to their new country, a small minority has become a fifth column in the United Kingdom.

Al Qaeda and bin Laden had even bigger plans for the fifth anniversary of 9/11 in 2006, again involving British Pakistani citizens. About twenty jihadis were to simultaneously blow up, over the North Atlantic, jumbo jets en route to airports in North America. Six of the terrorists had already recorded their martyrdom videos and had developed a bomb that could be brought aboard an aircraft hidden in soft drinks, which when mixed together would create an explosion on board the jet. They had selected flights to Chicago, New York, San Francisco, Montreal, and Toronto for the event.

A key player in the 2006 plot was a dual British and Pakistani citizen named Rashid Rauf, who is married to the daughter of JeM founder Maulana Masood Azhar, discussed in preceding chapters. Rauf shuttled back and forth between the terrorists in London and Pakistan, where he received directions on how to proceed from an Egyptian al Qaeda operative close to Zawahiri. The British foiled the plot, and he was arrested in Pakistan. But in December 2007 Rauf escaped from jail, in circumstances that strongly suggested an inside job. There is also evidence that part of the funding for the 2006 plot came from LeT.[60]

The jihadist sanctuaries in Pakistan have been linked to scores of other plots since 9/11. For example, Pakistan is where Amir Azizi was operating and was killed in December 2005. He was the Moroccan behind the March 11, 2003, attack on Madrid's subway system, which killed or wounded more than 2,000 people.[61] More such attacks continued to come from Pakistan after Bush and Mush were gone.

Osama bin Laden's dream, or nightmare, of a global jihad has come true, with most of the carnage occurring after he fled into Pakistan in late 2001. Since then he has been in hiding. Most sources still put him in Pakistan, although some say he is in Afghanistan and Iran. In truth, very few know. His voice is heard from time to time promising more terror, but the largest manhunt in human history has so far failed to find him.

CHAPTER FIVE

GLOBAL JIHAD

ONCE MORE A MEETING with Pakistani officials was being held at the Willard Hotel near the White House, now at the end of July 2008. This one was between Senator Barack Obama, the soon-to-be presidential candidate, and the new prime minister of Pakistan, Syed Yousaf Raza Gillani. The conference room was arranged with two large chairs facing each other at an angle and four smaller chairs off to the sides for aides. Gillani brought with him the Pakistani ambassador to the United States, Husain Haqqani, and his information minister, Sherry Rehman. I knew them both and think of them as friends. I was with one of Obama's traveling aides, Mark Limpert. As the campaign's team chief for South Asia, my job was to brief the senator in advance of the meeting and then take notes for the record.

This was, in effect, Obama's first official interaction with the Pakistani government, with which he is now trying to disrupt, dismantle, and defeat al Qaeda. Obama was not yet president and could not assume he would be, so he had to speak as a senator, although he was clearly more than that already. His interest in Pakistan related in part to his work on the Kerry-Lugar-Obama legislation that the Democrats had introduced in the Senate in 2008 and that was designed to bring constancy and consistency to U.S.-Pakistani relations and end the cycle of romance and divorce repeating itself for the past fifty years or more. The bill promised to triple economic aid to Pakistan to $1.5 billion a year and maintain that level for ten years, regardless of political changes in Pakistan or the bilateral relationship. It had a special democracy bonus, which mandated an automatic additional $1 billion in aid each year if the president could certify to Congress that Pakistan had a democratically elected government in office. I had worked with Senator Kerry's staff to draft the bill. Unlike Bill Clinton and many of his other predecessors at the negotiating table, Obama had something to offer and wanted Gillani's reaction.

Obama began by noting that Pakistan is an important country by every measure. The second largest Muslim country in the world. A nuclear power. A great friend of the United States for many years. He welcomed the return of democracy to Pakistan and explained that he had been urging the Bush administration for over a year to do more to restore democracy there. The Kerry-Lugar-Obama bill would be a visible and serious way for America to help.

The senator then turned to the legacy of terrorism bestowed on Pakistan's new government, explaining he understood how difficult the challenge was. If al Qaeda succeeded in staging a mass-casualty attack on America from Pakistan, the impact on their relations would be enormous. Therefore it was crucial to work together to ensure that such an assault did not occur. The safe haven al Qaeda and its allies had developed in Pakistan must be shut down. This would be among his highest priorities if he was elected to the presidency in November 2008.

The prime minister laid out just how difficult the problem had become inside Pakistan but stressed that the new government was determined to act. He had instructed Chief of Army Staff Ashfaq Parvez Kayani (former director general of the Inter-Services Intelligence Directorate [ISI]) to work closely with the Americans on fighting terrorism and militancy. The army faced daunting terrain and complex tribal issues in the Federally Administered Tribal Areas (FATA), but Pakistan was now bent on doing whatever was necessary to fight extremism, he said.

Obama also brought up India and the need to find a path to better relations between India and Pakistan. The tensions between the two were fueling an arms race that neither could afford but that hurt Pakistan most. The security of Pakistan's nuclear arsenal was another concern.

The two men spoke for almost an hour. A new chapter in the saga of Pakistani-American embraces had begun.

MUMBAI EXPLODES

After Obama was elected, but before his inauguration, an incident in South Asia presented the first national security challenge of his presidency—the multiple attacks in Mumbai, India, on November 26–29, 2008. Ten terrorists of the Pakistan-based Lashkar-e-Tayyiba (LeT) organization had perpetrated one of the most significant acts of international terrorism since 9/11. Not only did they put a city of 14 million people under siege, but they also captured the attention of the global media for sixty hours, fulfilling the first objective of any such attack: to terrorize one's target audiences.

The attack was meticulously planned and the terrorists well trained and equipped. It severely disrupted a budding rapprochement between India and Pakistan, probably one of its major goals, and highlighted the emergence of LeT as a major player in the global Islamic jihadist movement. Indeed, the targets of the killers—Indians, Westerners (including Americans), Israelis, and Jews—are also the prey of the global Islamic jihad and al Qaeda.

In July 2009 the lone survivor of the terrorist team, Mohammad Ajmal Amir Qasab, surprised prosecutors in his Mumbai trial by confessing in open court that he and his nine comrades had been recruited by LeT; had been trained at LeT camps in Pakistan on commando tactics; had been equipped by LeT with AK-56 automatic assault rifles (the Chinese version of the Russian AK-47), hand grenades, global positioning systems (GPS), cell phones, and other equipment; and were dispatched by senior members of the LeT from Karachi, Pakistan, in a small boat with orders to hijack an Indian boat at sea to take them into Mumbai. There, the group split into four teams and attacked their prearranged targets: the city's central train station, a hospital, two famous five-star hotels frequented by Western visitors as well as the cream of Indian society, a Jewish residential complex visited by Israelis, and a famous restaurant also known for attracting foreigners. The terrorists set small bombs behind the targets to add to the confusion and terror after they had fired indiscriminately into crowds at the various sites.[1]

Throughout the siege, the terrorists stayed in touch with their LeT masters back in Pakistan by phone. The Indian authorities have released the chilling transcripts of their calls, showing the masterminds guiding and encouraging the killers, even ordering them to kill specific hostages.

Qasab identified the leader of the operation as a senior LeT official, Zaki Rehman Lakhvi, who oversaw Qasab's own training and was actually present when the team left Karachi. In preparation, a group of LeT members completed three months of intense exercises with small arms, whereupon Qasab was selected for more specialized training for the attack itself, which included studying videos and photos of the targets on a laptop computer. The team then waited another three months while the LeT leadership determined the best timing for the attack.

Qasab's account is by and large consistent with other evidence India has presented since November 2008. Of course, Lashkar-e-Tayyiba, which is formally banned in Pakistan but operates relatively freely, has denied any role in the attack, while its senior officials claim to have no knowledge of the attackers. Thus the LeT's motives in Mumbai must be gleaned from the circumstances surrounding the attack rather than from the masterminds directly. Who ordered the assault is not known, but whoever it was obviously had powerful political leverage in Pakistan and powerful protectors.

The targets, as just mentioned, certainly match those of the global Islamic jihadist movement, led symbolically, at least, by bin Laden and al Qaeda. Bin Laden and his deputy, Ayman Zawahiri, have long urged the Islamic community to wage jihad against Muslim oppressors such as the Crusader-Zionist-Hindu alliance. The timing is also significant. In the fall of 2008 India and Pakistan's tense relationship was finally showing signs of easing after a post-partition history of three major wars and several smaller campaigns—and nuclear testing on both sides. In February 1999 then Indian prime minister Atal Behari Vajpayee and his Pakistani counterpart, Nawaz Sharif, met in Lahore to look for ways to defuse tensions. They specifically set up a back channel for quiet negotiations on the most difficult issue dividing the two, namely Kashmir. As Sharif has described it, the goal was to end their arms race and resolve their underlying differences.[2]

The process begun in Lahore then moved forward in bits and pieces, with some major setbacks along the way. The Kargil War in the summer of 1999, initiated by the Pakistani army leader and future dictator Pervez Musharraf, halted it altogether for some time. Musharraf had opposed the Lahore process, actually snubbing the Indian prime minister by not showing up for the events planned in honor of his unprecedented trip. Instead, the next spring Musharraf ordered the Pakistani army to take positions inside Indian-controlled territory across the Line of Control (LOC) in Kashmir near the town of Kargil, a move that sparked a limited war between India and Pakistan in mid-1999. The LeT, an enthusiastic supporter of the Kargil venture, was very critical of Sharif when he ordered the army to withdraw back behind the LOC.

The process was further damaged by the December 13, 2001, terrorist attack on India's parliament, which led to the mobilization of more than a million soldiers along the border and the threat of war again. This terror attack came after Musharraf had taken power in a coup.

Ironically, Musharraf would in time become the principal agent of the peace process. After trying limited war, nuclear blackmail, and terror, Musharraf finally settled on the back channel, which by 2008 achieved significant progress with the new Indian prime minister, Manmohan Singh. It even survived other major acts of terror such as the attack on Mumbai's subway and train system in July 2006, which killed more than 200 (fewer died in 2008). The details of the back channel talks have been covered in depth by Steve Coll, and none of the parties have denied the accuracy of his report.[3] Musharraf himself has confirmed the story.[4]

The back channel did not settle all the issues dividing the two sides, but it did produce an understanding that a deal would involve two key ideas. First, the LOC would become an international border with only minor, mutually agreed-upon adjustment. Second, the border would be a soft one; that is, it would permit maximum movement of Kashmiris between the two states. Local issues such as tourism and the environment would be handled by the local governments of Pakistani Azad Kashmir and Indian Jammu and Kashmir. India would claim victory in the LOC's final status, Pakistan in its irrelevance.

With the collapse of Musharraf's political position in 2007–08, the back-channel talks stalled. The Indian government became leery that Musharraf could deliver, rightly noting that he had done very little to prepare the Pakistani people and army for a deal. But the process regained some traction when Benazir Bhutto's widowed husband, Asif Ali Zardari, came to power and showed public signs of dramatically altering Pakistan's posture on terrorism, nuclear strategy, and India. In a number of press interviews, Zardari vowed that the Pakistani army and the ISI had for years been breeding terrorist groups like LeT, that they had been playing a double game of appearing to fight terror while actually sponsoring it, and that terrorism was a cancer that might destroy Pakistan.

In the summer of 2008 Zardari declared India was not Pakistan's inevitable enemy and proposed, in a striking reversal of Islamabad's strategy, that Pakistan should adopt a policy of "no first use" of nuclear weapons. At the same time, his administration took some small but important steps to open trade across the LOC in Kashmir for the first time in decades and to expand transportation links between India and Pakistan. Many in Pakistan, particularly in the army and the jihadist camp, were appalled at Zardari's statements and decried these small but important confidence-building steps.

It is reasonable to assume, therefore, that one of LeT's key targets in Mumbai, if not the key target, was this peace process itself. The organization succeeded, at least for some time, in stopping it. Singh was forced by the horror of Mumbai to suspend the dialogue. Almost certainly, those dark forces in Pakistan that sent the LeT team to Mumbai had intended that outcome, if not an all-out war with India.

Perhaps the most shocking element of the Mumbai attack was the role played by an American, David Coleman Headley, of Pakistani descent. Headley pleaded guilty in March 2010 to conspiracy to commit murder on the basis of his role in the Mumbai attack. Headley was born Daood Sayed Gilani in Washington, D.C., in 1960. He got into trouble with the law as a youth and was arrested on drug charges. His half-brother is a spokesman for Prime Minister Gillani's office. In 2002, according to his guilty plea, he joined Lashkar-e-Tayyiba on a visit to Pakistan. Over the next three years he traveled to Pakistan five times for training in weapons handling, surveillance, and other terrorist skills.[5] In 2005 LeT told him to change his name to David Headley so that he could travel more easily in India without attracting attention on his American passport.

Beginning in 2005, Headley was told to travel from the United States to India and conduct surveillance for the Mumbai attacks. He made five such trips between 2005 and 2008, each time stopping in Pakistan on the way back to obtain further instructions from LeT and to report his surveillance results. On visiting each of the targets, he recorded their locations with GPS and carefully studied the surrounding security. By the very nature of the task, he became one of the plot's masterminds. He had a co-conspirator in Chicago, Tahawwur Hussain Rana, a Canadian citizen, who helped devise a cover story that Headley worked for a travel agency. Rana also traveled to Mumbai and stayed in the Taj Hotel to help with the reconnaissance mission.

The Headley-Rana activities underscore the meticulous planning that lay behind the Mumbai attack. After his confession and sentencing to life in prison, Headley was interviewed by the Indians. According to information leaked in the Indian press, he confessed to them that the ISI was also deeply involved in the plot, providing naval commando training and the boat the terrorists used. The transcript of the Indian interrogation shows that the ISI gave Headley $25,000 to set up his travel office in Mumbai, provided him with special intelligence training, tasked him to scout an Indian nuclear facility for a possible attack, and was fully aware of all the targets selected for the Mumbai attack including the Jewish Chabad House where six American Jews were murdered. These accusations remain unproven but raise the most profound and disturbing questions about the army's role in Mumbai, as discussed later in this chapter.

By the beginning of 2009, Pakistan's new civilian government under Zardari and Gillani faced not just the consequences of Mumbai but also a growing Taliban insurgency inside the country. The various factions, both in the Pashtun belt in FATA and North-West Frontier Province and in the Punjabi heartland, were coalescing and seizing control of territory to set up mini-emirates. The most dangerous of these lay in the Swat Valley just north of Islamabad, but the problem went far beyond Swat.

Reluctantly and belatedly, Zardari directed General Kayani to take on the Taliban militants. The Taliban, backed by al Qaeda, struck back, sending suicide bombers across Pakistan, even into the very heart of the Pakistani Pentagon in Rawalpindi. The battle became a national struggle between the various Taliban factions and the army, working closely with the ISI. The army "cleaned" areas such as the Swat Valley, but whether it could "hold and build" local institutions to keep the Taliban from coming back was very unclear.[6]

In 2009 the war escalated. According to the Pakistani Institute for Peace Studies, nearly 25,000 Pakistanis were killed or injured in militancy-related violence (in Afghanistan the number was 8, 800). Although two-thirds of the violence occurred in the FATA and North-West Frontier Province, major violence wracked every Pakistani city from Kashmir to Karachi.[7] The army also lost hundreds of soldiers, and thousands more were wounded. The ISI alone lost more than seventy officers in the carnage.[8] Yet the Taliban forces grew in strength even in the midst of the army's offensives. By 2010 the Pashtuns had an estimated 50,000 armed jihadists in the frontier zones.[9]

Public attitudes shifted as a result. No longer in denial, many Pakistanis had now come to see the jihadists as a serious threat to their lives and to the survival of their country, although anti-Americanism still ran high.[10] By mid-2009 the Taliban were being denounced in several segments of society. This made it politically easier for the army and the government to fight the militants.

But some groups were off-limits. For the most part, the Afghan Taliban remained immune from action. Although a few senior leaders were caught in January 2010, no major sustained crackdown followed, and the Quetta shura continued to operate. Lashkar-e-Tayyiba also continued to operate above the law despite intense pressure from Washington and New Delhi to bring the masterminds of Mumbai to justice and break up the organization. As one Pakistani general told me in 2010, that would be like attacking part of the Punjabi family and was not about to happen. Indeed, the Pakistani army and LeT recruit in the very same villages and towns in Punjab.

OBAMA TAKES CHARGE

Few, if any, presidents have inherited so many problems from their predecessor as Barack Hussein Obama: two wars, al Qaeda, and a range of other international problems, all of which paled next to the collapsing global financial system and domestic economy in recession and headed, it seemed, for depression. Moreover, the first foreign policy challenge of his presidency—the Mumbai attack—occurred even before he was inaugurated.

Although Obama was careful to respect the "one president at a time" rule, he had to condemn the attack. He also called Prime Minister Singh to convey his regret at the terrible loss of life in India and to praise India's restraint. I prepared Obama's points for the call. Singh said it was a "ray of sanity" in the midst of terror, which he said originated in Karachi. He had told Zardari, he added, that Pakistan must take action. For Obama, it was a taste of the challenges awaiting him. In truth, they amounted to a disaster in both Afghanistan and Pakistan.

A war in Afghanistan that should have ended in 2003 or 2004 with the defeat of al Qaeda and the Taliban had been under-resourced and neglected. As a consequence, both al Qaeda and the Taliban under Mullah Omar staged remarkable comebacks, perhaps among the most remarkable in modern history. Al Qaeda found new sanctuary in Pakistan and in eastern Afghanistan, developed new capabilities in Iraq and Saudi Arabia, and became the world's first truly global terrorist group. The Afghan Taliban had gone from being in the "dustbin of history," as former Secretary of Defense Donald Rumsfeld had mistakenly prophesied, to posing a deadly threat to the North Atlantic Treaty Organization (NATO) forces in command of the mission in Afghanistan in 2006.

Across the border in Pakistan, the situation was even more dangerous and dire. The country with the world's fastest-growing nuclear arsenal was enmeshed in a virtual civil war, with a bewildering array of militant groups becoming more and more violent. And while the jihadist Frankenstein was threatening the survival of Jinnah's state, Pakistan was also hosting the Quetta shura and the Taliban senior leadership. In fact, Pakistan controls the supply lines for both sides in the war. The Taliban depend on their safe havens in Pakistan to refit and resupply; NATO depends on Karachi for more than 80 percent of the supplies it needs in Afghanistan. Pakistan also remains in a tense confrontation with India; another Mumbai could easily lead to war, and that one could go nuclear.

These were among the key conclusions I drew when the president asked me to chair a strategic review of policy toward Afghanistan and Pakistan in January 2009. I brought into the White House two brilliant aides to help draft and prepare the report. One was a colleague from my NATO days who had worked on Afghanistan from that vantage point for years. The other was an expert on Pakistan from the U.S. Central Intelligence Agency (CIA) whom I had also known for years. We had many other smart people from across the government helping, of course, but it was those two who did almost all the drafting.

My cochairs for the interagency working group asked to coordinate the report and get input from across the U.S. government were Under Secretary of Defense for Policy Michelle Flournoy and Special Representative for Afghanistan and Pakistan, Ambassador Richard Holbrooke. A third key player in the process was the commander in chief (CINC) for

Central Command, which actually runs the war in Afghanistan, General David Petraeus.

The first step was to meet with the Afghans and Pakistanis. Their countries were the ones we were studying and trying to help. Both governments sent teams headed by their foreign ministers to Washington for discussions, first bilaterally and then trilaterally. I chaired those sessions in the Old Executive Office Building next to the White House. We met for a week in a restored nineteenth-century office originally used by the secretary of war. Surrounded by murals and photographs of an earlier era in American history, the Afghans and Pakistanis provided their critical insights into the situation and their ideas on what to do next. Both sides had brought their intelligence chiefs along—Director General Ahmad Shuja Pasha of the ISI and his Afghan counterpart, Amarullah Salih—so their respective services could help us arrive at the facts. Despite occasional controversy, we agreed more than we disagreed.

Once the cochairs and I had agreed on the main elements of the review, it underwent an exhaustive examination by the Deputies Committee of the National Security Council (NSC) chaired by Tom Donilon and then the principals, including National Security Adviser General Jim Jones, Secretary of State Hillary Clinton, Secretary of Defense Bob Gates, Director of National Intelligence Dennis Blair, and Director Leon Panetta of the CIA. Vice President Joe Biden and White House Chief of Staff Rahm Emanuel were also deeply involved in the process.

Not everyone agreed on every point, which is as it should be. These are tough issues, and opinions on them should vary. In the end, a clear majority agreed with the conclusions in the report, and I submitted it to the president on Air Force One for his consideration and comment. He met with his team several times to hear all points of view. On March 27, 2009, he addressed the nation from the Old Executive Office Building and laid out his new strategy. A few days later, he left for Europe to present it to our NATO allies in Strasburg, France, at a summit held to celebrate the alliance's sixtieth anniversary.

The day the president laid out the strategy to the American people, the White House asked me to appear on the PBS-syndicated *Charlie Rose Show,* a nationally respected talk show. Asked how I evaluated the threat from al Qaeda after having been in government for sixty days versus how

I had seen it when I wrote my book *The Search for al Qaeda,* I said the threat was more dangerous than I had suspected. Charlie Rose seemed taken aback and asked if it was really that serious. My answer was similar to the president's remarks of that morning: the most dangerous place in the world for America was the border badlands between Pakistan and Afghanistan, where al Qaeda and its allies were planning (and still are planning) to attack America.

In his address, the president also laid out his goal in Afghanistan and Pakistan: to disrupt, dismantle, and defeat al Qaeda and destroy its sanctuaries. To do so meant helping to stabilize both states, supplying resources for that effort as appropriate and mobilizing broad international support for it. Both Afghanistan and Pakistan endorsed the president's new approach, and the NATO allies and other troop-contributing countries in the International Security Assistance Force in Afghanistan also supported it. Back home, Obama received unusually strong bipartisan support from Congress.

From the beginning of the review process, President Obama had told me he intended to revisit the issue periodically, particularly the key assumptions and the data, to ensure America was not on autopilot in South Asia. In this he was clearly affected by memories of the Vietnam War, during which President Lyndon Johnson stubbornly stuck with a policy long after it no longer suited the challenge on the ground. There are enormous differences between the Vietnam War of the 1960s and 1970s and the challenge of the current conflict in Afghanistan. For one, the Viet Cong never attacked New York and Washington. But the president is right to constantly rethink assumptions and review progress.

In the fall of 2009 he held a series of meetings with NSC principals to look again at the status of the conflict. His new commander on the ground in Afghanistan, General Stanley McChrystal, had delivered a devastatingly accurate and bleak appraisal of the war based on his survey. An already difficult situation looked even worse. Bob Woodward, the dean of Washington's journalist community, received a leaked copy of the report and the *Washington Post* published it. The review of McChrystal's report led the president to order 30,000 more troops to Afghanistan. He reaffirmed that the goal of the U.S. effort was to defeat al Qaeda. He expressed the intention to try to begin drawing down foreign forces in

Afghanistan by mid-2011 but with the caveat that much would depend on the situation on the ground.

By the end of 2010, the war in Afghanistan will be the longest in American history, with U.S. involvement there and in Pakistan expanding. Pressure is building on al Qaeda and its allies. But the global jihad is also growing and developing in many ways. The threat of global jihad remains as dire as I told Charlie Rose.

JIHAD UNLEASHED

The National Counter Terrorism Center uses the term "global Islamic jihad" to designate the movement begun by Abdallah Azzam and Osama bin Laden three decades ago, the core belief of which is that America is the fundamental enemy of Islam and can only be defeated by violence and terror. The vast majority of the world's one and a half billion Muslims reject this ideology as the antithesis of their religion. Every year the Brookings Institution holds a conference in Doha, Qatar, called the U.S. Islamic World Forum to encourage dialogue between America and the Islamic world, or ummah. The government of the Emirate of Qatar is a generous sponsor of and host to the forum. I am a convener of the U.S. Islamic World Forum. Every year we also commission polls in the Islamic world on key issues, and every year they consistently show that majorities of Muslims around the world have a negative view of al Qaeda and its ideology. Indeed, the trend is against the terrorists.

But a small minority is all that it takes to commit mayhem and carnage. Al Qaeda's call for global jihad does resonate with a minority in the ummah. In the past year or so, it has even found resonance with Muslims who are American citizens. David Headley is an early recruit; others have followed.

The global Islamic jihad now has at least five faces or components that are important to understand if one is to appreciate its strength and its threat: (1) al Qaeda's old core senior leadership in Pakistan; (2) al Qaeda's allies in Pakistan and Afghanistan; (3) its franchises in the other parts of the ummah; (4) its cells and sympathizers in the Islamic diaspora in Europe, North America, Australia, and elsewhere; and (5) the idea of global jihad itself. Each play a vital role in perpetuating jihad.

At the center of the old core are Osama bin Laden and Ayman Zawahiri, known in the intelligence community as High-Value Targets Number One and Number Two. They are the subjects of the largest manhunt in human history, with large bounties on their heads. Both give occasional statements to al Qaeda's media arm, As Sahab, or to other outlets such as Qatar's Al Jazeera news network. The voices of these two are occasionally heard on tape and a photograph released, but in truth, no one knows where they are. The best bet is Pakistan.

Surrounding them are the remains of the old cadre, now replenished with new recruits coming to join the caravan. Many of the old veterans have been captured and arrested by the ISI or the CIA. Some have been detained by Jordanian, Saudi, Egyptian, and other intelligence services. Some have died in firefights or in drone attacks in Pakistan, Yemen, or Iraq. These losses have disrupted al Qaeda's operations, but not enough to prevent it from still launching attacks on the United States and its allies abroad.

By one count, the person in the number three position has been killed or captured ten times since 2001, or at least ten times in that period the intelligence community has said it has done so. However, al Qaeda has never identified a number three in its chain of command, so it is difficult to be certain. In any case, those killed and captured have been significant operatives, but they have been quickly replaced by al Qaeda's bench and by new recruits.[11]

One important operative eliminated in May 2010 is Mustafa Uthman abu Yazid, most likely killed by a drone. Declared a martyr following his death, Yazid was an Egyptian who had worked with Zawahiri since the early 1980s. Both were part of the plot to assassinate Egyptian president Anwar Sadat in 1981. They formed a militant group called Egyptian Islamic Jihad in the mid-1980s and merged it into al Qaeda in 1998. Yazid was directly involved in the 9/11 plot and helped raise funds for al Qaeda. As Stuart Levey, under secretary of the treasury for intelligence and terrorism, has noted, "More than anyone else, Yazid possessed links to the deep-pocketed donors in the Arabian Peninsula who have historically formed the backbone of al Qaeda's financial support network."[12] Yazid created al Qaeda's Pakistan Bureau to forge alliances with groups like LeT and individuals like Ilyas Kashmiri.[13] At the time of his death, he was also al Qaeda's operational commander, or amir, for Afghanistan. In that capacity, he participated with the senior leadership in many plots.

To illustrate how deadly that core remains today, in early 2009 an American citizen of Afghan descent named Najibullah Zazi traveled to Pakistan intending to join the Afghan Taliban and fight the NATO forces. The Taliban recognized his value and instead persuaded him to work for al Qaeda. He was then trained in bomb-making by Rashid Rauf, the British citizen who had been the key link between al Qaeda and the August 2006 plot to blow up multiple airliners over the Atlantic on the fifth anniversary of 9/11. Yazid was involved in Zazi's training and indoctrination as well. Another Afghan American and a Bosnian American joined the plot.

The three planned to blow themselves up on New York City subway trains on the first Monday after the 9/11 anniversary in 2009. They were to strike at 9 a.m., the peak of rush hour, and attack the trains as they moved through Times Square, Grand Central, and the Port Authority stations. The FBI arrested them before they could execute their plan, and Zazi has since pleaded guilty.

A plot that did succeed struck at the CIA in Afghanistan. In 2009 a Jordanian using the nom de guerre Abu Dujannah al Khorasani, an Arabic name for Afghanistan and neighboring regions, persuaded the Jordanian General Intelligence Department (GID) to take him on as a double agent against al Qaeda. Under his real name, Human Khalil Abu Mulal al Balawi, he had previously been a propaganda specialist for al Qaeda's franchise in Iraq and its dead leader Abu Musaib al Zarqawi, so his story seemed plausible. Khorasani went from Jordan to Pakistan and on his arrival contacted the GID, claiming to have information on the location of Zawahiri.

The bait was dangled. But Khorsani was actually a triple agent, still working for al Qaeda. On December 30, 2009, he blew himself up once inside the CIA's base in Khost, Afghanistan, killing seven CIA officers and the Jordanian intelligence specialist who was his case officer. The Jordanian was given a state funeral in Amman, which the king and queen attended to indicate the importance Jordan attaches to fighting al Qaeda. It was the second worst day ever in CIA history. In honor of the dead officers, memorial stars have been added to the wall of the main entrance to agency headquarters, alongside those for its 120 other fallen heroes.

Al Qaeda took credit for the attack, dedicating it to the memory of a leader of the Pakistani Taliban, Beitullah Mehsud, also said to have been killed in a CIA drone attack. Mehsud's successor appeared in a videotape of Khorasani in which Khorasani described his plans to bomb the CIA base and revealed that the GID officer had told him it was the GID that killed Abdallah Azzam in Peshawar in 1989 (see chapter 2). The Haqqani network of the Afghan Taliban also later said it, too, had a hand in the attack by helping Khorasani gain access to his target.

The operation demonstrated the intricate connections between al Qaeda and its allies in Pakistan and Afghanistan. This is the second face of al Qaeda and the global jihad today, the syndicate of terror in Pakistan that works with al Qaeda and shares at least in part its ideology and focuses on the same target list as al Qaeda.

The many groups that make up the Pakistani syndicate of terror have neither a single leader nor a single goal. Some are truly dedicated to global jihad, others to more local grievances. Over time, the Taliban militants in Pakistan have developed closer ties to al Qaeda, while the Afghan Taliban appear to be holding to Afghan-centered goals. Some groups in Pakistan like Lashkar-e-Janghvi and Sipah-e-Sohaba are more focused on sectarian warfare against Shia and Christians than on other goals. Lashkar-e-Tayyiba pursues it own dream of restoring the Mughal Caliphate even as it seeks to kill Crusaders and Jews in Mumbai, Pune, and other Indian cities.

Yet these various groups often cooperate closely on specific missions, as in the Khorasani operation, and overall the trend is toward greater cohesion and support among network components in the interest of global jihad. Secretary of Defense Bob Gates told Congress recently that "the Taliban and al Qaeda have become symbiotic, each benefiting from the success and mythology of the other."[14] Or as Pakistan's interior minister Rehman Malik has put it, "They—Lashkar-e-Janghvi, the Sipah-e-Sohaba Pakistan, and Jaish-e-Mohammad—are allies of the Taliban and al Qaeda" and do indeed pursue many of the same goals.[15]

For its part, al Qaeda makes no secret that its dream is to overthrow the Pakistani state and replace it with an Islamic emirate. In a 130-page treatise titled *The Morning and the Lamp: A Treatise Regarding the Claim That the Pakistani Constitution Is Islamic,* Zawahiri attacks Jinnah's vision of Pakistan for its non-Islamic character. One of al Qaeda's common themes is that Zardari, Gillani, and Kayani must be killed and the army must revolt and set up a proper jihadist state. In a June 2009 audio message, bin Laden accused Zardari of being no better than or different from Musharraf, and of being rewarded with more than his usual 10 percent for helping America, a clever reference to Zardari's nickname for corruption, Mr. Ten Percent. Bin Laden called on the Pakistani army to rebel and kill Zardari and Kayani, both stooges of an American-Jewish-Indian plot. The prospects for this are assessed in chapter 6.

An excellent example of how the network implements its terror plots can be seen in David Headley's activities after Mumbai. LeT first sent him back to India to look at more targets, including Israeli targets such as the offices of El Al airlines. But it also outsourced him to al Qaeda for another mission in Europe, which sent him to Denmark. His task was to conduct a surveillance of the offices of a Danish newspaper that had published cartoons mocking the prophet Muhammad. The cartoons had aroused a storm of anger in the Islamic world, where depictions of the prophet in any form are rare and ones making fun of him are scandalous. Al Qaeda had promised to make Denmark pay and had already attacked the Danish embassy in Pakistan. Headley made at least two trips to Denmark for a closer look at the newspaper's offices in Copenhagen. He even got inside using his travel-agent cover.

He reported back to al Qaeda in FATA, meeting with Ilyas Kashmiri, the former ISI asset who had defected to al Qaeda. Kashmiri told Headley that al Qaeda's "elders" were very interested in this project and that an al Qaeda cell already up and running in Europe was ready to conduct the operation. It would be a mini-Mumbai attack, seizing the newspaper's offices, then beheading all the captured employees with maximum publicity, and finally fighting to the death against the police and Danish security forces. According to his guilty plea, Headley had a meeting with the al Qaeda team in Europe.[16]

In October 2009 Headley was arrested at Chicago's O'Hare Airport before he could get on a flight back to Pakistan for a final planning session with Kashmiri. Danish authorities speculate that the plan was set to be executed in December 2009, when Copenhagen was to host the Climate Change Summit, and dozens of world leaders would have been in the city along with media outlets from around the world. His admissions provide extraordinary insight into the workings of the LeT and al Qaeda. What they fail to shed light on is the relationship between LeT and ISI.

Copenhagen was not the first LeT objective outside South Asia. In 2003 it recruited a French Muslim convert from the Caribbean island of Guadeloupe to carry out attacks in Australia. Willie Brigitte lived in one of the Muslim slums, or *banlieue,* of Paris and participated in the al Qaeda plot to kill Ahmad Shah Massoud in 2001 by helping the killers procure Belgian passports. In 2002 Brigitte traveled to Pakistan and spent four months in a LeT training camp before returning to Paris. The next year, at LeT direction, he moved to Sydney, where he got married and began keeping watch on a number of targets, including a nuclear reactor, military facilities, and an American intelligence base. Acting on a tip from French intelligence, the Australians arrested him and deported him to France, where he was convicted in 2007 of planning a mass-casualty terror attack.[17]

This network of terror is a handy force multiplier for al Qaeda. It can use LeT capabilities or Taliban capabilities to strike where its own may be limited. It can also draw on the 800,000-strong Pakistani diaspora in the United Kingdom and large communities in many European countries and throughout the Persian Gulf for both recruits and funds. About three-quarters of the Pakistanis in Britain are Kashmiris and thus even more susceptible to jihadist recruitment, given the violence and alienation in their homeland. As the network becomes progressively radicalized and adopts more of a global agenda, it grows more and more dangerous.

This became apparent on May 1, 2010, in Manhattan's Times Square. A naturalized American citizen of Pakistani origin, Faisal Shahzad, had constructed a primitive car bomb and left it on a street corner in the middle of New York's most congested area. Fortunately, an alert hot dog vendor saw smoke coming from the car and contacted the police. Shahzad was arrested two days later as he tried to catch a flight to Dubai. He has pleaded guilty to the attempted attack and said the Pakistani Taliban trained him in building a bomb over a period of five weeks in December and January 2010.[18] In a video made during his training but only released months after his failed attack, Shahzad said he was inspired to take on the mission after reading Abdallah Azzam's *In Defense of Muslim Lands.*[19]

Shahzad, like Headley, came from a relatively well-off family in Pakistan. Shahzad's father was an air vice marshal in the Pakistani air force, a very senior position. The network of terror is obviously attracting some of the best and brightest in the country and the diaspora.

The third element of today's global jihad, the al Qaeda franchises in the rest of the Islamic world, proclaim loyalty to Osama bin Laden and are considered to be responsible for operations in their part of the ummah. The local franchise gets broad strategic direction from al Qaeda's core but is almost fully autonomous in terms of operational activity and planning. Each also creates its own propaganda outlet. For example, al Qaeda in the Islamic Maghreb, or North Africa, has a propaganda outlet called al Andalus, the Arabic word for Spain and a symbol of al Qaeda's call for the return of Spain to Muslim rule.

The franchises vary tremendously in their strength and the danger they pose. Al Qaeda in Mesopotamia was the most effective franchise for a time and almost pushed Iraq into a full-scale civil war. Its strength has eroded seriously since 2007, largely because of its own mistakes. Al Qaeda in the Arabian Peninsula (AQAP) is the product of two previously independent franchises in Saudi Arabia and Yemen. The Saudis effectively suppressed the Saudi faction, so its remnants sought protection and safe haven in Yemen.

AQAP was responsible for the attempt to blow up Northwest Airlines flight 253 en route from Amsterdam to Detroit on Christmas Day 2009. The Nigerian suicide bomber failed to detonate his bomb as the plane was descending over southern Ontario and a Dutch tourist alertly raised the alarm. The attempt showed that al Qaeda remains fixated on the airline industry as a prime target.

AQAP is also closely aligned with a Yemeni American, Anwar al Awlaki, who is a popular Islamic lecturer. Three of the 9/11 terrorists attended his lectures in the United States before the attack. Awlaki was also in touch with Nidal Malik Hassan, the Palestinian American who killed thirteen and wounded thirty of his fellow soldiers at Fort Hood, Texas, on November 5, 2009, and with Umar Farouk Abdulmutallab, the Nigerian Christmas bomber.[20]

The Yemeni franchise was the first to stage attacks on the United States directly. Others have had plans to do so in the past but never turned them into action. The al Qaeda franchise in Southeast Asia, for example, plotted with Khalid Sheikh Muhammad to launch a second wave of attacks on the United States after 9/11, focusing on the West Coast. Indonesian recruits would have provided the terrorists, but Muhammad's capture aborted the plot. The targets were never finalized but included Los Angeles, Seattle, and possibly Vancouver.

Each franchise has its own dynamics. The Iraq franchise did not exist before the American invasion in 2003, matured rapidly into a major threat, and then declined almost as rapidly after it alienated the Arab Sunni community it claimed to represent by engaging in a bloodbath of violence. It did reach outside of Iraq to strike in Turkey and Jordan but since 2007 has been largely confined to Iraq.[21]

The Muslim diaspora in North America, Europe, and Australia contains jihadist cells that occasionally have contact with al Qaeda's core or that simply espouse its ideology and narrative. This is the fourth face of moden global jihad. Many of the jihadists in these cells are self-radicalized; that is, they become angry and extreme on their own, without being proselytized by al Qaeda or another terrorist group.

Many find the Internet an aid to self-radicalization as it enables them to contact extremist groups and obtain information on their websites or participate in jihadist chat rooms. Al Qaeda is well aware of this phenomenon and is quick to respond to nascent recruits. It may encourage a potential recruit to attend a mosque where one can meet other extremists.

The diaspora's disaffected Muslims first came to light in Europe when cells there attacked the subway systems in Madrid and London. They became the role models for al Qaeda's penetration of the European Islamic community. Al Qaeda only needs a handful of recruits to create devastation. Thus even if only 1 percent of the nonviolent communities in the United Kingdom or France are al Qaeda or Lashkar-e-Tayyiba sympathizers and potential terrorists, this amounts to a massive counterterrorism challenge.

Until recently it seemed the United States was devoid of the cell problem. As David Headley and Faisal Shahzad make clear, that is no longer true. In 2009 alone, at least ten jihadi cells and plots were reportedly uncovered inside the United States, an unprecedented number.[22] Terrorists who are American citizens with American passports are obviously harder to detect and are eagerly used by al Qaeda and its allies both to attack America and to facilitate terror outside the United States, as Headley dramatically demonstrated in India and Denmark.

Perhaps most important, the global Islamic jihad is a powerful idea: an ideology and a narrative. It is rooted in works of the 1960s by Sayid

Qutb and others. Abdallah Azzam provided the crucial input in the 1980s. Since then jihad thinking has been articulated by dozens of jihadist writers and in recent As Sahab videos and audio messages since 9/11. Al Qaeda still places Azzam at the center of jihadi ideology. When its operatives attacked a Japanese oil tanker in the Strait of Hormuz in July 2010, it claimed the attack in the name of the Abdallah Azzam brigades of the jihad.[23]

At the core of jihadism is the belief that Islam's real enemy today is the United States, which must be answered with violence against every American. An apocalyptic ideology, it predicts America can be weakened and finally defeated by means of bleeding wars in Iraq and Afghanistan and perhaps elsewhere like Yemen, just as the Soviet Union was worn down by the jihad in Afghanistan. Al Qaeda, the Taliban, and others constantly draw this analogy. For bin Laden and Zawahiri and many others, the mujahedin's fight was the formative experience of their lives and has shaped their worldviews ever since.

Although the idea of global jihad is shunned by most Muslims, a few groups are strongly drawn to it, as illustrated by the LeT attack on Mumbai and the Pakistani Taliban connection to the Times Square plot. These groups have adopted the set of targets pursued by al Qaeda. And some have now given jihad an American face, as is evident in the lectures of Anwar al Awlaki. Born in New Mexico, he can articulate the narrative in a way that connects better than ever before with the small extremist community inside North America. Today's inescapable reality is that the jihad is a truly global phenomenon. Pakistan remains the epicenter, and the future of the movement will depend more on Pakistan than on any other country. What could happen next in Pakistan could be a nightmare.

CHAPTER SIX

THINKING THE UNTHINKABLE
Implications of a Jihadist State in Pakistan

THE MAP ROOM ON the ground floor of the White House is often used by the president or first lady for sensitive meetings. It provides considerable privacy mixed with the intimacy of being inside one of the mansion's most historic rooms. President Franklin Delano Roosevelt used the room to follow the course of World War II, filling it with maps to monitor the struggle with fascism. The name endures, and one of FDR's maps remains in the room. In early May 1998, First Lady Hillary Clinton met with Benazir Bhutto in the map room for a private conversation and tea. At the first lady's request, I joined her.

It was only supposed to be a twenty-minute meeting, but it went on for almost an hour and half. Benazir did almost all the talking. General Zia ul-Haq, she began, had imprisoned her and persecuted her family in the 1980s. Now it was Prime Minister Nawaz Sharif persecuting her family and concocting false allegations of corruption against her and her husband, Asif Ali Zardari. She became emotional when recounting the details of Zardari's arrest on charges of killing her brother. He was suffering from several ailments in jail and urgently needed help. Sharif, she said, was using "draconian measures to squeeze, strangle and to suffocate us."[1]

Mrs. Clinton was diplomatically careful not to intervene in the internal affairs of Pakistan, but she did express her sympathy. As always, Benazir could be very impressive—"mesmerizing and hypnotic," wrote one of the *Washington Post* editors she called on that day.

The most riveting part of Benazir's discussion was her analysis of the rise of extremism in Pakistan, which she blamed on Zia for starting and the Inter-Services Intelligence Directorate (ISI) for nourishing. Extremists like Osama bin Laden were determined to kill her, and they had powerful protection in the ISI. As she would say often over the next decade, "I am what the terrorists most fear, a female, political leader fighting to bring modernity to Pakistan."[2]

By December 2007 Benazir Bhutto was convinced that al Qaeda could even be "marching on Islamabad in two to four years."[3] Her words are now close to being borne out. The growing strength of the network of terror in Pakistan raises the serious possibility (but not yet the probability) of a jihadist takeover of the country. A jihadist victory in Pakistan, meaning the takeover of the nation by a militant faction of the army or a militant Sunni Islamic movement led by the Taliban, would have devastating consequences, not only for Pakistan but also for South Asia, the broader Middle East, Europe, China, and the United States—in a word, for the entire planet. American options for dealing with such a state would be limited and costly.

Although this nightmare scenario is, thankfully, neither imminent nor inevitable, it is a real possibility that needs to be assessed. I endeavor to do so in this chapter, mainly by considering what such a state might look like, the implications of its creation, and two terrifying yet possible scenarios: a repeat of 9/11 and of Mumbai, both staged from Pakistan.

INSIDE PAKISTAN

A jihadist Pakistan would emerge through some combination of violence and intimidation. The simplest way would be another military coup led by a general who shares the worldview of Zia ul-Haq. A new Zia would move Pakistan toward accommodating the Taliban and al Qaeda instead of fighting them. Are there new Zias in the Pakistan military? Almost certainly yes, and undoubtedly in the army. Supporters clearly exist among former army officers like Hamid Gul, once head of the ISI. It is impossible for an outsider to determine how many officers are sympathetic to the jihadists, as most such individuals probably try hard not to let their views be known. What is evident is that many army recruits are from the same towns and villages in the Punjab as militant groups like Lashkar-e-Tayyiba (LeT). Former ambassador to Pakistan Bill Milam has noted that "the pool of young men the army recruits, Punjabi or Pashtun, are increasingly from the same socio/economic pool as the jihadi organizations recruit from. Jawans looking through their gun sights at their brothers or cousins may be more reluctant to shoot than at present."[4]

Officers with the most power and influence are the corps commanders, especially those in the key Punjab region. Some of them may well have connections with LeT. As recently as September 2009, the organization's founder and current leader, Hafez Saeed, was the featured guest at an iftar (evening meal when Muslims break the fast during Ramadan) hosted by a corps commander in Rawalpindi.[5]

A jihadist state could also emerge following an insurgent victory, but that would be much more difficult to achieve. The Taliban would need to reach out from the Pashtun tribal areas west of the Indus and gain significantly more support in the Punjabi heartland. Actually, there is good evidence this is happening. A coalescence of Islamist groups like the Pakistani Taliban and Lashkar-e-Tayyiba also seems to be developing, although differences remain. Taliban leaders might tap into the deep anger among landless peasants in the Punjab and Sindh to mobilize a mass movement similar, in some respects, to that which toppled the shah of Iran in 1978. I. A. Rehman, director of the Human Rights Commission of Pakistan, has noted that "the Taliban have people across Punjab and these terrorists are not fighting for small stakes. They are fighting to capture Pakistan, including Punjab."[6]

Suppose, for purposes of analysis, that a new Zia comes to power. The current civilian government would be swept out of office, and the army would accommodate the new Islamist leadership. A new government might be composed of representatives of the Pakistani Taliban movement, LeT, and possibly the Islamist political parties that have contested power in the past, such as the Jamaat-i-Islam. It might draw some support from breakaway elements of the two mainstream political parties, the Pakistan Muslim League (PML) and Pakistan Peoples Party (PPP), hoping to "moderate" the movement and to "tame" the Taliban.

However it came about, a new Islamic Emirate of Pakistan would move to purge the armed forces of potential countercoup plotters. It might also set up a new military force to act as a counterweight to the regular army, as the Revolutionary Guards do in Iran. The ISI would undergo special cleansing to eliminate threats to the regime.

A Pakistani emirate would welcome Osama bin Laden and Ayman Zawahiri from their hiding places of the past decade, although they would presumably keep a low profile to avoid being attacked by outside security services. Free of any significant constraints on their activities from the Pakistani authorities, al Qaeda, LeT, and a host of other terrorist groups would have much more room to operate, particularly if they have access to Pakistan's embassies from which to stage terrorist operations abroad.

As it purged the army of any dissident voices, the new regime would also take control of the nuclear arsenal. In response, many outside Pakistan would probably call on America to "secure" Pakistan's nuclear weapons, but since no outsider knows where most of them are located, such efforts would be in vain and pose a hollow threat to the regime. Even if force were used to capture some of the weapons, the emirate would retain most of its arsenal as well as the capacity to build more. It certainly would make their production an even higher priority than it already is.

At the same time, the Islamists would face significant internal opposition. Some in the officer corps would undoubtedly resist and perhaps try to stage a countercoup. The fifth of Pakistanis who are Shia would be extremely uneasy with a Sunni militant regime as well, and communal violence would probably intensify, causing turbulence in Islamabad's ties with Tehran. The muhajir Muttahida Qaumi Movement (MQM) in the Sindh's large cities—especially Pakistan's largest, Karachi—would probably resist and have to be defeated by force. The MQM party has the broad support of Muslims who fled India in 1947 and has become a secular and liberal force in recent years, but its appeal is limited to a minority and its leadership resides in London.

Large numbers of educated and Westernized Pakistanis would flee the emirate. Few ports would be willing to take them, however, as security services around the world would insist on tight visa controls. And in potential countries of refuge such as the United Kingdom or Norway, both of which already have large Pakistani émigré populations, opposition to taking in more Muslims would be strong.

Within Pakistan's borders, harsh Islamic penalties imposed for social reasons, land reforms, and the flight of many with capital would damage an already weak economy and discourage foreign investment and loans. The emirate would probably blame its economic difficulties on the outside world and use outside pressure as an excuse for even more draconian crackdowns inside.

REGIONAL IMPLICATIONS: AN ANGRY NEIGHBORHOOD

An Islamic takeover in Pakistan would make the North Atlantic Treaty Organization's (NATO's) current mission in Afghanistan virtually untenable. A jihadist Pakistan would be even more of a safe haven for the Afghan Taliban than now, and those in the Pashtun belt across the south and east would only grow stronger. Across the border, the commander of the faithful, Mullah Muhammad Omar, and his Quetta shura would take over at least southern and eastern Afghanistan. The non-Pashtun majority in Afghanistan—Tajiks, Uzbeks, and Shia—would certainly resist and seek NATO help but would be facing militants from both inside and outside the country.

Logistics are difficult in landlocked Afghanistan. Once the jihadists in Islamabad cut NATO off from Karachi, the point of arrival for more than half of its supplies, the alliance would have to depend on supply routes via Iran or the Central Asian states and Russia. Whether the infrastructure of those routes could even deliver sufficient supplies for the size of the foreign forces in Afghanistan now is uncertain. In any case, such an arrangement would make NATO's International Security Assistance Force in Afghanistan and the accompanying U.S. forces entirely dependent on the goodwill of Tehran or Moscow for their survival.

Pakistan's relations with Iran would probably deteriorate. Shia jihadist Iran and Sunni jihadist Pakistan would become enemies, each competing for influence on Afghanistan's battlefields. Both would also be tempted to meddle with each other's minorities. Baluchistan, already unstable on both sides of the border, would become another battlefield. As the Islamic Emirate of Pakistan suppressed its Shia minority, Tehran would be powerless to do anything but watch. Iran would certainly accelerate its nuclear weapons development program but would be years, if not decades, behind its neighbor.

A jihadist Pakistan would be particularly bad news for India, which would have little choice but to build up both its nuclear and conventional forces. Any chance for a peace agreement in Kashmir would be dead, and the new militant regime in Pakistan would increase support for the insurgency. The impact on the 150 million Muslims throughout the rest of India would be a great concern for the Indian security services, already stretched thin with the Naxalite-Maoist threat.

A major mass-casualty attack like the one on Mumbai in November 2008 could spark a war. India has shown remarkable restraint over the past decade in its response to provocations by the Pakistani army or militants in Pakistan, or both, such as the Kargil War in 1999, the attack on the Indian parliament in 2001, and the Mumbai raid. Of course, India lacks any good military option for retaliation that would avoid the risk of a nuclear Armageddon. But pressed hard enough, New Delhi may need to make some response.

The impact on Israel would also be huge. Pakistan has a long history of support for the Palestinian cause, but mostly at the rhetorical level. An Islamic state would become a more practical supporter of groups like Hamas, providing them with money and arms. Pakistani embassies could become safe havens for terrorists having an eye on Zionist as well as Crusader targets. Needless to say, Pakistan could also provide the bomb.

A militant Islamic state in Pakistan—the second largest Muslim country in the world and the only one with a nuclear arsenal—would have a massive ripple effect across the Muslim world, more profound that any previous Islamic takeover in relatively remote or marginal states such as Afghanistan, Sudan, Somalia, or Gaza. All of the existing regimes in the Islamic world would be alarmed at the prospect of Pakistani jihadists arriving in search of new refuges and training facilities. As a Sunni state, a jihadist Pakistan would also have far more resonance in the Muslim world than Shia Iran as Sunnis compose some 90 percent of Muslims.

The global Islamic jihad, spearheaded by al Qaeda, would proclaim that the liberation of the ummah was at hand. Pakistani diaspora communities in the United Kingdom and the Gulf States would see the risk of terrorism rise. Meanwhile the United States would have to take steps to curb the travel of citizens of Pakistani origin to their homeland.

Pakistan's military ally, China, would also be threatened by a Taliban state that might provide assistance to the Muslim minority in the west of China. The Chinese might try to use their arms-supply relationship to modulate Pakistani support for Islamic unrest, but it would be difficult to bargain with the regime in Islamabad.

Bangladesh, the other Muslim state in the subcontinent, would also feel the impact of a jihadist victory in its former partner. Islamic militancy has been on the rise in Bangladesh recently and might receive a substantial boost from an Islamic Emirate of Pakistan.

AMERICAN OPTIONS: BAD AND WORSE

A jihadist Pakistan would be the most serious threat the United States has faced since the end of the cold war. Aligned with al Qaeda and armed with nuclear weapons, such a state would be a nightmare, and all U.S. options for dealing with it would be bad.

Engagement would be almost impossible: the new leadership in Islamabad would have no faith and little interest in any dialogue with the Crusaders and Zionists. If the United States retained an embassy in Pakistan, it would be at constant risk of attack, if not from the regime itself, then from jihadi allies like al Qaeda. Islamabad would almost certainly demand an immediate and complete withdrawal of all foreign forces from neighboring Afghanistan and consider any counterterrorist operations on its territory cause for retaliation elsewhere against American interests. In an international forum, Pakistan would outdo Iran as the leader of the anti-Israel cause and would increase demands on India to turn over all of Kashmir.

U.S. options to change the regime by means of a coup or by assisting dissidents such as the MQM would be limited. The United States is so unpopular in Pakistan today that its endorsement of a politician is the kiss of death. Benazir Bhutto learned this lesson the hard way. The Pakistani Shia community would look to Iran, not America, for help.

Military options would be unappealing at best and counterproductive at worst. The United States would discover the same difficult choices Indian leaders have looked at for a decade. Striking terrorist training camps achieves virtually nothing since they can easily and cheaply be rebuilt. The risk of collateral damage—real or invented—probably creates more terrorists than a raid kills. Even a successful operation creates new martyrs for the terrorists' propaganda machines.

A naval blockade to coerce behavioral change would mean imposing humanitarian suffering on the greater population. It would also prompt terrorist reprisals in and outside of South Asia. Combined with air strikes, it might impose real costs on the jihadist regime but is unlikely to topple it and would be hard to sustain.

Invasion in the Iraq manner of 2003 would require a land base nearby. Landlocked Afghanistan would be a risky base from which to work; Iran is a nonstarter. India might be prepared in some extreme scenario to attack with American forces, but that would rally every Pakistani to the extremists' cause.

The Pakistanis would, of course, use their nuclear weapons to defend themselves. While they do not have delivery systems capable of reaching America, they could certainly destroy cities in Afghanistan, India, and, if smuggled out ahead of time by terrorists, perhaps in the United States. A win in such a conflict would be Pyrrhic indeed.

The hardest problem would arise the day after. What would the United States do with a country twice the size of California and burdened with enormous poverty, 50 percent illiteracy, and intense hatred by its populace for all that America stands for, especially after U.S. soldiers have fought a nuclear war to occupy it?

The worst thing about the military option is that the United States might be forced to pursue it if al Qaeda launched another 9/11-magnitude attack on the country from a jihadist Pakistan. A jihadist Pakistan would be highly unlikely to turn over bin Laden for justice after a new "Manhattan raid," and sanctions would be a very unsatisfying response to the killing of thousands of Americans, or even worse, if al Qaeda had acquired one of Pakistan's bombs.

In short, a jihadist, nuclear-armed Pakistan is a scenario that must be avoided at all costs. That means working with the Pakistan of today to try to improve its very spotty record on terrorism and proliferation. While many (on both sides of the U.S.-Pakistan dialogue) are pessimistic that cooperation/engagement between America and Pakistan will succeed, there is every reason to try, given the alternatives.

9/11 REDUX?

On May 1, 2010, a naturalized American citizen, Faisal Shahzad, set a car bomb in New York City's Times Square. According to one analysis, had the bomb exploded, the blast would have reached speeds of 12,000 to 14,000 feet per second. Anyone standing within 1,400 feet of the explosion—a distance of about five city blocks—could have been hit by shrapnel or flying shards of glass.[7] Broadway would have looked like Tel Aviv or Baghdad.

Shahzad was born in Pakistan, has pleaded guilty to the crime, and confirmed that the Pakistani Taliban taught him how to make the bomb.

The Taliban has claimed responsibility for his attempted attack. As mentioned earlier, Shahzad's father is a retired air vice marshal in the Pakistani air force, a very senior rank, but his sympathies for the jihad are unknown. Less than a month after Shahzad's failed plot, the *Washington Post* reported the U.S. military was examining options for a military response to a mass-casualty attack in America that might be staged or supported by jihadists in Pakistan.[8]

As in the scenario of a jihadist Pakistan, U.S. options here would be bad and worse. A purely diplomatic response—summoning the Pakistani leadership to Washington for intense discussions to achieve renewed assurances that Pakistan would "do more" to fight terror—would be necessary but probably insufficient to satisfy domestic calls for action. The White House would come under immense political pressure to take unilateral action.

A limited military excursion into the Federally Administered Tribal Areas (FATA), perhaps into North Waziristan, would be a doable mission, but one fraught with risks. It would clearly violate Pakistani sovereignty and provoke an outcry in Islamabad, even if the Zardari government tacitly accepted it as a political necessity. It would have to be a temporary mission unless the United States wanted to take long-term responsibility for administering some Pakistani territory and expand the already huge burden of the Afghan war and constant friction with Islamabad. Yet a short in-and-out mission is not likely to have any lasting impact on Taliban or al Qaeda capabilities. In any case, few of America's NATO and International Security Assistance Force (ISAF) allies in Afghanistan would want to join in a new mission across the border, and it would be difficult to persuade the United Nations to legitimize any such endeavor.

A larger military mission to purge all of Pakistan of terrorism would require an invasion. As noted earlier, it would be a mission from hell. No president should contemplate this outcome as anything but a nightmare scenario. There are no good choices.

MUMBAI REDUX?

When the city of Mumbai was attacked in November 2008 by a Lashkar-e-Tayyiba cell based in Karachi, India responded by suspending dialogue with Pakistan. It is important to note what India did not do then, as well as what it did do. Although the Indian air forces were put on increased alert during and immediately after the attacks, there was no general mobilization of the Indian army, as occurred after the December 2001 attack on the parliament, nor were any military strikes made on LeT targets in Pakistan. With its air force and advance ground units also on alert, Pakistan apparently feared some type of military retaliation, but as India's air force commander later disclosed, his units "exercised restraint and did not give Pakistan any excuse for a misadventure."[9]

India's restraint is especially significant in light of an intense effort by its military after 2001 to develop the capability to strike Pakistan quickly in the wake of another terrorist incident like the Mumbai massacre without requiring a lengthy national military mobilization. Announced in 2004, this new doctrine for rapid response to a provocation is called the Cold Start approach. Since its initiation, Indian forces have trained and conducted exercises to carry out a limited military attack on Pakistan.[10]

India's main opposition party, the Bharatiya Janata Party (BJP), applied intense pressure for just such a response amid the run-up to the national elections in May 2009. Instead, Prime Minister Manmohan Singh and the rest of the ruling Congress Party leadership chose a political course, which BJP leaders repeatedly criticized as being too weak and likely to incite further terror. The argument did not resonate with Indian voters, however, as they kept the Congress Party in office and gave it an even larger mandate than it had won previously. Yet it was clear that another mass-casualty attack like Mumbai would put intense political pressure on New Delhi to opt for a firmer response, even military action.

It is safe to assume India's national security bureaucracy is exploring its options should another terrorist attack be mounted from Pakistan. The principal constraint on New Delhi is, of course, Pakistan's nuclear capability. Any military response, no matter how limited, carries the risk of escalating to a larger military engagement and possibly even a nuclear crisis. The Kargil War in 1999 threatened to move in precisely that direction had India chosen to expand the battlefield to other points on the Indian-Pakistani frontier. The 2002 standoff between the two countries after the attack on the parliament demonstrated again that each country's growing nuclear arsenal put severe constraints on its conventional military options in a crisis.

Should other attacks like Mumbai or the one on India's parliament occur in the next few years, Indian patience may well wear thin. The nuclear constraint and danger of a major war may not be enough to dissuade Singh or his successors from a violent response to a made-in-Pakistan attack. India has several options here. One would be to implement Cold Start by ordering a series of air strikes and limited ground operations targeting LeT and other training camps and installations inside Pakistani-controlled Kashmir or in Pakistan proper, perhaps around the LeT's Lahore strongholds.

Another option would be a naval blockade or quarantine of Karachi, especially if the city is again a launch pad for terror. Karachi is Pakistan's only major port and outlet to the sea. Oil imports crucial to the country's economy come through Karachi. Any disruption in those supplies would have an immediate impact on Pakistan and force Islamabad to either bow to India's demands or fight back. India considered such a blockade during the 1999 Kargil War, and its navy prepared to impose one as a means to increase the pressure on Pakistan. Fortunately, New Delhi decided not to do so.[11]

Karachi, as already noted, is also the port of entry for the bulk of supplies going to U.S. and NATO forces in Afghanistan, including ammunition, food, and water. A blockade would therefore have immediate consequences for the war effort in Afghanistan. India might see NATO's vulnerability as added leverage, however, since the alliance would put pressure on Pakistan to comply with Indian demands and thus have the blockade lifted.

A third option would be for India to flex its own nuclear muscle. It could test a bomb (or bombs) again in the Thar Desert bordering Pakistan. Such a test would be a symbolic way to signal Pakistan that terror must be curbed or it could lead to devastation. The 1998 tests were widely approved in India and won the then BJP government tremendous popular support early in its administration. Nuclear testing could also be used preemptively in conjunction with a Cold Start attack or a blockade to deter Pakistan from escalating.

But all of these options entail significant risks, which is why they have not been implemented before. Each could escalate to a full-scale conflict if Pakistan responds in kind. And each could invite international censure. Ironically, a nuclear test may be less risky in terms of escalation but the most likely to produce global outrage. However, India's patience is not eternal.

Pakistanis contend that India has already settled on another option, which is to increase support for unrest and instability inside Pakistan, in effect, to respond in kind. Islamabad accuses India of helping Baluchi rebels in Pakistan's southwestern province, channeling aid through New Delhi's consulates in neighboring Iran and Afghanistan. So far Pakistan has not produced a smoking gun to verify Indian malfeasance. But if India is not already providing aid to the Baluchis, another Mumbai certainly would make it a more attractive course of action.

The dire possibilities outlined in this chapter are of great concern to the international community, especially in the wake of the Mumbai horror. Led by the United States, France, and the United Kingdom, the international community was quick to condemn the Mumbai attacks in a statement issued by the UN Security Council just after they occurred. In June 2009 the United Nations added four LeT officials to the Consolidated List of Individuals associated with Osama bin Laden and al Qaeda and created by UN Security Council Resolution 1267 (passed in May 2005), which obligates all states to freeze the funds and assets of these officials. The U.S. Department of the Treasury followed suit by targeting the four in July 2009 for an asset freeze.

Should another attack occur, the United States and the rest of the international community would undoubtedly urge restraint on India again and try to press Pakistan to "do more." But that tactic will not work forever. It amounts to playing Russian roulette in South Asia. Sooner or later a Pakistan-based terror attack on India is going to lead to Armageddon.

For the past sixty years, American policy toward Pakistan has oscillated wildly. At times—under the Eisenhower, Nixon, Reagan, and George W. Bush administrations—the United States was enamored of Pakistan's dictators and embraced its policies without question. At other times—under Jimmy Carter, George H. W. Bush, and Bill Clinton—the United States imposed sanctions on Pakistan, blaming it for provoking wars and developing nuclear weapons. In the love-fest years, Washington would build secret relationships (which gave rise to the U2 base in Peshawar and the mujahedin war in the 1980s) and throw billions of dollars at Pakistan with little or no accountability. In the scorned years, Pakistan would be démarched to death, and Washington would cut off all military and economic aid. Both approaches failed dismally.

Throughout the relationship, America endorsed every Pakistani military dictator, despite the fact that they started wars with India and moved their country ever deeper into the jihadist fold. John F. Kennedy entertained the first dictator, Ayub Khan, at Mount Vernon in the only state dinner ever held at the home of the nation's first family. Richard Nixon turned a blind eye to the murder of hundreds of thousands of Bangladeshis to keep his friends in Pakistan's army in power, a strategy that ultimately failed. Ronald Reagan entertained Zia ul-Haq even as Zia was giving succor to the Arab jihadists who would become al Qaeda. George W. Bush allowed Pervez Musharraf to give the Afghan Taliban a sanctuary from which to kill American and NATO soldiers in Afghanistan.

In contrast, George Bush senior sanctioned a democratic Pakistan for building a bomb that Reagan knew Pakistan was building. Bill Clinton sanctioned Pakistan for testing the bomb after India goaded it into doing so (he had little choice since Congress had mandated automatic sanctions for testing).

One obvious lesson of these past interactions is that the U.S.-Pakistan relationship needs to be on a more constant and consistent footing. To that end, the United States must engage reliably with the Pakistani people, support their democratic process, and address their legitimate security concerns. Candor needs to be the hallmark of an enduring commitment to civilian rule in Pakistan.

None of this will be easy. Pakistan is a complex and combustible society undergoing a severe crisis, which America helped create over the years. If the United States does not come to Pakistan's aid now, it may have to deal with an extremist Pakistan sooner rather than later, or witness a repeat of 9/11, this time originating from Pakistan. Even worse, a crisis in the subcontinent could lead to a nuclear war in South Asia. These all-too-possible nightmare scenarios should impel the United States to focus on the current state of Pakistan. It needs to do better in Pakistan. Some solutions are discussed in the next chapter.

CHAPTER SEVEN

HELPING PAKISTAN

THE OLD EXECUTIVE OFFICE Building (OEOB), now officially renamed the Eisenhower Executive Office Building, is one of Washington's architectural and historic gems. Originally called the State, War, and Navy Building, it was built in 1871 in the style of Napoleon III's Paris to house the national security infrastructure of the post–Civil War federal government. A magnificent example of America's self-confidence and ambition in the aftermath of its bloodiest war, the building stood as a symbol in stone of the nation's transformation into a world power. The Departments of State, War, and Navy filled its spaces until the end of World War I. Today it houses several key presidential offices, including most of the staff of the National Security Council (NSC). I have called it home for some nine years under four presidents.

In February 2009 I chaired a day-long meeting in one of the OEOB's most beautiful rooms, the restored Office of the Secretary of War, its ceiling adorned with murals depicting captured flags from America's wars and its walls decorated in rich Victorian style with paintings of secretaries of war from the nineteenth century. My guest was the foreign minister of Pakistan, Makhdoom Shah Mehmood Qureshi, who led a team of senior officials for the first in-depth review of U.S.-Pakistan relations under the Obama administration. Qureshi is a charming and articulate diplomat, with a good sense of humor, grace, and a quiet determination to advance his country's interests. I was joined by Under Secretary Michelle Flournoy, Ambassador Richard Holbrooke, and a team of experts from across the government. Qureshi was joined by Ambassador Husain

Haqqani, Lieutenant General Ahmad Shuja Pasha, director of Pakistan's Inter-Services Intelligence Directorate (ISI), and other key officials.

I was there to listen to them, to hear their views of the situation in Afghanistan and in their country. I knew a "trust deficit" existed between our two countries, arising from decades of mistrust. I also knew many Pakistanis believed America was not a reliable ally. I told them I understood that—because the truth is, America has not been a reliable ally of Pakistan and certainly not a reliable ally of Pakistani democracy. This chapter, to a large extent, is based on what I have heard Pakistanis say about what they think of America and what they would like America to do to help their country in its deadly struggle with global Islamic extremism.

Without doubt, Pakistan faces a challenging host of problems quite apart from the jihadist threat, the primary focus of this book. Among the most dramatic are its population explosion and declining water resources. Start with demographics. At independence in 1947 Pakistan had a population of 39 million (not counting those in today's Bangladesh). In 2009 UN estimates put the figure at 180.8 million, making it the sixth most populous country in the world. It is a very young nation: 53.8 percent are below the age of nineteen and 37.7 percent are between twenty and thirty-nine. If fertility rates remain constant, the population will reach 460 million by 2050. Even with a modest decline, the figure would still probably hit about 335 million by 2050. Urbanization is also on the rise, changing lifestyles from rural isolation to urban slums in megacities like Karachi. Although most Pakistanis are poor, a 30-million-strong middle class is also present. Nor should it be overlooked, as noted in earlier chapters, that Pakistan is now the second largest Muslim country in the world; by 2050 it will be the largest, surpassing Indonesia.[1]

As for Pakistan's water problem, it is already severe and shows no signs of abating, especially under the pressure of a rapidly growing population and urbanization. Between 1951 and 2007 per capita water availability decreased from 5,000 to 1,100 cubic meters a year. The country probably slipped below the 1,000-cubic-meter level in 2010. By 2025 water availability will drop to less than 700 cubic meters per capita. To compound the problem, more and more of Pakistan's water is becoming polluted. An estimated 250,000 child deaths each year can be attributed to waterborne diseases and polluted water. Pakistan is now one of the most water-stressed countries in the world.[2] Some are using water shortages as another reason for violence against India. In March 2010 Hafez Saeed, the founder and leader of Lashkar-e-Tayyiba, accused India of stealing water from Pakistan in Kashmir, insisting, "If India continues with her water terrorism, Pakistan must keep open the option of using force."[3]

Ironically, extreme monsoons and flooding in the summer of 2010 inundated Pakistan with too much water. Millions lost their homes and infrastructure was devastated in an area the size of England. While Pakistan was suffering, President Asif Ali Zardari traveled to France and England for a state visit. He even paid a short visit to the Bhutto family chateau in Mesnil Lieubray, in Normandy, originally built in the sixteenth century for the widow of King Philippe VI. The stark contrast between Zardari visiting his chateau and Pakistan drowning underscored the gap between the nation's leaders and its people.

These and most of Pakistan's other challenges are certainly too much for the United States and the international community to solve. The United States and Europe face massive economic problems themselves in the wake of the financial crisis of 2008, and both are heavily committed in Afghanistan. In any case, only Pakistanis can determine their country's future and decide whether to allow the global Islamic jihad to envelop them or whether to develop a strong and healthy democracy.

Strange to say, the United States may have been making it harder for Pakistanis to develop a healthy democracy that can effectively fight terror. As I have argued in the preceding chapters, much that it has done since partition has had this unanticipated effect. One reason is that American policy has often tilted toward encouraging military interference in the civilian government's conduct of policy and all but encouraged military dictatorship. Most recently, Washington worked behind the scenes to secure an extension in the tour of duty of Chief of Army Staff Ashfaq Parvez Kayani, which was due to expire in mid-2010. The Gillani government, which had its own reasons for keeping Kayani in office, gave him an unprecedented three-year extension. In a sense, Kayani has become the power behind the throne in Pakistan.

Rebuilding Trust

The first objective of American policy toward Pakistan must be to try to reverse its deep distrust of America, made all too clear in poll after poll and outpourings of the Pakistani press. Sixty-three years of history verify that America is an unreliable friend of Pakistan. Reinforcing that conclusion for most Pakistanis are the stronger ties the United States and India have developed under Presidents Bill Clinton, George W. Bush, and Barack Obama.

A particularly insightful poll by the University of Maryland in mid-2009 found that more than two-thirds of Pakistanis (69 percent) had negative views of the current U.S. government, that is, the Obama administration. This was just a few months after Obama had announced his new Afghanistan and Pakistan strategy, emphasizing that "the United States has great respect for the Pakistani people. They have a rich history and have struggled against long odds to sustain their democracy."[4]

Asked if the United States is a positive player on the world stage, only 10 percent of the respondents said yes, whereas almost 70 percent saw it as a negative player. Especially illuminating, almost 90 percent believe the United States wants to weaken and divide the ummah, and almost 60 percent share al Qaeda's views of the United States as a country hostile to Islam (though only a quarter said they support al Qaeda's attacks on America). On democracy, the overwhelming majority believe the United States only supports democracy if it means a government that does what America wants; only 7 percent believe the United States supports democracy unconditionally.[5]

A Gallup poll for Al Jazeera later in 2009 showed similar results. Half believed the United States poses the greatest danger to Pakistan today, 18 percent named India in this regard, and only 11 percent the Taliban and al Qaeda.[6] Any country that outpolls India as the bad guy in Pakistan is surely in a deep hole.

In a more recent poll, conducted by Pew in June 2010, only 8 percent of Pakistanis reported confidence in President Obama, while 18 percent put their trust in Osama bin Laden. Overall, the United States still is viewed negatively. In contrast, 79 percent of Pakistanis have a favorable view of China.[7] In a second Pew poll in July, 59 percent saw America as an enemy, only 11 percent as a partner.[8]

This deep distrust of American intentions, even toward a president who has backed democracy in Pakistan and called for a new day in the relationship, is a major hurdle to helping Pakistan meet the challenges of the jihadist infrastructure. Pakistani opinion depicted in newspapers or on numerous television news programs only further illustrates the extent to which intense anti-Americanism in the country twists the truth. Conspiracy theories abound in the media blaming America for all of Pakistan's problems. At the extreme end are "think tanks" that routinely deny any Pakistani role in terror and accuse America of being the real perpetrator of attacks like the Mumbai raid in 2008. Others blame Israel, which they say wanted to provoke a war between India and Pakistan so as to destroy Pakistan's nuclear arsenal. According to one Pakistani think tank, America, India, and Israel did it together.[9]

Suspicion of American motives pervades the army and the government alike. A graphic illustration of this was Pakistan's reaction to the Kerry-Lugar legislation of September 2009 tripling aid to Pakistan. The intent of the legislation was, as Obama put it, to "build schools and roads and hospitals and strengthen Pakistani democracy . . . so to avoid the mistakes of the past."[10] Pakistanis almost universally denounced it. Editorials focused exclusively on the bill's hortatory language, calling for a full investigation of A. Q. Khan's history of proliferation and for an end to support for Lashkar-e-Tayyiba (LeT). The fact that America was tripling economic aid for a country far away when it was itself in the grips of the worst recession in decades was lost in the commentary. Senator John Kerry even issued a statement saying the aid came without conditions, but the cacophony of criticism continued. Much of the negative editorial comment was orchestrated by Kayani, the army, and the ISI, who were especially offended by the criticism of their ties to terror and proliferation.

As should be clear by now, Pakistanis and Americans have entirely different narratives about their bilateral relationship. Pakistan speaks of America's continual betrayal, of America promising much and delivering little. America finds Pakistan duplicitous, saying one thing and doing another. Americans want Pakistan to focus on the global threat, be it communism or jihadism. Pakistanis want to concentrate on the threat next door, India.

These attitudes will not change overnight, or even in a few years. They are the legacy of the history of America's ties with Pakistan. Only time will change them. American policy toward Pakistan must now be built on the principle of unwavering support for democracy, even if the United States is averse to some policies of Islamabad's democratic governments.

It is imperative to send that message consistently and constantly. Backing up the message with real assistance, like the Kerry-Lugar bill, is even more important, as discussed later in the chapter.

The United States has one significant factor on its side. Terrorist attacks against Pakistanis in their own cities have turned many, but far from all, against the jihadist Frankenstein. This trend is apparent in part in polling data from the University of Maryland showing that in 2007 only a third of Pakistanis viewed the "activities of Islamist militants" in Pakistan as a critical threat, whereas in 2009 the figure rose to four out of five (81 percent). A similar number (82 percent) pointed to al Qaeda's activities in Pakistan as a critical threat.[11] While many still agree with much of al Qaeda's view of America, and a quarter back its attacks on Americans, the majority are no longer in denial about the extremist threat to their own freedoms.

A survey in June 2010 by the Pakistani Institute for Peace Studies showed similar changes.[12] Despite growing religiosity in the national population, as indicated by strong support for women wearing the veil (57 percent) or other manifestations of Islamic piety, the majority polled were opposed to acts of terrorism from the Taliban and other extremists. The murder of Benazir Bhutto was widely opposed. On the other hand, support for jihad in Kashmir against India remained strong (56 percent). The overall change in opinion has made it easier for the civilian government and the army to conduct limited counterterrorist offensives in the Swat Valley and Waziristan but may also help explain the administration's reluctance to crack down on LeT.

President Obama noted this shift in his second major address on Pakistan in December 2009: "In the past there have been those in Pakistan who argued that the struggle against extremism is not their fight, and that Pakistan is better off doing little or seeking accommodation with those who use violence. But recently as innocents have been killed from Karachi to Islamabad, it has become clear that it is the Pakistani people who are the most endangered and public opinion has turned."[13]

The shift is far from complete, however, and could yet turn the wrong way. Some polls show it may be reversing already. But it is consistent with trends in public opinion in other Islamic countries, notably in Indonesia and Jordan, where al Qaeda's violent attacks against fellow Muslims produced a strong backlash. The challenge in Pakistan is to try to use this backlash productively to destroy the terrorist network.

One key American tactic—using drones or unmanned aerial vehicles to attack terrorist targets inside Pakistan—has had the opposite effect. While some Pakistanis are pleased when a Taliban leader is killed in a drone operation, the vast majority are deeply angered by the drone operations, which they see as an infringement on their country's sovereignty and territorial integrity. According to the Maryland poll, nearly all Pakistanis oppose the drone attacks, with 82 percent calling them unjustified and rejecting them under any circumstances.[14] Pakistani generals, some of whom have even helped identify drone targets, find the drone attacks deeply humiliating since they vividly demonstrate the army's inability to defend the country. How to reconcile these opposing goals of rebuilding trust and attacking the terrorist enemy is a daunting policy challenge.

ATTACKING TERROR—ALONE AND TOGETHER

The United States began using drones to target al Qaeda and its allies in Pakistan in 2004, but it was not until 2007 that the attacks became frequent. The Bush administration developed the drone program when it belatedly became aware that Pervez Musharraf was not fully engaged in the war against extremism. Initially, the Pakistanis were notified in advance of any drone attack, but this changed when it became apparent that some if not all of the targets were being tipped off.[15] According to a comprehensive study and mapping of these operations by the New America Foundation, all drone attacks take place in the border region along the Federally Administered Tribal Areas (FATA), none in Baluchistan or the Punjab.[16]

Although these are covert operations, both the Bush and Obama administrations have publicly taken credit for them while trying to avoid directly claiming responsibility. The CIA director at the time, Michael Hayden, said that several senior al Qaeda officials had been killed by such operations and that "the ability to kill key members of al Qaeda keeps them off-balance in their best safe haven along the Afghanistan-Pakistan border."[17] President Obama significantly increased the rate of drone operations in 2009 and provided more resources to make them effective. The New America Foundation database shows fifty-one attacks in 2009. This is more drone attacks than in the Bush administration's eight years in office.[18]

The drones work. They have killed senior al Qaeda and Taliban operatives. Beitullah Mehsud, the first head of the Pakistan Taliban, was killed by one in 2009, and Mustafa Muhammad Uthman abu Yazid, the head of al Qaeda operations in Afghanistan, was killed in May 2010. The White House took credit for Yazid's death, noting that he was involved in the December 2009 attack on the CIA base in Khost. The under secretary of the treasury, Stuart A. Levey, wrote an op-ed piece for the *Washington Post* referring to Yazid's death as a "major blow" because he was a key link to "the deep-pocketed donors in the Arabian peninsula and beyond who have historically formed the backbone of al Qaeda's financial support network."[19]

As Levey points out, the drones have also disrupted al Qaeda's operational activity—its planning and training, and even financial transactions. These effects are reflected in the slower pace of al Qaeda's propaganda. Ayman Zawahiri, the group's most active public speaker who used to appear in al Qaeda propaganda tapes constantly, was not heard for eight months after the Khost attack. In the first eight months of 2010 he appeared in only a handful of messages, a sign his operational tempo has been disrupted by the drones. But by August he was back on the airwaves, so the disruption was not permanent.

One should also recognize that the drone campaign often does less than promised. Operatives allegedly killed in attacks have had a frustrating tendency to reappear. Mehsud's successor in the Pakistani Taliban was said to have died from wounds in a drone attack, only to show up a few weeks later looking quite healthy in a video promising more attacks on America. Muhammad Ilyas Kashmiri was said to have perished in an attack and then summoned David Headley to meet him in Pakistan. Rashid Rauf, the architect of the 2006 airline plot in England, may or may not be dead. While the campaign is putting considerable pressure on al Qaeda, admits the CIA's Leon Panetta, the U.S. Intelligence community still considers al Qaeda and its allies the greatest threat to America and has had no information on bin Laden's whereabouts since "the early 2000s."[20]

Pakistan is an active partner in the drone operations. Pakistani newspapers and London's *Sunday Times* revealed in early 2009 that some are actually flown from a Pakistani air base. Satellite photos of the base published by the *Times* clearly showed the drones at the airfield.[21] Official Pakistani protests against the drone attacks must therefore be viewed with some skepticism. Nonetheless, the attacks do alienate the majority of Pakistanis.

There is no simple or good solution to this policy dilemma. The drones are needed to thwart terrorism. Obama was right to increase their use. But it is also essential to avoid becoming drone addicted, using them so indiscriminately as to make them counterproductive. This is a fine line to maneuver.

The best solution, of course, would be for the Pakistani government and the army, in particular, to adopt a comprehensive counterterrorism policy and take down the entire terror network operating in Pakistan today. A strategic shift of this nature would be the best solution to the nightmares of a jihadist Pakistan and another 9/11 or Mumbai.

ENGAGEMENT, RED LINES, AND VERIFICATION

The only way to change Pakistani behavior is to engage Pakistan. The United States has tried unilateral and multilateral sanctions and isolation; they did not work. It has tried congressionally imposed ultimatums and conditions-based aid; they did not work either. Military operations are another option, but they are not likely to work and would certainly be costly.

Engagement should be based on several principles. First, it should always proceed in a manner that strengthens Pakistan's civilian-elected leadership. That means going first to the prime minister, who, after a constitutional amendment in 2010, wields more power in Pakistan than the president. A national consensus supported this very significant change, which has made the elected prime minister the real head of government. This is a major accomplishment for Pakistan, a vindication of the country's long struggle to build a civilian authority that has real clout.

This change is a good one for engagement purposes. President Asif Ali Zardari is deeply unpopular in Pakistan. Allegations of past corruption continue to plague him. Recall that he was nicknamed Mr. Ten Percent for allegedly receiving a 10 percent kickback on every contract signed during each of his wife's terms as prime minister. He is still head of state, but his powers are much diminished.

The United States must be careful not to build a relationship with an individual. That was the mistake the younger Bush made with Musharraf, the consequences of which are still being felt. America's diplomats should be reaching out to all nonviolent political forces in Pakistan. That certainly includes Nawaz Sharif and his Muslim League, but it should also include the Muttahida Qaumi Movement (MQM) and its rising stars, such as the former mayor of Karachi, Syed Kamal, who did much to improve life in the country's largest city. To reiterate, U.S. policy should support the democratic process, not an individual leader or party—it should help the civilian leadership gain authority and strength, not undermine it.

With the Pakistani army chipping away at them for decades, the democratic institutions of the country have had a long hard struggle. The longest period of civilian rule has lasted all of eleven years, while the army's civilian power only grows: according to *The Economist*, the army has amassed a $20 billion business empire and is now the country's largest land developer.[22] Ayesha Siddiqa, author of a brilliant and controversial book, *Military Inc.*, estimates that a senior general's net worth averages about $1.7 million today.[23] While that may be an exaggeration and many Pakistani generals are repelled by the corruption around them, the army needs to stay in the barracks and out of politics.

It would be naïve, however, not to recognize that Pakistan's military leaders still have much of the real power in government. That means strong military-to-military and intelligence-to-intelligence networks are vital to an effective engagement approach, though it must avoid circumventing Pakistan's political leaders in the process. One goal of engagement with the army and ISI would be to make clear America's opposition to another coup.

When dealing with Pakistan, Washington has always been tempted to first seek out the chief of army staff (COAS) for a rapid decision. Bill Clinton sent his chairman of the Joint Chiefs to see General Jehangir Karamat in 1998 when the United States was firing cruise missiles at bin Laden. Prime Minister Nawaz Sharif showed up at the meeting unexpectedly, so was brought into the loop despite Washington's inclination to deal directly with the COAS. Failing to engage with the democratically chosen leadership erodes the power of those the United States most wants to succeed and help: the civilians elected to office.

The role of the current COAS, General Ashfaq Parvez Kayani, is a case in point. As director general of the ISI from 2004 to 2007, he was in charge when the Afghan Taliban received critical support from the ISI. During his watch, the LeT planned the attack on Mumbai, which Indian officials claim was supervised by the ISI at every stage. Yet since becoming COAS, Kayani has ordered the army to carry out the most significant antimilitant offensives in the country's history, in the Swat Valley and in the FATA. Kayani rightly points out that more Pakistani soldiers and ISI officers have died fighting the Taliban in Pakistan than NATO has lost in Afghanistan. Zardari and Yousaf Raza Gillani extended Kayani's tour as COAS an unprecedented three years because of his leadership in the fight against extremism. One observer, a retired brigadier general who knows Kayani well, has noted that he "has indeed become indispensable (but) this situation cannot but continue to weaken civilian institutions in the long run." Worse, "it can result in a desire for self-perpetuation as happened to many of Kayani's predecessors as absolute power can become a powerfully addictive aphrodisiac."[24] This is a course America needs to steer away from.

A second principle is to encourage leaders of both countries to be candid in their interactions and draw red lines. America and Pakistan are not always going to agree. That is how states interact; they have different interests and agendas. Disagreement does not have to mean acting disagreeably. Washington and Islamabad should work on narrowing their differences but should not expect them all to be resolved. Sometimes they should agree to disagree.

But Washington should also be abundantly clear that there are behaviors it cannot tolerate, the most important being collusion with terror. All of Pakistan's leadership must recognize that the days of double-dealing need to end, which they may be starting to do now that Pakistan itself is a victim of terror and its leaders have been attacked by al Qaeda.

Two red lines in particular need to be drawn. The first involves the Afghan Taliban. Pakistan's safe haven for the Quetta shura and the Haqqani network must be shut down. Pakistan indicates it is no longer offering the Afghan militants refuge and is at war with the Pakistani Taliban. It claims rightly that it has more troops on the Afghan border to prevent militancy than NATO has on the Afghan side. And it correctly notes that more Pakistani soldiers have died fighting the Taliban than Americans or Europeans.

But suspicions linger about ties between the ISI and the Afghan Taliban. Most recently, interviews with more than a dozen current and former senior Taliban leaders reported by the London School of Economics revealed that ties with the ISI are still extensive and include training, arming, financing, and advising the Taliban. Some of those interviewed claimed to have attended ISI training schools and camps as recently as early 2010. Others said former and active-duty ISI officers not only help them plan attacks on NATO but at times even participate in the operations inside Afghanistan. Furthermore, ISI representatives are said to attend meetings of Mullah Omar's Quetta shura, still "playing a double game of astonishing magnitude."[25]

Pakistan has denied these allegations, arguing that the report is based solely on Afghan sources. But the former head of Afghan intelligence, Amarullah Salih, a brilliant and professional intelligence officer who ran Afghan intelligence for six years, has publicly charged that Afghanistan's "enemy number one" is Pakistan.[26] Salih says the top Taliban leadership is hiding out in Karachi and is being financed, armed, and protected by the ISI, with its inner circle "totally under Pakistani control."[27] Given the history of ISI ties to the Taliban, these reports need to be taken seriously.

Even when the Pakistanis have taken action against parts of the Afghan Taliban, they appear more intent on keeping the militants under Islamabad's control than on defeating them. In early 2010 in Karachi, the ISI, with CIA assistance, arrested Mullah Baradar, the Taliban's operational commander, and shortly thereafter detained a dozen other Taliban officials. But then the arrests halted. Later the Pakistanis said that those detained had been considering peace negotiations with the Karzai government in Kabul and that the arrests were a warning to the Taliban not to try to negotiate independently of Pakistan. One Pakistani official told the *New York Times* that the ISI had used the CIA in the operation because "they are so innocent" in their understanding of the complexities of Pakistani policy. Baradar now is under house arrest in an ISI safe house, while the others have all been released and are back to fighting NATO forces in Afghanistan.[28]

The second red line is Lashkar-e-Tayyiba, which still operates with impunity in Pakistan. Far too little has been done to break up its capability since Mumbai. Indian officials who have debriefed David Headley, the American mastermind of Mumbai, have been quoted anonymously in India as saying Headley told them the ISI was involved in the plot at "each and every stage."[29] The ISI, they said, bought the boat the terrorists used to travel from Karachi to Mumbai, and Pakistani naval commandos taught the terrorists frogman assault tactics. This may be an exaggeration, but again the track record of ISI-LeT relations suggests it cannot be dismissed. Another Mumbai-like attack could be a disaster for America and South Asia.

LeT is also becoming more active in Afghanistan. It has long sent operatives to train there but now is actively engaged in insurgent and terror attacks on Indian targets in Afghanistan and even clashes with NATO forces. Again some evidence suggests the attacks are coordinated and controlled by the ISI. Equally significant, LeT's operational ties to the Afghan Taliban, especially the Haqqani network, are intensifying.[30]

Thus in its dialogue with Islamabad, the United States needs to be candid and direct, making clear that violation of U.S. red lines will have consequences. These consequences should fall directly on the ISI. Instead of imposing sanctions on all of Pakistan, Washington could specifically target ISI officers, up to and including the director general, if it had evidence of continued support for terror. Such targeted sanctions could consist of threatening arrest if these ISI members traveled abroad or taking action against their individual and corporate financial holdings. International arrest warrants and placement on UN terrorism lists could be used as punishment. Alternatively, Washington could make clear that its intelligence relationship with Pakistan will be adversely affected if double-dealing continues. It has done so with other intelligence agencies in the past. In the 1980s, for example, most intelligence cooperation with Israel was briefly suspended when it was found to be running an American spy named Jonathan Pollard inside the United States Navy.

The third principle of the engagement approach emphasizes internal verification and stock taking. A general, diplomat, or station chief deeply engaged in a dialogue with a foreign partner may often be tempted to suggest that his or her side's ends are being met. It is only human to suppose one's interlocutor is working toward the same end and is really cooperating. Anecdotal reporting on "my latest trip" to Islamabad is almost always upbeat. No one wants to fail. Similarly, embassies and stations tend to adopt the views of the people they work with. So the U.S. embassy in Kabul is likely to be more skeptical of the ISI claim that it has given up its ties to the Taliban than the embassy in Islamabad.

But good policy should not be based on impressions. The president should task the director of national intelligence (DNI) to prepare, perhaps quarterly, an all-source intelligence report on Pakistan's role in terror, conveying both the good news and the bad. The DNI should be in charge because he is supposed to coordinate the views of the entire intelligence community. The CIA has a vested interest in its relationship with the Pakistani security services, the military has a vested interest in its ties to the army, and the State Department has a vested interest in promoting bilateral ties. All should be involved in the intelligence process, but the DNI should run the show and demand the data—good, bad, and ugly—needed to assess Pakistan's behavior in relation to terror. He then should report directly to the president and NSC principals.

Sound intelligence does not ensure good policy, nor does it provide policy answers to difficult issues. However, periodic, comprehensive intelligence reports do make it harder for policymakers to ignore facts they find unpleasant. As this book has shown, that problem has bedeviled U.S. ties with Pakistan from the start. Key members of Congress should be given access to the intelligence as well, to ensure Capitol Hill is doing its job of overseeing intelligence and advising policy.

Even when based on these principles, engagement will be difficult. There will be no romance like the Charlie Wilson–Zia ul-Haq relationship here. The time has come to be serious about how America engages Pakistan.

To move in that direction, it will be essential to view Pakistan in its regional South Asian context. For years the State Department and other parts of the U.S. government considered South Asia a stepchild of their interests in the Near East. The senior diplomat for South Asia was the assistant secretary for the Near East and spent most of his time in the Middle East, with only occasional interaction with South Asia. By 1990 many on Capitol Hill were coming to recognize that too little attention was being directed to a part of the world of increasing importance to U.S. interests.

In 1992 Congress told the State Department to create a separate South Asia Bureau with its own assistant secretary, whereupon State urged the White House to veto the legislation. I was the NSC desk officer responsible for South Asia at the time and persuaded Brent Scowcroft not to veto. Congress was right then and still is. Pakistan, India, and Afghanistan should be part of one executive bureau across the U.S. government. There should not be a special Afghanistan-Pakistan section at State or the NSC, South Asia should be separated from Central Command and Pacific Command in the military, and the region should be treated holistically.

Like good intelligence, good organization does not guarantee good policy. However, a poorly constructed bureaucracy is almost always a recipe for bad policy. A new military command that puts Pakistan and India under the same commander in chief (CINC) of South Asia Command (SACOM) would help improve strategic thinking about South Asia enormously. No longer would one CINC talk to the Pakistanis and another to the Indians. The United States already has a base in the region to call home, the British island of Diego Garcia.

An empowered assistant secretary for South Asia could deal with Pakistan's obsession, India. He or she would routinely travel between Kabul, Islamabad, and New Delhi. President Obama was right to recognize that the Afghanistan war could not be effectively prosecuted without dealing with the Pakistani dimension of the conflict. But Pakistan cannot be effectively assisted without dealing with the issue that dominates Pakistan's strategic calculus: as always, India.

Developing Capability

Pakistan's ability to fight the global jihad is severely hampered by weak capacities both in the military and in the economic arenas. If Pakistan is to be a healthy state that does not nurture extremism and incubate terror, it needs help in developing the capability to do so. America should not do this alone. Many others should be part of the effort.

For a half-century or more, the Pakistani military has been structured and armed for one overriding mission: war with India. The fact that it has lost all its wars with India has only reinforced the imperative to do more, and to do better the next time. Pakistani officers spend much of their time in staff schools studying the past wars and creating schemes for the next one. The subject of Musharraf's thesis at the Royal College of Defence Studies in London, for example, was how to fight India in a small war, a preview of his Kargil adventure.

Consequently, Pakistan has devoted little attention to developing the strategies, tactics, and equipment for fighting counterinsurgency and counterterrorism. When it has fought such a campaign, in Baluchistan in the 1970s, for example, it has employed conventional forces in largely conventional ways and relied on massive firepower to win.

This is starting to change. The campaigns in the Swat Valley and South Waziristan have brought new thinking and new tactics, and with them new opportunities for U.S. help. General David Petraeus, the commander of Central Command until he was reassigned to Afghanistan, has been engaged in finding ways to help the Pakistani army and air force develop a more effective approach to fighting the Pakistani Taliban militants. This is a smart step in the right direction.

American efforts could be particularly effective if directed at improving Pakistani air mobility. A key to successful counterinsurgency is the ability to rapidly deploy soldiers and equipment to hot spots. That means helicopters and lots of them. That is how the United States has fought insurgents for decades. It was loss of air control and thus loss of air mobility that doomed the Soviet Fortieth Army in the 1980s.

One Friday in February 2009, during the strategic review of policy toward Pakistan, I received a call from the Oval Office asking me to come over quickly. I walked briskly from the OEOB to the West Wing and went in to see the president. He said he only had a minute but had been thinking about Pakistan a lot. Was I thinking of out-of-the-box solutions to the problems of Pakistan? Had I consulted with other experts on the Pakistani army about its obsession with India and how to change that? I assured him I was doing both.

One of the experts I work with most is Shuja Nawaz, the author of *Crossed Swords,* a definitive work on the Pakistani army. I called him that day and asked what single thing could do more than any other to help the Pakistani army fight militancy. Helicopters, he replied. It may not be out of the box, but it is the right answer. Advice and expertise are helpful, but the real sign of support is equipment, especially for air mobility.

However, the Americans are not providing them. After being in Washington for two years, Pakistan's ambassador, Husain Haqqani, says all he has to show for it is "eight second-hand Mi-17 transport helicopters for a war that requires helicopters to root out al Qaeda and the Taliban." Pakistan, Haqqani added, is losing lives "because we don't have the right equipment."[31] Pakistan's wish list focuses on helicopters, including gunships like the Apache and utility and cargo helos like the Black Hawk and Huey.

Meanwhile India worries that the same helicopters so useful in FATA could be used against its interests in Kashmir. There is no way to avoid that policy problem. If the United States remains firm in its red lines about Pakistan's ties to terrorism, the danger will ease, although not be resolved.

Pakistan also needs its own drones, equipped with intelligence-collection and weapons systems. If it is to take more ownership of the war against al Qaeda, it should have the platforms and weapons needed to wage that war. In time Washington's own drone campaign could convert to a joint campaign, making Pakistan more responsible and accountable for the counterinsurgency.

On the economic side, the Kerry-Lugar bill has already tripled economic assistance for Pakistan. Despite the negative press it received in Pakistan, the bill should provide a significant boost to key sectors of the economy, including education, water, and energy. It would be even more useful if supplemented with an automatic democracy bonus, an idea Congress had been toying with earlier. This would commit the United States to adding another billion dollars a year in aid every year the president could certify that Pakistan was a democracy. This, in turn, would provide an incentive to keep the army out of politics.

A sector in dire need of help is education. According to a recent Brookings study, illiteracy in Pakistan is actually increasing, and the education infrastructure resembles that of a poor sub-Saharan nation. Girls in particular are undereducated, although the problem affects both genders and all parts of the country. Spending on education has been insufficient for decades, often because of the army's demands for the country's wealth. It is not just the religious schools, the madrassas, that teach hate. The public school system does so as well, targeting India and America in particular. The new civilian government has promised to increase spending on education considerably, and the United States should help it do so.[32]

But financial aid has its limitations. Even though $1.5 billion dollars a year is a significant amount, especially when America faces major economic problems itself, this is far from enough to turn the Pakistani economy around in the face of a fast-growing population and scarce resources. Recovering from the floods of 2010 alone will take billions in aid. Many economists argue Washington could do much more for Pakistan by modifying its trade policy to allow more Pakistani-made textiles to be sold in the United States. Some 60 percent of Pakistan's exports today consist of textiles, but far too few get into the American market because of high tariffs. The Atlantic Council notes that typical tariffs on Pakistan textiles in the United States are 11.4 percent, which is nearly three times the average rate of 4 percent.[33]

Musharraf pressed George W. Bush for free trade and tariff changes but did not get far. A new report published by Pakistan experts at the Council on Foreign Relations recommends that Obama and Congress aggressively pursue a free trade deal with Pakistan. This, it concludes, would have the largest impact on job creation, especially among women, and would help revitalize economic growth. Others have reached the same conclusion.[34]

With its acute energy shortfall, Pakistan's energy sector is also in desperate need of help. According to a Brookings colleague, the energy crisis has now reached a point where it "threatens this nuclear-armed nation's economic and political stability."[35] Small towns and villages are experiencing power outages lasting 20–22 hours a day, while large cities like Karachi, Lahore, Faisalabad, Peshawar, and Quetta are routinely without power for half of every day. Power demand is about 14,600 megawatts whereas supply is only at 10,200 megawatts.[36] Much could be done to improve supply by upgrading Pakistan's energy grid and infrastructure. Some energy support is expected from the United States, which in 2010 pledged $1 billion in aid for the sector. Hydropower traditionally accounts for a major part of Pakistan's energy production and should continue to be an important source, unless threatened by the nation's current water scarcity.

Pakistan also wants to produce energy through civilian nuclear power plants. At the top of its agenda is a civilian nuclear power deal like the one George W. Bush negotiated for India and Obama supported as a senator. Understandably, this proposal has met with very strong opposition in the United States and in other members of the International Atomic Energy Agency (IAEA) and the Nuclear Suppliers Group (NSG), which would have to approve any such deal. It was difficult enough to get the India deal through Congress, the IAEA, and NSG. Moreover India has a virtually spotless record of not selling its nuclear technology to other countries.

By contrast, Pakistan probably has the world's worst record as a nuclear proliferator. Only six years ago it was caught red-handed trying to sell nuclear technology to Libya. It provided Iran with its first centrifuge technology. The A. Q. Khan network has rightly been characterized as the most dangerous proliferation apparatus ever, not just selling Pakistan's technology to others but also stealing technology from countries around the world to help build Pakistan's bombs.[37]

A. Q. Khan has been under house arrest since 2004, but he remains a national hero. Thus it is highly unlikely that any Pakistani government would take the deeply unpopular step of forcing him to reveal to the IAEA or CIA further details of his past activities. And no Pakistani government is likely to want to have Khan reveal how its predecessors aided, abetted, and directed his proliferation activities. The army and ISI, which directly assisted him for years, would be the least interested in coming clean.

Given this history of proliferation and an unwillingness to reveal secrets of past technology exchanges, Pakistan is unlikely to achieve the nuclear deal it desires in the foreseeable future. Nonetheless, there may be a good reason to engage Pakistan seriously regarding such a deal and what it would take to win the approval of Congress, the IAEA, and NSG.

That reason is not difficult to find: Pakistan today has the fastest-growing nuclear arsenal in the world, with no constraints on its development other than technology and resources. The global proliferation regime is doing nothing to curb this expansion. Only two countries have large nuclear arsenals with no international oversight: Pakistan and Israel. A global proliferation regime that leaves them outside is not going to achieve President Obama's goal of a world without nuclear weapons. Somehow, Pakistan must be brought into a system that imposes at least some constraints on its arsenal and provides some incentive for it to cap this growth.

The U.S.-India civilian nuclear deal is far from perfect and has been rightly criticized for allowing India to keep most of its reactors outside of IAEA oversight. But it does provide some measure of restraint on India's nuclear program. Pakistanis deeply resent the deal, which they say rewards the country that began the nuclear arms race in South Asia by testing a bomb in 1974 and in 1998. They correctly argue that their own program began as an attempt to catch up with India. It is another sign of American double standards toward Pakistan, many say. India gets a nuclear deal with America; Pakistan is told it will never qualify.

Washington should try a different approach, though it may be a long process: try to find the basis for a civilian nuclear power deal. This would open the door to greater dialogue on Pakistan's past and to more transparency about where it is going. The process itself would have value even if the odds of ever reaching a deal are slim.

If the United States does not do it, China will. It is already committed to building two new power reactors in Pakistan and wants to sign a China-Pakistan civilian power deal that balances the U.S.-India deal.

Building Peace in South Asia

Remarkably, Pakistan is separated from its two biggest neighbors by very long borders that are still unsettled and unrecognized by those neighbors. These disputed borders explain in part why the military has been such a dominant player in the country's politics. Its military leaders can make a convincing case that the country faces serious national security threats on multiple fronts and must therefore devote much of its budget to preparing for war. The military has for decades made those problems worse by supporting terror and schemes like Kargil and Operation Gibraltar. But the fact remains that Pakistan needs to find a peaceful resolution to its border disputes with Afghanistan and India. American diplomacy should focus on this critical issue: Pakistan's relations with these two neighbors.

The Afghan-Pakistan border, 1,610 miles long, lies in the heart of al Qaeda's sanctuary in South Asia. Known as the Durand Line, this border was unilaterally imposed by the British colonial government in 1893 and thus has never been recognized by any Afghan government. Because the line divides the Pashtun and Baluchi peoples, it has never been popular in Afghanistan, which has always been reluctant to formally give up its claim to a larger "Pashtunistan."

The government of President Hamid Karzai is no more likely to accept the line than its predecessors could. But the United States should work with Kabul and Islamabad to reach a public agreement that the line cannot be modified or altered without the consent of both governments. Acceptance of the de facto permanence of the border would set the stage for greater willingness on both sides to police the line and to regard it as a real international frontier. It would clearly not stop smuggling and infiltration overnight, or even over several years, but it would provide a basis for long-term cooperation between Kabul and Islamabad, something lacking in the past.

Since the United States has so much at stake in the stabilization of this border and in preventing the region around it from remaining an al Qaeda safe haven, Washington should be prepared to endorse an agreement between Pakistan and Afghanistan. Pakistan, in turn, would need to address the insecurity of its badlands in the north and responsibly administer them like any other part of the country. Former U.S. ambassador to Afghanistan Ronald Neuman has rightly characterized the current situation as "borderline insanity" and suggested that resolving its ambiguity is part of the "big think" solution to the threat posed from the badlands.[38]

To effectively promote and encourage border stabilization, the United States has to stay in Afghanistan and continue to lead the International Security Assistance Force (ISAF) there. Americans are understandably frustrated that this war has become the longest in its history, with no end in sight. Pointing to the Karzai government's many weaknesses, some argue that the war is unwinnable. It is certainly true that five years of neglecting it while invading Iraq have set back the chances for success immeasurably and perhaps fatally.

But the alternatives to staying the course in Afghanistan are much worse. A precipitous withdrawal, perhaps under the fig leaf of some kind of political deal with the Taliban, would only lead the Tajik-Uzbek-Shia Northern Alliance and the Pashtuns of the south to resume their civil war. Outsiders would inevitably be drawn in. Al Qaeda would thrive in the vacuum. Afghanistan could look like Lebanon in the 1980s or Somalia today, a lawless land with civil war and terrorists everywhere.

Most important, NATO's defeat in Afghanistan would be seen across the Muslim world as al Qaeda's and jihad's victory. It would be a global game changer. The NATO alliance would probably die a slow death afterward. Nowhere would that resonate more powerfully than next door in Pakistan. Abdallah Azzam and Osama bin Laden will have won, and the global jihad will have been triumphant. The prospects of a jihadist takeover in Pakistan would increase significantly.

The other critical issue for American diplomacy to address is the underlying problem that drives Pakistan's relationship with terror: India and Kashmir. The Pakistani state and its army have been obsessed with India since its creation in 1947. The ISI built much of the modern jihadist infrastructure in South Asia precisely to fight India asymmetrically, either directly in Kashmir or to defend Pakistan's strategic depth in Afghanistan.

From the Pakistani perspective, an optimal resolution of Kashmir would be a union of the province, or at least the Muslim-dominated Valley of Kashmir and the capital of Srinagar, with Pakistan. Once Kashmir was "reunited" with Pakistan, there would be no need for nuclear weapons or for a jihadist option to compel Indian withdrawal from the valley. This is precisely the outcome that Pakistani leaders have in mind when they urge American leaders to devote diplomatic and political energy to the Kashmir issue.

Of course, it is a completely unrealistic scenario. India has made it clear that it will not withdraw from Kashmir. On the contrary, India argues it has already made a major concession by de facto accepting the partition of the state between itself, Pakistan, and China. India is probably prepared to accept the Line of Control, in effect the cease-fire line of 1948, as the ultimate border with Pakistan, but not a fundamental redrawing of borders to put the valley under Pakistan's sovereignty.

There is a way to resolve the Kashmir problem more realistically. The basis for such an approach would be to use the Indo-Pakistani bilateral dialogue. That dialogue has already produced a series of confidence-building measures between the two countries, reopening transportation links, setting up hot lines between military commands, and holding periodic discussions at the foreign secretary level on all the issues that divide the two. Unfortunately, the dialogue has not seriously addressed the Kashmir issue because of the significant gulf between the two parties and India's refusal to negotiate while still a target of terrorist attacks planned and organized in Pakistan. But the two have gone far in the back-channel talks on how to resolve Kashmir.

The United States has long been reluctant to engage more actively in the Kashmir dispute in light of the Indian posture that outside intervention is unwarranted and that Kashmir is a purely bilateral issue. Faced with the likelihood of Indian rejection of outside intervention, American diplomacy has put the Kashmir problem in the "too hard" category and left it to simmer. The results are all too predictable. The Kashmir issue periodically boils over, and the United States and the international community have to step in to try to prevent a full-scale war. This was the case during the Kargil crisis in 1999, after the terrorist attack on the Indian parliament in December 2001, and again in 2002 when India mobilized its army for war on the Pakistani border.

A unique opportunity for quiet American diplomacy to help advance the Kashmir issue to a better, more stable solution may exist now. The U.S.-India nuclear deal has created a more stable and enduring basis for relations between the two countries than at any time in their history. The deal removes the central obstacle to closer strategic ties between Washington and New Delhi—the nuclear proliferation problem, which held back the development of their relationship for two decades.

In the new era of U.S.-Indian strategic partnership, Washington should quietly but forcefully encourage New Delhi to be more flexible on Kashmir. It is clearly in the American interest to try to defuse a lingering conflict that has generated global terrorism and repeatedly threatened to create a full-scale military confrontation on the subcontinent. It is also in India's interest to find a solution to a conflict that has gone on too long. Since the Kargil War in 1999, the Indians have been more open to an American role in Kashmir because they sense Washington is fundamentally in favor of a resolution to maintain the status quo, which favors India.

The key will be whether the United States can make clear to Pakistan that its red lines about terror are real, especially the red line on Lashkar-e-Tayyiba. If Prime Minister Singh can see real evidence of LeT being broken up and dismantled in Pakistan, then he can reenter and advance the back channel with the political clout to secure a peace breakthrough.

The United States currently has better relations with both India and Pakistan than at any other time in the past several decades. Its rapprochement with India, begun by President Clinton and advanced by President Bush, is now supported by an almost unique bipartisan consensus in the American foreign policy establishment and Congress. President Obama has already hosted Singh at the White House for a state dinner and traveled to New Delhi in November 2010. At the same time, the sanctions that poisoned U.S.-Pakistani ties for decades have been removed by new legislation passed with bipartisan support. Obama has begun a strategic partnership dialogue with Islamabad. It is a unique and propitious moment.

A Kashmir solution would have to be structured around a formula for making the Line of Control both a permanent and normal international border (perhaps with some minor modifications) and a permeable frontier between the two parts of Kashmir so that the Kashmiri people could live more normal lives. A special condominium might be created to allow the two constituencies to work together on issues specific to the region, such as transportation, the environment, sports, and tourism. The two currencies of India and Pakistan could become legal tender on both sides of the border, for example, an idea recently floated in India.

Given the history of mistrust that pervades both sides, the two states are unlikely to be able to reach such an agreement on their own. A quiet American effort led by the president to promote a solution is probably essential to move the parties toward an agreement. This should not be a formal, public initiative—discretion and privacy are essential. I urged Obama to do just this on Air Force One and in the strategic review.

Resolution of the Kashmiri issue would go a long way toward making Pakistan a more normal state and one less preoccupied with India. It would also remove a major rationale for the army's disproportionate role in Pakistan's national security affairs. That in turn would help to ensure the survival of genuine civilian democratic rule in the country. A resolution of the major outstanding issue between Islamabad and New Delhi would reduce the arms race between them and the risk of nuclear conflict. With the desire to fight asymmetric warfare against India eliminated, Pakistan would also be discouraged from making alliances with the Taliban, Lashkar-e-Tayyiba, and al Qaeda. Former ambassador Bill Milam, a seasoned South Asia hand, has insightfully stressed that the "India-Centricity of the Pakistani mindset is the most important factor and variable" in the future of the country.[39]

Such an agreement would not resolve all the tensions between the two neighbors or end the problem of the Taliban in Afghanistan. But more than anything else, it would set the stage for a different era in the subcontinent and for more productive interaction between the international community and Pakistan. It could set the stage for a genuine rapprochement between India and Pakistan and nurture trade and economic interaction that could transform the subcontinent for the better. This is the big idea America needs to promote in south Asia.

CONCLUSION

We flew more than twenty-two hours and refueled in the air three times to get from Tampa to Islamabad in May 1998. Strobe Talbott and I had boarded General Tony Zinni's plane in a desperate effort to persuade Pakistan not to follow India's lead and test nuclear weapons. At Pakistan's Foreign Ministry and army headquarters we had already been told our mission was futile and that America was a "fair-weather friend," but we still felt we had to try to deter Prime Minister Nawaz Sharif from testing.

We began in a large meeting with the prime minister and his aides. Sharif was offered a multibillion-dollar aid package, a promise to repeal the Pressler Amendment, and a state visit to Washington if he would show restraint. Let India be the guilty party for testing, we urged him. Sharif understood the argument and appreciated the proposal. He asked to see Strobe alone.

Face-to-face, Sharif told Strobe it was impossible for him not to test. Pakistan could not be outdone by India. At the same time, he understood our points and agreed with much of what we had said. Nawaz, Strobe later said, seemed akin to Shakespeare's Hamlet, almost pathetically unable to decide what to do. The only way he could survive in office if he did not test, Sharif asserted, was if the United States would do something to resolve Kashmir. He repeatedly stressed that all hinged on Kashmir. Barring that, he would have to test. Otherwise, Sharif warned, the next time Strobe came to Islamabad the prime minister would be a jihadist with a "long beard."[40]

None of the policy options laid out in this chapter will be easy to implement and none can guarantee that the global Islamic jihad movement will be defeated in Pakistan. After all, Pakistan has been nurturing jihad for more than three decades, at least since Abdallah Azzam moved to Peshawar in the 1980s. An extremely powerful jihadist Frankenstein is now roaming the world, with equally powerful protectors in Pakistani society, right up to the very top. Who cannot fear that the "long beards" will prevail?

Yet just in 2008 Pakistanis ousted a military dictator without major violence and elected a civilian leadership. They have begun to tackle part of the jihadist infrastructure at great cost to their lives and wealth. The battle for the soul of Pakistan is under way.

The stakes in this endeavor are enormous. The future of the global jihad will be decided in Pakistan more than anywhere else in the world. As difficult as the mission remains, there is every reason for Pakistanis and Americans to transform what has long been a deadly embrace into a union of minds with a common purpose: to defeat the jihad monster.

KEY PERSONS AND TIMELINE

JIHADIS

Abdallah Azzam, Palestinian writer and proponent of the Afghan jihad who was assassinated in 1989.

Osama bin Laden, Saudi son of wealthy Yemeni construction mogul, fought in Afghan war in 1980s, and founded al Qaeda.

David Headley, American citizen of Pakistani descent who scouted targets for the Lashkar-e-Tayyiba attack on Mumbai in 2008 and for al Qaeda in Copenhagen in 2009; has pleaded guilty and is in jail.

Gulbudin Hekmatayar, Afghan warlord who has led Pashtun resistance to the Soviet and American forces in eastern Afghanistan.

Muhammad Ilyas Kashmiri, Pakistani who led campaign against India in Kashmir in the 1990s with ISI assistance, then joined al Qaeda.

Mullah Muhammad Omar, Afghan who founded the Taliban and became commander of the faithful leading the Islamic Emirate of Afghanistan.

Sayid Qutb, Egyptian writer who preached for jihad and was executed by the government of Gamal Abdel Nasser.

Rashid Rauf, British citizen of Pakistani descent who planned the 2006 airline plot and the 2009 plot to attack the New York City subway system.

Hafez Saeed, Pakistani who founded Lashkar-e-Tayyiba with Abdallah Azzam and today leads its successor, Jamaat ud Dawa.

Abu Musaib al Zarqawi, Jordanian who created al Qaeda in Iraq and was killed in 2006.

Ayman al Zawahiri, Egyptian doctor who was imprisoned for his role in assassination of Anwar Sadat and is bin Laden's deputy in al Qaeda.

PAKISTANIS

Benazir Bhutto, twice prime minister of Pakistan who returned from exile in 2007 and was assassinated by al Qaeda.

Zulfikar Bhutto, prime minister and president of Pakistan who was executed by Zia ul-Haq in 1977.

Syed Yousaf Raza Gillani, prime minister of Pakistan since 2008.

Zia ul-Haq, chief of army staff who overthrew Zulfikar Bhutto in 1977 and Islamized Pakistan's army and society; killed in airplane crash in 1988.

Muhammad Ali Jinnah, founder of Pakistan and its first leader, who died in 1948.

Ayub Khan, chief of army staff who overthrew civilian government in 1958 and created first military dictatorship, leading country into 1965 war with India.

Yahya Khan, second military dictator who led country into 1971 civil war and then war with India that created Bangladesh.

Pervez Musharraf, chief of army staff who overthrew Nawaz Sharif in 1999 and was removed from power by parliament in 2008.

Nawaz Sharif, twice prime minister of Pakistan, ousted by Musharraf's coup and returned from exile in Saudi Arabia in 2007 and leads Pakistan Muslim League.

Asif Ali Zardari, president of Pakistan since 2008 and husband of Benazir Bhutto.

DIRECTORS GENERAL OF THE ISI

Major General R. Cawthome, 1948–56
Brigadier Riaz Hussain, 1959–66
Major General (then Brigadier) Mohammad Akbar Khan, 1966–71
Lieutenant General (then Major General) Ghulam Jilani Khan, 1971–78
Lieutenant General Muhammad Riaz, 1978–80
Lieutenant General Akhtar Abdur Rahman, 1980–March 1987
Lieutenant General Hamid Gul, March 1987–May 1989
Lieutenant General Shamsur Rahman Kallu, May 1989–August 1990
Lieutenant General Asad Durrani, August 1990–March 1992
Lieutenant General Javed Nasir, March 1992–May 1993
Lieutenant General Javad Ashraf Qazi, May 1993–95

Lieutenant General (then Major General) Naseem Rana, 1995–October 1998
Lieutenant General Ziauddin Butt, October 1998–October 1999
Lieutenant General Mahmud Ahmad, October 1999–October 2001
Lieutenant General Ehsan ul Haq, October 2001–October 2004
Lieutenant General Ashfaq Parvez Kayani, October 2004–October 2007
Lieutenant General Nadeem Taj, October 2007–October 2008
Lieutenant General Ahmad Shuja Pasha, October 2008–Present

Short Timeline of Events in Pakistan

1947   Pakistan gains independence from British Empire, fights first war with India over Kashmir.

1958   Ayub Khan overthrows civilian government, creates first military dictatorship.

1965   Second Pakistani war with India ends in stalemate.

1971   Third Pakistani war with India ends in Pakistan's defeat, creation of Bangladesh, and removal of second military dictator, Yahya Khan.

1977   Zia ul-Haq overthrows Zulfikar Bhutto and rules as third military dictator.

1979   Soviet invasion of Afghanistan starts mujahedin war.

1988   Soviet forces evacuate Afghanistan, Zia dies in airplane crash.

1990   President George H. W. Bush invokes Pressler Amendment, cutting off all aid to Pakistan.

1994   Taliban movement created in Afghanistan, takes Kabul in 1996.

1999   Pakistan and India fight war in Kargil, Musharraf overthrows Nawaz Sharif.

2001   September 11 attacks, U.S. intervention in Afghanistan.

2007   Benazir Bhutto assassinated after returning home from exile.

2008   Musharraf removed from office, Benazir's husband, Asif Ali Zardari, becomes president.

Notes

Preface

1. Stephen P. Cohen, *The Future of Pakistan Project* (Brookings, 2010), p. 8.

2. Evan F. Kohlman, *Al Qaeda's Jihad in Europe: The Afghan Bosnian Network* (Oxford: Bers, 2004), p. 9.

3. "Remarks by the President on a New Strategy for Afghanistan and Pakistan," White House, Office of the Press Secretary, March 27, 2009.

4. Peter Lavoy, ed., *Asymmetric Warfare in South Asia: The Causes and Consequences of the Kargil Conflict* (Cambridge University Press, 2009), p. 88.

5. Jack Devine, "Where Is Osama bin Laden?" *Washington Post*, October 10, 2010, p. A19.

6. John Brennan, "Securing the Homeland by Renewing America's Strengths, Resilience and Values," speech to the Center for Strategic and International Studies, Washington, May 26, 2010.

Chapter One

1. Afghanistan was not part of the British Empire in India nor is it part of today's Pakistan. Ali may have meant what is better known as the North-West Frontier Province, which like much of Afghanistan is populated by Pashtun Muslims. Or he may have sought to unite Afghanistan and Pakistan.

2. Stanley Wolpert, *Shameful Flight: The Last Years of the British Empire in India* (Oxford University Press, 2006), p. 1.

3. Stanley Wolpert, *Jinnah of Pakistan* (Oxford University Press, 1984), p. 9. See also the portrait of Jinnah in Alex Von Tunzelmann, *Indian Summer: The Secret History of the End of an Empire* (New York: Picador, 2007), p. 94.

4. Jaswant Singh, *Jinnah: India – Partition – Independence* (New Delhi: Rupa, 2009), p. 79.

5. William Dalrymple, *The Last Mughal: The Fall of a Dynasty, Delhi, 1857* (New York: Penguin, 2007), p. 485.

6. Wolpert, *Jinnah of Pakistan*, p. 156.

7. Fouad Ajami, "With Us or against Us," *New York Times*, Book Review, January 7, 2007, p. 14.

8. Seyyed Vali Reza Nasr, *The Vanguard of the Islamic Revolution: The Jama'at-i Islami of Pakistan* (University of California Press, 1994), pp. 19–20.

9. Alyssa Ayres, *Speaking Like a State: Language and Nationalism in Pakistan* (Cambridge University Press, 2009), pp. 25–26.

10. Ibid., p. 42.

11. Seth Jones, *In the Graveyard of Empires: America's War in Afghanistan* (New York: Norton, 2009), p. 30.

12. Shuja Nawaz, *Crossed Swords: Pakistan, Its Army, and the Wars Within* (Oxford University Press, 2008), p. 255.

13. Arvin Bahl, *From Jinnah to Jihad: Pakistan's Kashmir Quest and the Limits of Realism* (New Delhi: Atlantic, 2007), p. 67.

14. Hassan Abbas, *Pakistan's Drift into Extremism: Allah, the Army and America's War on Terror* (London: M. E. Sharpe, 2005), p. 57.

15. How many died in the 1971 campaign is a disputed figure. Several experts have studied the data and tend to confirm the Bangladeshi claims. See Rounaq Jahan, "Genocide in Bangladesh," in *Century of Genocide: Eyewitness Accounts and Critical Views,* edited by Samuel Totten, William Parsons, and Israel Charny (New York: Routledge, 2004), pp. 295–319.

16. Abbas, *Pakistan's Drift*, p. 67.

17. Nawaz, *Crossed Swords,* p. 17.

18. Arthur Herman, *Gandhi and Churchill: The Epic Rivalry That Destroyed an Empire and Forged Our Age* (New York: Bantam Books, 2008), p. 499.

19. Tunzelmann, *Indian Summer*, p. 153.

20. Dennis Kux, *The United States and Pakistan, 1947–2000: Disenchanted Allies* (Johns Hopkins University Press, 2001), p. 56.

21. Kux, *The United States and Pakistan,* p. 61.

22. Ibid., p. 76.

23. Ibid., pp. 91–92.

24. Tariq Ali, *The Duel: Pakistan on the Flight Path of American Power* (Toronto: Scribner, 2008), p. 59

25. Abdul Qadeer Khan, interview on the "Islamabad Tonight" program broadcast by Aaj New Television in Karachi, August 31, 2009. Translated by the Open Source Center.

CHAPTER TWO

1. For details of Casey's trip, see Charles Cogan, "Partners in Time: The CIA and Afghanistan since 1979," *World Policy Journal* 10 (Summer 1993): 73–82. Chuck was the CIA's Near East and South Asia Division chief in the Directorate

of Operations at the time and accompanied Casey on all his visits to the region. Bob Gates also recounts the first Zia-Casey meeting in his book, cited in n. 2.

2. Robert M. Gates, *From the Shadows: The Ultimate Insider's Story of Five Presidents and How They Won the Cold War* (New York: Simon and Schuster, 1996), p. 349.

3. There are many accounts of Pakistan's pursuit of nuclear weapons. Pervez Hoodbhoy, a Pakistani scientist, has offered an excellent overview in "Pakistan's Nuclear Trajectory Past, Present and Future," in *Pakistan: Reality, Denial and the Complexity of the State* (Berlin: Heinrich-Böll-Stiftung, 2009), pp. 111–39.

4. For A. Q. Khan's story, see, for example, Douglas Frantz and Catherine Colins, *The Nuclear Jihadist: The True Story of the Man Who Sold the World's Most Dangerous Secrets . . . and How We Could Have Stopped Him* (New York: Hachette, 2007); and International Institute for Strategic Studies, *Nuclear Black Markets: Pakistan, A. Q. Khan and the Rise of Proliferation Markets; A Net Assessment* (London, 2007).

5. William B. Milam, *Bangladesh and Pakistan: Flirting with Failure in South Asia* (Columbia University Press, 2009), p. 73.

6. His Royal Highness Prince Hassan bin Talal, interview with the author, April 11, 2010.

7. Jordan repaid Pakistan in 1971 by sending ten F104 jet fighters to help fight the Indians. See Aparna Pande, *Explaining Pakistan's Foreign Policy: Escaping India* (New York: Routledge, forthcoming), p. 282.

8. Seyyed Vali Reza Nasr, *The Vanguard of the Islamic Revolution: The Jama'at-i Islami of Pakistan* (University of California Press, 1994), p. 189.

9. Shuja Nawaz, *Crossed Swords: Pakistan, Its Army, and the Wars Within* (Oxford University Press, 2008), p. 361.

10. Steve Coll, *Ghost Wars: The Secret History of the CIA, Afghanistan, and Bin Laden, from the Soviet Invasion to September 10, 2001* (New York: Penguin, 2004), p. 180.

11. Ayesha Siddiqa, *Military Inc.: Inside Pakistan's Military Economy* (London: Pluto Press, 2007), p. 186.

12. Mohammad Yousaf and Mark Adkin, *The Bear Trap: Afghanistan's Untold Story* (London: Leo Cooper, 1992), p. 22; and Mohammad Yousaf, *Silent Soldier: The Man behind the Afghan Jehad, General Akhtar Abdur Rahman Shaheed* (Lahore: Jang, 1991), p. 27. *The Bear Trap* is the definitive account of the ISI's war from a Pakistani perspective; Yousaf was the ISI's Afghan bureau chief from 1983 to 1987, and the book is dedicated to General Akhtar Rahman.

13. Daveed Gartenstein-Ross, "Religious Militancy in Pakistan's Military and Inter-Services Intelligence Agency," in *The Afghanistan-Pakistan Theater: Militant Islam, Security and Stability* (Washington: FDD Press, 2010), p. 33.

14. Yousaf, *Silent Soldier,* pp. 16, 70.

15. Fouad Ajami, "With Us or against Us," *New York Times,* Book Review, January 7, 2007, p. 14.

16. Seyyed Vali Reza Nasr, "International Politics, Domestic Imperatives and Identity Mobilization: Sectarianism in Pakistan, 1979–1998," *Comparative Politics* 32 (January 2000): 171–90.

17. Nawaz, *Crossed Swords,* pp. 372–73. Prince Turki has also confirmed this account in an interview with this author.

18. Nawaz, *Crossed Swords,* p. 386.

19. Ibid., p. 375.

20. Carlotta Gall of the *New York Times* interviewed the ISI trainer, Colonel Imam, in 2010. I am indebted to her for this information on Mullah Omar's ISI background. Colonel Imam also mentioned training Omar to Christina Lamb in "The Taliban Will Never Be Defeated," *London Sunday Times,* June 7, 2009. Imam claims the ISI trained more than 95,000 Afghans.

21. S. M. A. Hussaini, *Air Warriors of Pakistan* (Lahore: Ferozsons, 1989), p. 25.

22. Yousaf and Adkin, *Bear Trap,* pp. 191–95.

23. Yousaf, *Silent Soldier,* p. 42.

24. Gregory Feifer, *The Great Gamble: The Soviet War in Afghanistan* (New York: HarperCollins, 2009), p. 130. Feifer's book is the best account available on the Soviet side of the war.

25. Yousaf and Adkin, *Bear Trap,* p. 97.

26. Arif Jamal, *Shadow War: The Untold Story of the Jihad in Kashmir* (Brooklyn: Melville House, 2009), pp. 107–11.

27. Ibid., p. 115.

28. The authoritative account of the CIA relationship with the mujahedin and the decisions within the agency and the White House is Gates's *From the Shadows*; see esp. p. 147. For added insight and color, see George Crile's masterpiece, *Charlie Wilson's War: The Extraordinary Story of How the Wildest Man in Congress and a Rogue CIA Agent Changed the History of Our Times* (New York: Atlantic Monthly Press, 2003).

29. Gates, *From the Shadows,* p. 321; Cogan, "Partners in Time," p. 76.

30. Cogan, "Partners in Time," p. 79.

31. Crile, *Charlie Wilson's War,* pp. 502–03.

32. Zvi Rafiah, interview with the author, May 10, 2010. Zvi was Charlie's Israeli contact.

33. Efraim Halevy, interview with the author, November 20, 2008.

34. The best biography of Azzam is Thomas Hegghammer, "Abdallah Azzam," in *Al Qaeda in Its Own Words,* edited by Gilles Kepel and Jean-Pierre Milelli (Harvard University Press, 2009), pp. 81–102.

35. Shaul Mishal, *West Bank, East Bank: The Palestinians in Jordan, 1949–1967* (Yale University Press, 1978).

36. Zaki Chehab, *Inside Hamas: The Untold Story of Militants, Martyrs and Spies* (London: Tauris, 2007), p. 193.

37. Lawrence Wright, *The Looming Tower: Al Qaeda and the Road to 9/11* (New York: Alfred A. Knopf, 2006), p. 102.

38. Matthew Levitt, *Hamas: Politics, Charity and Terrorism in the Service of Jihad* (Yale University Press, 2006), p. 150.

39. Hegghammer, "Abdallah Azzam," p. 108.

40. Ahmed Rashid, *Taliban: Militant Islam, Oil and Fundamentalism in Central Asia* (Yale University Press, 2001), p. 132.

41. John Wilson, "Lashkar e Tayyeba," Pakistan Security Research Unit Brief 12 (University of Bradford, 2007); and Ashley J. Telis, "Bad Company—Lashkar-e-Tayyiba and the Growing Ambition of Islamist Militancy in Pakistan," Congressional Testimony (Carnegie Endowment for International Peace, March 11, 2010).

42. Chehab, *Inside Hamas*, p. 193.

43. Asaf Maliach, "Bin Ladin, Palestine and al Qaida's Operational Strategy," *Middle Eastern Studies* 44 (May 2008): 355.

44. Paul McGeough, *Kill Khalid: The Failed Mossad Assassination of Khaled Mishal and the Rise of Hamas* (London: New Press, 2009), p. 405.

45. Benazir Bhutto, *Reconciliation: Islam, Democracy and the West* (New York: Harper, 2008), p. 56.

46. Roger Hardy, *The Muslim Revolt: A Journey through Political Islam* (Columbia University Press, 2010), pp. 156–59.

47. Rashid, *Taliban*, p. 130.

48. Brynjar Lia, *Architect of Global Jihad: The Life of Al Qaida Strategist Abu Mus'ab al-Suri* (London: Hust, 2007).

49. Norm Cigar, *Al-Qa'ida's Doctrine for Insurgency: 'Abd Al-'Aziz Al-Muqrin's A Practical Course for Guerrilla War* (Washington: Potomac, 2009).

50. Maliach, "Bin Laden, Palestine," p. 364.

51. Hegghammer, "Abdallah Azzam," pp. 96–97.

52. Maliach, "Bin Laden, Palestine," p. 357.

53. Shaheed Abu Dujannah al Khorasani, hero of the raid of the Shaheed Amir Beitullah Mehsud, a February 2010 interview, translated by the Nine Eleven Finding Answers (NEFA) Foundation.

54. Yousaf and Adkin, *Bear Trap*, p. 234.

55. Barbara Crossette, "Who Killed Zia?" *World Policy Journal* 22 (Fall 2005): 94–102.

56. Nawaz, *Crossed Swords*, pp. 393–405.

CHAPTER THREE

1. Benazir Bhutto, *Daughter of the East: An Autobiography* (London: Hamish Hamilton, 1988), pp. 76–78.

2. Ibid., p. 252.

3. Mohammad Yousaf and Mark Adkin, *The Bear Trap: Afghanistan's Untold Story* (London: Leo Cooper, 1992), p. 220.

4. Arif Jamal, *Shadow War: The Untold Story of the Jihad in Kashmir* (Brooklyn: Melville House, 2009), p. 128.

5. Benazir Bhutto, *Reconciliation: Islam, Democracy and the West* (New York: HarperCollins, 2008), pp. 195–201.

6. Bhutto, *Daughter of the East,* p. 400.

7. Arnaud de Borchgrave, "Army Back on Top," *Washington Times,* March 30, 2010.

8. UN Commission of Inquiry, "Report into the Facts and Circumstances of the Assassination of Former Pakistani Prime Minister Mohtarma Benazir Bhutto," April 2010, pars. 38, 218.

9. Jamal, *Shadow War,* p. 136.

10. Zahid Hussain, *Frontline Pakistan: The Struggle with Militant Islam* (Columbia University Press, 2007), p. 54.

11. Jamal, *Shadow War,* p. 13.

12. Ibid., p. 137.

13. Ibid., pp. 147–57.

14. Arif Jamal, "South Asia's Architect of Jihad: A Profile of Commander Mohammad Ilyas Kashmiri," *Militant Leadership Monitor* (Jamestown Foundation) 1 (January 30, 2010): 8–10.

15. P. R. Chari, Pervaiz Iqbal Cheema, and Stephen P. Cohen, *Four Crises and a Peace Process: American Engagement in South Asia* (Brookings, 2007), p. 86.

16. Ibid., pp. 91–98.

17. Husain Haqqani, *Pakistan: Between Mosque and Military* (Washington: Carnegie Endowment for International Peace, 2005), p. 220.

18. Abdul Qadeer Khan, discussing Pakistan's nuclear program on TV talk show, Karachi Aaj Television, August 31, 2009, translated by Open Source Center.

19. "Nawaz Sharif Met Osama Three Times, Former ISI Official," *Daily Times Monitor* (Lahore), June 23, 2005.

20. Haqqani, *Pakistan: Between Mosque and Military,* p. 228.

21. The most thorough investigation is by Asif's brother. See Shuja Nawaz *Crossed Swords: Pakistan, Its Army, and the Wars Within* (Oxford University Press, 2008), esp. appx. 3, "Investigation into the Death of General Asif Nawaz," pp. 599–605. Nawaz states that there was no direct evidence linking Prime Minister Sharif to the death, but the mystery remains.

22. Haqqani, *Pakistan: Between Mosque and Military,* p. 229.

23. Abdul Salam Zaeef, *My Life with the Taliban,* translated and edited by Alex Strick van Linschoten and Felix Kuehn (Columbia University Press, 2010), p. 123.

24. Ibid., p. 171.

25. Jamal, *Shadow War,* pp. 184–85.

26. Ibid., p. 185. As on most things about Pakistani politics, there is a great debate about whether Benazir was actually ever asked to consider the Kargil operation on her watch. For a look at the argument on both sides, see Peter R.

Lavoy, ed., *Asymmetric Warfare in South Asia: The Causes and Consequences of the Kargil Conflict* (Cambridge University Press, 2010), pp. 76–79.

27. Lavoy, *Asymmetric Warfare*, pp. 241–42.

28. See Bruce Riedel, "American Diplomacy and the 1999 Kargil Summit at Blair House," in ibid., pp. 130–43.

29. For a detailed study of the Pressler and Brown Amendments and their legislative history, see Rebecca K. C. Hersman, *Friends and Foes: How the Congress and the President Really Make Foreign Policy* (Brookings, 2000), pp. 67–84.

30. Robert Gates, "Helping Others Defend Themselves," *Foreign Affairs*, May/June 2010, p. 3.

31. Ibid., p. 3.

32. Ahmed Rashid, *Taliban: Militant Islam, Oil and Fundamentalism in Central Asia* (Yale University Press, 2001), p. 166.

33. Ibid., p. 164.

34. Bill Richardson, *Between Worlds: The Making of an American Life* (New York: Putnam, 2005), p. 226.

35. Rashid, *Taliban*, p. 138.

36. Bruce Riedel, *The Search for al Qaeda: Its Leadership, Ideology, and Future* (Brookings, 2010), p. 68.

37. Defense Intelligence Agency cable, "Veteran Afghanistan Travelers Analysis of Al Qaeda and the Taliban," October 2, 2001, declassified by the National Security Archives (www.gwu.edu/nsarchiv/NSAEBB/NSAEBB97/tal28.pdf).

38. Riedel, "American Diplomacy and the 1999 Kargil Summit," pp. 130–43.

39. Tariq Fatemi, interview with the author, June 29, 2010. Tariq was the note-taker.

40. A senior UAE official, interview with the author, May 21, 2009.

41. *Mullah Mohammad Omar Mujahid* (Azzam Publications, 2010).

42. In his memoirs, Pervez Musharraf confirms Omar was trained in Pakistan and recovered from his eye wound in a Pakistani hospital, but he puts that hospital in Peshawar rather than Quetta. Pervez Musharraf, *In the Line of Fire: A Memoir* (New York: Free Press, 2006), p. 210.

43. Rashid, *Taliban*, p. 183.

44. Gilles Dorronsoro, *Revolution Unending: Afghanistan, 1979 to the Present* (Columbia University Press, 2005), p. 236.

45. The 9/11 Commission picked Khalis but said Hekmatayar was also involved. National Commission on Terrorist Attacks upon the United States, *The 9/11 Commission Report* (U.S. Government Printing Office, 2004), p. 65. Rashid, *Taliban*, p. 133, suggests the shura.

46. *The 9/11 Commission Report*, p. 62.

47. Roy Gutman, *How We Missed the Story: Osama bin Laden, the Taliban and the Hijacking of Afghanistan* (Washington: United States Institute for Peace, 2008), p. 92.

48. Ibid., p. 98.

49. Dorronsoro, *Revolution Unending*, p. 305.

50. Peter Bergen, *The Osama bin Laden I Know: An Oral History of al Qaeda's Leader* (New York: Free Press, 2006), p. 164.

51. James Risen, "U.S. Seeks Means to Bring Suspect from Afghanistan," *New York Times*, August 30, 1998.

52. Luke Harding, "Taliban Will Not Hand Over Bin Laden," *Manchester Guardian*, March 31, 2001.

53. On the license plates, see *The 9/11 Commission Report*, p. 66. On Ariana, see Steve Coll, *The Bin Ladens: An Arabian Family in the American Century* (New York: Penguin Books, 2006), p. 482.

54. Peter Bergen, *Holy War, Inc.: Inside the Secret World of Osama bin Laden* (New York: Simon and Schuster, 2002), p. 165. See also Robert Crews and Amin Tarzi, eds., *The Taliban and the Crisis of Afghanistan* (Harvard University Press, 2008), p. 105.

55. *The 9/11 Commission, Report*, p. 110; and Gutman, *How We Missed the Story*, p. 92.

56. Gutman, *How We Missed the Story*, p. 241.

57. Jean-Louis Bruguiere, *Ce que je n'ai pas pu dire* (What I have never been able to tell) (Paris: Robert Laffont, 2009), p. 342.

58. Gutman, *How We Missed the Story*, p. 193.

59. *The 9/11 Commission Report*, pp. 174–75.

60. Riedel, *The Search for al Qaeda*, chap. 5, "The Stranger: Zarqawi," pp. 85–115.

61. *The 9/11 Commission Report*, pp. 176–79.

62. Neelesh Misra, *173 Hours in Captivity: The Hijacking of IC 814* (New Delhi: HarperCollins, 2000), p. 47.

63. Ibid., pp. 149, 170.

64. Gutman, *How We Missed the Story*, p. 192.

65. Embassy of India, "Information on Hijacked Indian Airlines Flight IC 814."

66. Jaswant wrote later that the hijacking was in many ways the precursor for the 9/11 operation since it involved al Qaeda, the Taliban, and ISI. Jaswant Singh, *In Search of Emergent India: A Call to Honor* (Indiana University Press, 2007), p. 204.

CHAPTER FOUR

1. Bill Clinton, *My Life* (New York: Knopf, 2004), p. 903.

2. Bill Clinton, Greeting to the People of Pakistan, White House, Office of the Press Secretary, March 25, 2000.

3. Former Afghan foreign minister Abdallah Abdallah, interview with the author, May 17, 2010.

4. Pervez Musharraf, *In the Line of Fire: A Memoir* (New York: Free Press, 2006), p. 11.

5. Musharraf's memoir is a key source on his life but has to be viewed with some care. An excellent short biography is by Fouad Ajami, "With Us or against Us," *New York Times*, Book Review, January 7, 2007, pp. 14–15. It tells how Musharraf was recruited to the Bush administration's war on terror.

6. "Musharraf Wept When East Pak Fell," *Times of India*, April 24, 2006.

7. Ahmed Rashid, *Descent into Chaos: The United States and the Failure of Nation Building in Pakistan, Afghanistan, and Central Asia* (New York: Viking, 2008), p. 48.

8. Robert L. Grenier, interview with the author, May 18, 2010.

9. Reported in Adrian Levy and Catherine Scott-Clark, *Deception: Pakistan, the United States and the Secret Trade in Nuclear Weapons* (New York: Walker, 2007), p. 6.

10. The story is reviewed in Richard Clarke, *Against All Enemies: Inside America's War on Terror* (New York: Free Press, 2004).

11. Clarke's memo was declassified after a Freedom of Information request and can be accessed at the National Security Archives website. The subject is Presidential Policy Initiative/Review—The Al Qida Network.

12. George Tenet, *At the Center of the Storm: My Years at the CIA* (New York: HarperCollins, 2007), pp. 140–41.

13. Ambassador Wendy Chamberlin, interview with the author, August 24, 2010.

14. Zahid Hussain, *Frontline Pakistan: The Struggle with Militant Islam* (Columbia University Press, 2007), p. 43.

15. Grenier interview, May 18, 2010.

16. "India Helped FBI Trace ISI-Terrorist Link," *The Times of India*, October 9, 2001.

17. Grenier interview, May 18, 2010.

18. Musharraf, *In the Line of Fire*, p. 202.

19. Ibid.

20. Pervez Musharraf, interview with the author, September 30, 2009.

21. The dispersal of Al Qaeda and Taliban fighters in 2002 is covered best by Anne Stenersen, "Al Qaeda's Allies," Policy Paper (Washington: New America Foundation, April 2010).

22. Grenier interview, May 18, 2010.

23. John Kiriakou, *The Reluctant Spy: My Secret Life in the CIA's War on Terror* (New York: Random House, 2009), pp. 106–22.

24. Musharraf, *In the Line of Fire*, p. xxx.

25. Jaswant Singh, *In Service of Emergent India: A Call to Honor* (Indiana University Press, 2007), p. 204. I have also interviewed Jaswant several times on the incident.

26. B. Muralidhar Reddy, "Jaish behind Parliament Attack: Ex-ISI Chief," *The Hindu*, July, 3, 2004.

27. I am indebted to Ambassador Wendy Chamberlain for this insight.

28. Singh, *A Call to Honour*, p. 238.

29. Rashid, *Descent into Chaos*, p. 113.

30. Musharraf, *In the Line of Fire*, pp. 1–7.

31. The back-channel discussions are reported by Steve Coll, "The Back Channel: India and Pakistan Negotiate on Kashmir," *New Yorker*, March 2, 2009, pp. 38–51.

32. Stephen P. Cohen, "How America Helped Wreck Pakistan," *Current History*, April 2010, p. 140.

33. Tenet, *Center of the Storm*, p. 285.

34. For an excellent analysis of the Bush Freedom Agenda, see Tamara Cofman Wittes, *Freedom's Unsteady March: America's Role in Building Arab Democracy* (Brookings, 2008); the Bush quotations are from pp. 3–4.

35. "Dictatorship Non-Existent in Pakistan: U.S.," *Pakistan Tribune*, April 1, 2006.

36. Helene Cooper and Mark Mazzetti, "Backstage, U.S. Nurtured Pakistan Rivals' Deal," *New York Times*, October 20, 2007.

37. UN Commission of Inquiry, "Report into the Facts and Circumstances of the Assassination of Former Pakistani Prime Minister Mohtarma Benazir Bhutto," April 2010, par. 205.

38. Ibid., par. 219.

39. Ibid., par. 208.

40. Ibid., executive summary.

41. Ibid., par. 218.

42. Adnan R. Khan, "Land of the Generals," *Maclean's* Magazine, July 5, 2010, p. 46.

43. Hussain, *Frontline Pakistan*, p. 43.

44. Jean Pierre Filiu, *Les neuf vies d'al Qaida* (The nine lives of al Qaeda) (Paris: Fayard, 2009), p. 109.

45. Alan Cullison, "Inside al Qaeda's Hard Drive," *The Atlantic Online*, September 2004.

46. Filiu, *Les neuf vies*, p. 108.

47. Musharraf, *In the Line of Fire*, p. 208.

48. Sally Neighbour, *The Mother of Mohammed: An Australian Woman's Extraordinary Journey into Jihad* (Melbourne University Press, 2009), p. 272.

49. Guy Lawson, "Omar Bin Laden's Twisted Journey," *Rolling Stone*, February 4, 2010, p. 70.

50. Gary C. Schroen, *First In: An Insider's Account of How the CIA Spearheaded the War on Terror* (New York: Ballantine, 2005).

51. Richard Haass, "We're Not Winning; It's Not Worth It," *Newsweek*, July 18, 2010.

52. Stenersen, "Al Qaeda's Allies."

53. Syed Saleem Shazad, "Al Qaeda's Guerrilla Chief Lays Out Strategy," *Asia Times,* October 15, 2009.

54. Matt Waldman, "The Sun in the Sky: The Relationship between Pakistan's ISI and Afghan Insurgents," Discussion Paper 18 (London School of Economics, Crisis States Research Centre, June 2010).

55. Christina Lamb, "Taliban Leader Killed by SAS Was Pakistani Officer," *London Sunday Times,* October 12, 2008.

56. Nick B. Mills, *Karzai: The Failing American Intervention and the Struggle for Afghanistan* (New York: Wiley, 2007), p, 216.

57. Jane Perlez and Salman Masood, "Terror Ties Run Deep in Pakistan, Mumbai Case Shows," *New York Times,* July 27, 2009.

58. Bruce Riedel, *The Search for al Qaeda* (Brookings, 2008), p. 32.

59. Stephen Tankel, *Lashkar e Taiba: From 9/11 to Mumbai* (London: International Centre for the Study of Radicalization and Political Violence, 2009), pp. 12–18.

60. Ibid., p. 18.

61. Fernando Reinares, "The Madrid Bombings and Global Jihadism," *Survival* 52 (May 2010), pp. 23–24.

CHAPTER FIVE

1. The details of the attack have been widely reported. For a good summary, see Angel Rabasa and others, "The Lessons of Mumbai," Occasional Paper (Santa Monica, Calif.: RAND, 2009). This work includes a useful chronology of the incident. Qasab's confession was reported by the BBC, among others. See *BBC News,* "Excerpts from Mumbai Suspect's Confession," July 20, 2009.

2. See Nawaz Sharif, interview, "Vajpayee May Have Dealt Differently with Jaswant Singh," *Hindustan Times,* August 23, 2009. Sharif says, "Look at the colossal damage that we have done to our own economies by the arms race."

3. Steve Coll, "The Back Channel: India and Pakistan Negotiate on Kashmir," *New Yorker,* March 2, 2009.

4. See Pervez Musharraf, interview, "Obama Is Aiming at the Right Things," *Der Spiegel,* July 6, 2009.

5. See the guilty plea agreement in *United States of America* v. *David Coleman Headley,* 09 CR 830-3, U.S. District Court, Northern District of Illinois, March 2010. The prosecutor was Patrick Fitzgerald.

6. Sameer Lalwani, "Pakistan's COIN Flip: The Recent History of Pakistani Military Counterinsurgency Operations in the NWFP and FATA" (Washington: New America Foundation, April 2010).

7. Pakistan Institute for Peace Studies, *Pakistan Security Report 2009* (Islamabad, 2010).

8. See the National Counterterrorism Center's Worldwide Incidents Tracking System database.

9. Lalwani, "Pakistan's COIN Flip," estimates between 40,000 and 60,000. Former Pakistani information minister Sherry Rehman told me 50,000 in an interview, June 5, 2010.

10. The PEW Global Attitudes Project, "Pakistani Public Opinion: Growing Concerns about Extremism, Continuing Discontent with U.S." (Washington, 2009), p. 8.

11. Craig Whitlock and Greg Miller, "Al Qaeda Likely to Replace Leader," *Washington Post,* June 2, 2010.

12. Stuart A. Levey, "How al Qaeda Will Miss Its Moneyman," *Washington Post,* June 6, 2010.

13. Zafar Imran, "Al Qaeda's Ambitions in Pakistan: Changing Goals, Changing Strategies," *Terrorism Monitor* 8 (August 5, 2010).

14. Statement of Secretary of Defense Robert Gates, before Senate Armed Services Committee, December 2, 2009.

15. Jane Perlez, "Official Admits Militancy Has Deep Roots in Pakistan," *New York Times,* June 3, 2010.

16. *United States of America* v. *David Coleman Headley.*

17. Stephen Tankel, *Lashkar e Taiba: From 9/11 to Mumbai* (London: International Centre for the Study of Radicalization and Political Violence, 2009); and Jean-Louis Bruguiere, *Ce que je n'ai pas pu dire* (What I have never been able to tell) (Paris: Editions Robert Laffont, 2009).

18. Andrea Elliot, "Militant's Path from Pakistan to Times Square," *New York Times,* June 22, 2010.

19. "Pakistani Taliban Release Video of Times Square Bomber Faisal Shahzad," Flashpoint Global Partners, August 2, 2010.

20. Ramzy Martine, ed., *The Battle for Yemen: Al Qaeda and the Struggle for Stability* (Washington: Jamestown Foundation, 2010).

21. An excellent study of the Iraqi franchise based on its own documents is Brian Fishman, *Dysfunction and Decline: Lessons Learned from Inside al Qa'ida in Iraq,* Harmony Project (West Point, N.Y.: West Point Combating Terrorism Center, 2009).

22. Bruce Hoffman, "Why al Qaeda Is Winning," *National Interest,* no. 107, May/June 2010.

23. "Militant Group Claims Credit for Suicide Attack on Japanese Oil Tanker," Flashpoint Partners, August 3, 2010.

CHAPTER SIX

1. The Clinton meeting with Bhutto is reported in Chidanand Rijghatt, "Daughter of the East Goes to Washington with Her Cup Full of Woes," *Indian Express,* May 10, 1998; and Helene Cooper and Mark Mazzetti, "Backstage, U.S. Nurtured Pakistan Rivals' Deal," *New York Times,* October 20, 2007.

2. Gail Sheehy, "A Wrong Must Be Righted," *Parade*, December 27, 2007.

3. Ibid.

4. William Milam, "Factors Shaping the Future," *The Future of Pakistan Project* (Brookings, 2010).

5. Wilson John, "General Hafiz Saeed," Observer Research Foundation Analysis, December 1, 2009.

6. Karin Brulliard, "Pakistan Conflicted over Fighting Extremists in Its Heartland," *Washington Post*, June 22, 2010.

7. Howard Chua-Eoan, "Broadway Bomber," *Time* Magazine, May 17, 2010.

8. Greg Miller, "Options Studied for a Possible Pakistan Strike," *Washington Post*, May 29, 2010.

9. Rahul Singh, "India, Pak Were on Brink of War after 26/11," *Hindustan Times*, June 1, 2009.

10. See Walter C. Ladwig III, "A Cold Start for Hot Wars? The Indian Army's New Limited War Doctrine," *International Security* 32 (Winter 2007/08): 158–90.

11. V. P. Malik, *Kargil from Surprise to Victory* (New Delhi: HarperCollins, 2007), pp. 130–31, 249–50. Malik was chief of army staff and chairman of the Chiefs of Staff Committee during the war.

CHAPTER SEVEN

1. Michael Kugelman, "Don't Drop That Bomb on Me," paper presented at Woodrow Wilson International Center for Scholars, Washington, June 9, 2010.

2. World Wide Fund for Nature–Pakistan, *Pakistan's Waters at Risk: A Special Report* (Lahore, 2007).

3. "India Imposed War on Pak by Constructing Illegal Dams, Saeed," *Times of India*, March 7, 2010.

4. Remarks by the President on a New Strategy for Afghanistan and Pakistan, White House, Office of the Press Secretary, March 27, 2009.

5. Clay Ramsay and others, "Pakistani Public Opinion on the Swat Conflict, Afghanistan and the U.S.," World Public Opinion, University of Maryland, July 1, 2009.

6. Owen Faye, "Pakistanis See U.S. as Biggest Threat," Al Jazeera Exclusive Gallup Pakistan Poll, August 13, 2009.

7. "Obama More Popular Abroad than at Home, Global Image of U.S. Continues to Benefit," 22-Nation Pew Global Attitude Survey, June 17, 2010.

8. "America's Image Remains Poor: Concern about Extremist Threat Slips in Pakistan," Pew Research Center Global Attitudes Project, July 29, 2010.

9. Zaid Hamid, *Mumbai: Dance of the Devil, Hindu Zionists, Mumbai Attacks and the Indian Dossier against Pakistan* (Rawalpindi: Brass Tacks Security Think Tank and Defence Analysis Consulting, 2009).

10. Remarks by the President, March 27, 2009.

11. Ramsay and others, "Pakistani Public Opinion on the Swat Conflict."

12. "Radicalization in Pakistan: Understanding the Phenomenon," Pakistan Institute for Peace Studies, June 6, 2010.

13. "Remarks by the President to the Nation on the Way Forward in Afghanistan and Pakistan," White House, Office of the Press Secretary, December 1, 2009.

14. Ramsay and others, "Pakistani Public Opinion on the Swat Conflict."

15. Shuja Nawaz, *Pakistan in the Danger Zone: A Tenuous U.S.-Pakistan Relationship* (Washington: Atlantic Council, 2010), p. 6.

16. Peter Bergen and Katherine Tiedemann, "The Year of the Drone," Counterterrorism Strategy Initiative Policy Paper (Washington, February 2010). Database updated periodically.

17. "Upbeat CIA Assessment on al Qaeda Challenged," Agence France-Presse, May 31, 2008.

18. Bergen and Tiedemann, "Year of the Drone."

19. Stuart A. Levey, "How al Qaeda Will Miss Its Moneyman," *Washington Post,* June 6, 2010.

20. Scott Shane, "Pakistan's Plan on Afghan Peace Leaves U.S. Wary," *New York Times,* June 28, 2010.

21. Jeremy Page, "Google Earth Reveals Secret History of U.S. Base in Pakistan," *London Times,* February 19, 2009.

22. Banyan, "Land of the Impure," *The Economist,* June 19, 2010.

23. Adnan R. Khan, "Land of the Generals," *Maclean's* Magazine, July 5, 2010.

24. Shaukat Qadir, "Still an Uncertain Future," The Futures of Pakistan Project (Brookings, 2010).

25. Matt Waldman, "The Sun in the Sky: The Relationship between Pakistan's ISI and Afghan Insurgents" (London School of Economics Crisis States Research Centre, June 2010).

26. Carlotta Gall, "Report Says Pakistani Intelligence Agency Exerts Great Sway on Afghan Taliban," *Washington Post,* June 13, 2010.

27. Joshua Partlow, "Afghan Leaders Leaving Karzai's Side," *Washington Post,* July 23, 2010.

28. Dexter Filkins, "Pakistanis Tell of Motive in Taliban Leaders' Arrests," *New York Times,* August 23, 2010.

29. Diwakar Mohan and Vishwa Mohan, "ISI Guided LeT at Every Step for 26/11," *The Times of India,* June 10, 2010.

30. Alissa Rubin, "Militant Group Expands Attacks in Afghanistan," *New York Times,* June 16, 2010.

31. "Haqqani Links Quicker Action with U.S. Equipment," *The News International* (Pakistan), June 17, 2010.

32. Rebecca Winthrop and Corinne Graff, *Beyond Madrasas: Assessing the Links between Education and Militancy in Pakistan* (Brookings, 2010).

33. Nawaz, *Pakistan in the Danger Zone,* p. 21.

34. Council on Foreign Relations, "Study Group Report on U.S. Policy toward Afghanistan and Pakistan" (New York, forthcoming).

35. Charles K. Ebinger and Kashif Hasnie, "'Power'-less Pakistan," Brookings Opinion Paper (www.brookings.edu/opinions/2010/0519).

36. Ibid.

37. A. Q. Khan has been the subject of several excellent studies. A good place to start is the International Institute for Strategic Studies, *Nuclear Black Markets: Pakistan, A. Q. Khan and the Rise of Proliferation Networks, A Net Assessment* (London, 2007).

38. Ronald E. Neuman, *The Other War: Winning and Losing in Afghanistan* (Washington: Potomac Books, 2009).

39. William Milam, "Factors Shaping the Future," The Futures of Pakistan Project (Brookings, 2010).

40. Strobe Talbott, *Engaging India: Diplomacy, Democracy and the Bomb,* rev. ed. (Brookings, 2006), p. 65.

BIBLIOGRAPHY

Abbas, Hassan. *Pakistan's Drift into Extremism: Allah, the Army, and America's War on Terror*. London: M. E. Sharpe, 2005.

Ahmed, Akbar S. *Resistance and Control in Pakistan*. London: Routledge, 1991.

Ali, Tariq. *The Duel: Pakistan on the Flight Path of American Power*. Toronto: Scribner, 2008.

Ayres, Alyssa. *Speaking Like a State: Language and Nationalism in Pakistan*. Cambridge University Press, 2009.

Bahl, Arvin. *From Jinnah to Jihad: Pakistan's Kashmir Quest and the Limits of Realism*. New Delhi: Atlantic, 2007.

Bearden, Milton. *The Black Tulip: A Novel of War in Afghanistan*. New York: Random House, 1998.

———. *The Main Enemy: The Inside Story of the CIA's Final Showdown with the KGB*. New York: Random House, 2003.

Benjamin, Daniel, and Steven Simon. *The Age of Sacred Terror: Radical Islam's War against America*. New York: Random House, 2003.

Bergen, Peter. *The Osama bin Laden I Know: An Oral History of al Qaeda's Leader*. New York: Free Press, 2006.

Berman, Eli. *Radical, Religious, and Violent: The New Economics of Terrorism*. Massachusetts Institute of Technology, 2009.

Bhutto, Benazir. *Daughter of the East: An Autobiography*. London: Hamish Hamilton, 1988.

———. *Reconciliation: Islam, Democracy, and the West*. New York: HarperCollins, 2008.

Bhutto, Fatima. *Songs of Blood and Sword: A Daughter's Memoir*. London: Jonathan Cape, 2010.

Bruguiere, Jean-Louis. *Ce que je n'ai pas pu dire* (What I have never been able to tell). Paris: Editions Robert Laffont, 2009.

Chari, P. R., Pervaiz Iqbal Cheema, and Stephen P. Cohen. *Four Crises and a Peace Process: American Engagement in South Asia*. Brookings, 2007.

Chehab, Zaki. *Inside Hamas: The Untold Story of Militants, Martyrs, and Spies*. London: Tauris, 2007.

Cigar, Norman. *Al-Qa'ida's Doctrine for Insurgency: 'Abd Al-'Aziz Al-Muqrin's A Practical Course for Guerrilla War*. Washington: Potomac, 2009.

Clarke, Richard A. *Against All Enemies: Inside America's War on Terror*. New York: Free Press, 2004.

Clinton, Bill. *My Life*. New York: Knopf, 2004.

Cohen, Stephen Philip. *The Idea of Pakistan*. Brookings, 2004.

———, ed. *The Futures of Pakistan Project*. Brookings, forthcoming.

Coll, Steve. *The Bin Ladens: An Arabian Family in the American Century*. New York: Penguin Books, 2006.

———. *Ghost Wars: The Secret History of the CIA, Afghanistan, and Bin Laden, from the Soviet Invasion to September 11, 2001*. New York: Penguin, 2004.

Crews, Robert, and Amin Tarzi, eds. *The Taliban and the Crisis of Afghanistan*. Harvard University Press, 2008.

Crile, George. *Charlie Wilson's War: The Extraordinary Story of How the Wildest Man in Congress and a Rogue CIA Agent Changed the History of Our Times*. New York: Grove Press, 2004.

Dalrymple, William. *The Last Mughal: The Fall of a Dynasty, Delhi, 1857*. New Delhi: Penguin, 2007.

Dorronsoro, Gilles. *Revolution Unending: Afghanistan, 1979 to the Present*. Columbia University Press, 2005.

Dreyfus, Robert. *Devil's Game: How the United States Helped Unleash Fundamentalist Islam*. New York: Metropolitan Books, 2005.

Evans, Duane. *North from Calcutta*. New York: Pecos, 2007.

Feifer, Gregory. *The Great Gamble: The Soviet War in Afghanistan*. New York: HarperCollins, 2009.

Filiu, Jean-Pierre. *Les Neuf Vies d'Al Qaida* (The nine lives of al Qaeda). Paris: Fayard, 2009.

Fishman, Brian. *Dysfunction and Decline: Lessons Learned from Inside al Qa'ida in Iraq*. Harmony Project. West Point, N.Y.: West Point Combating Terrorism Center, 2009.

Franz, Douglas, and Catherine Collins. *The Nuclear Jihadist: The True Story of the Man Who Sold the World's Most Dangerous Secrets . . . and How We Could Have Stopped Him*. New York: Hachette, 2007.

Gartenstein-Ross, Daveed, and Clifford May, eds. *The Afghanistan-Pakistan Theater: Militant Islam, Security and Stability*. Washington: FDD Press, 2010.

Gates, Robert M. *From the Shadows: The Ultimate Insider's Story of Five Presidents and How They Won the Cold War*. New York: Simon and Schuster, 1996.

Ghani, Ashraf, and Clare Lockhart. *Fixing Failed States: A Framework for Rebuilding a Fractured World*. Oxford University Press, 2008.

Gutman, Roy. *How We Missed the Story: Osama bin Laden, the Taliban and the Hijacking of Afghanistan*. Washington: United States Institute for Peace, 2008.

Habeck, Mary R. *Knowing the Enemy: Jihadist Ideology and the War on Terror*. Yale University Press, 2006.

Haider, Ziad. *The Ideological Struggle for Pakistan*. Hoover Institution Press, 2010.

Hamid, Zaid. *Mumbai: Dance of the Devil, Hindu Zionists, Mumbai Attacks and the Indian Dossier against Pakistan*. Rawalpindi: Brass Tacks Security Think Tank and Defence Analysis Consulting, 2009.

Haqqani, Husain. *Pakistan: Between Mosque and Military*. Washington: Carnegie Endowment for International Peace, 2005.

Hardy, Roger. *The Muslim Revolt: A Journey through Political Islam*. Columbia University Press, 2010.

Harrison, Selig S. *Pakistan: The State of the Union*. Washington: Center for International Policy, 2009.

Hayes, Geoffrey, and Mark Sedra, eds. *Afghanistan: Transition under Threat*. Wilfrid Laurier University Press, 2008.

Hegghammer, Thomas. *Jihad in Saudi Arabia: Violence and Pan Islamism since 1979*. Cambridge University Press, 2010.

Herman, Arthur. *Gandhi and Churchill: The Epic Rivalry That Destroyed an Empire and Forged Our Age*. New York: Bantam Books, 2008.

Hersman, Rebecca. *Friends and Foes: How Congress and the President Really Make Foreign Policy*. Brookings, 2000.

Hewitt, Vernon. *Towards the Future? Jammu and Kashmir in the 21st Century*. London: Cromwell Press, 2001.

Hoffman, Bruce. "Why al Qaeda Is Winning," *National Interest*, No. 107, May/June 2010.

Hopkins, B. D. *The Making of Modern Afghanistan*. Cambridge University Press, 2008.

Hussain, Zahid. *Frontline Pakistan: The Struggle with Militant Islam*. Columbia University Press, 2007.

———. *The Scorpion's Tale*. New York: Free Press, 2010.

Hussaini, Syed Masood Akhtar. *Air Warriors of Pakistan*. Lahore: Ferozsons, 1992.

International Institute for Strategic Studies. *Nuclear Black Markets: Pakistan, A. Q. Khan, and the Rise of Proliferation Networks*. London, 2007.

Jamal, Arif. *Shadow War: The Untold Story of Jihad in Kashmir*. Brooklyn: Melville House, 2009.

Jones, Owen Bennett. *Pakistan: Eye of the Storm*. Yale University Press, 2002.

Jones, Seth G. *In the Graveyard of Empires: America's War in Afghanistan*. New York: Norton, 2009.

Kaplan, Robert D. *Soldiers of God: With Islamic Warriors in Afghanistan and Pakistan*. New York: Vintage, 2001.

Kepel, Giles, and Jean-Pierre Milelli, eds. *Al Qaeda in Its Own Words*. Harvard University Press, 2008.

Khan, Yasmin. *The Great Partition: The Making of India and Pakistan*. Yale University Press, 2007.

Kiriakou, John. *The Reluctant Spy: My Secret Life in the CIA's War on Terror*. New York: Random House, 2009.

Kohlmann, Evan. *Al Qaida's Jihad in Europe: The Afghan Bosnian Network*. Oxford: Berg, 2004.

Kux, Dennis. *The United States and Pakistan, 1947–2000: Disenchanted Allies*. Johns Hopkins University Press, 2001.

Lamb, Alastair. *Kashmir: A Disputed Legacy 1846–1990*. Oxford University Press, 1992.

Lavoy, Peter R., ed. *Asymmetric Warfare in South Asia: The Causes and Consequences of the Kargil Conflict*. Cambridge University Press, 2010.

Lawrence, Bruce, ed. *Messages to the World: The Statements of Osama bin Laden*. London: Verso, 2005.

Levitt, Matthew. *Hamas: Politics, Charity and Terrorism in the Service of Jihad*. Yale University Press, 2006.

Levy, Adrian, and Catherine Scott-Clark. *Deception: Pakistan, the United States and the Secret Trade in Nuclear Weapons*. New York: Walker, 2007.

Lia, Brynjar. *Architect of Global Jihad: The Life of al Qaida Strategist Abu Mus'ab al Suri*. London: Hurst, 2007.

Luce, Edward. *In Spite of the Gods: The Rise of Modern India*. New York: Anchor, 2008.

Malik, V. P. *Kargil from Surprise to Victory*. New Delhi: HarperCollins, 2007.

Marston, Daniel, and Chandar Sundaram, eds. *A Military History of India and South Asia*. Indiana University Press, 2007.

Martine, Ramzy, ed. *The Battle for Yemen: Al Qaeda and the Struggle for Stability*. Washington: Jamestown Foundation, 2010.

McGeough, Paul. *Kill Khalid: The Failed Mossad Assassination of Khaled Mishal and the Rise of Hamas*. London: New Press, 2009.

Milam, William B. *Bangladesh and Pakistan: Flirting with Failure in South Asia*. Columbia University Press, 2009.

Mills, Nick. *Karzai: The Failing American Intervention and the Struggle for Afghanistan*. New York: Wiley, 2007.

Mishal, Shaul. *West Bank, East Bank: The Palestinians in Jordan, 1949–1967*. Yale University Press, 1978.

Misra, Neelesh. *173 Hours in Captivity: The Hijacking of IC 814*. New Delhi: HarperCollins, 2000.

Musharraf, Pervez. *In the Line of Fire: A Memoir*. London: Free Press, 2006.

Nasr, Seyyed Vali Reza. *The Vanguard of the Islamic Revolution: The Jama'at-I Islami of Pakistan*. University of California Press, 1994.

National Commission on Terrorist Attacks upon the United States. *The 9/11 Commission Report*. U.S. Government Printing Office, 2004.

Nawaz, Shuja. *Crossed Swords: Pakistan, Its Army, and the Wars Within*. Oxford University Press, 2008.

———. *Pakistan in the Danger Zone: A Tenuous U.S.-Pakistan Relationship*. Washington: Atlantic Council, 2010.

Neighbour, Sally. *The Mother of Mohammed: An Australian Woman's Extraordinary Journey into Jihad*. Melbourne University Press, 2009.

Netherlands National Coordinator for Counterterrorism. *Ideology and Strategy of Jihadism*. Amsterdam: NCTb, 2009.

Neumann, Ronald. *The Other War: Winning and Losing in Afghanistan*. Washington: Potomac Books, 2009.

O'Hanlon, Michael E., and Hassina Sherjan. *Toughing It Out in Afghanistan*. Brookings, 2010.

Pande, Aparna. *Explaining Pakistan's Foreign Policy: Escaping India*. New York: Routledge, forthcoming.

Persico, Joseph. *Casey: The Lives and Secrets of William J. Casey from the OSS to the CIA*. New York: Viking, 1990.

Rashid, Ahmed. *Taliban: Militant Islam, Oil, and Fundamentalism in Central Asia*. Yale University Press, 2001.

———. *Descent into Chaos: The United States and the Failure of Nation Building in Pakistan, Afghanistan, and Central Asia*. New York: Viking, 2008.

Richardson, Bill. *Between Worlds: The Making of an American Life*. New York: Putnam, 2005.

Riedel, Bruce. *The Search for Al Qaeda: Its Leadership, Ideology, and Future*. Brookings, 2008.

Roe, Andrew M. *Waging War in Waziristan: The British Struggle in the Land of Bin Laden, 1849–1947*. University Press of Kansas, 2010.

Roy, Olivier. *Globalized Islam: The Search for a New Ummah*. Columbia University Press, 2004.

Schaffer, Howard. *The Limits of Influence: America's Role in Kashmir*. Brookings, 2009.

Scheuer, Michael. *Osama Bin Laden*. Oxford University Press, forthcoming.

Schroen, Gary C. *First In: An Insider's Account of How the CIA Spearheaded the War on Terror*. New York: Ballantine, 2005.

Sevan, Emmanuel. *Radical Islam: Medieval Theology and Modern Politics*. Yale University Press, 1985

Siddiqa, Ayesha. *Military Inc.: Inside Pakistan's Military Economy*. London: Pluto Press, 2007.

Singh, Jaswant. *In Search of Emergent India: A Call to Honor*. Indiana University Press, 2007.

———. *Jinnah: India – Partition – Independence*. New Delhi: Rupa, 2009.

Talbott, Strobe. *Engaging India: Diplomacy, Democracy, and the Bomb*, rev. ed. Brookings, 2006.

Talbott, Strobe, and Chanda Nayan, eds. *The Age of Terror*. New York: Basic Books, 2001.

Tankel, Stephen. *Lashkar e Taiba: From 9/11 to Mumbai*. London: International Centre for the Study of Radicalization and Political Violence, 2009.

Tenet, George. *At the Center of the Storm: My Years at the CIA*. New York: HarperCollins, 2007.

Tunzelmann, Alex von. *Indian Summer: The Secret History of the End of an Empire*. New York: Picador, 2007.

Winthrop, Rebecca, and Corinne Graff. *Beyond Madrasas: Assessing the Links between Education and Militancy in Pakistan*. Brookings, 2010.

Wittes, Tamara Cofman. *Freedom's Unsteady March: America's Role in Building Arab Democracy*. Brookings, 2008.

Wolpert, Stanley. *Jinnah of Pakistan*. Oxford University Press, 1985.

———. *Shameful Flight: The Last Years of the British Empire in India*. Oxford University Press, 2006.

Woodward, Bob. *Veil: The Secret Wars of the CIA, 1981–1987*. London: Simon and Schuster, 1987.

———. *Bush at War*. London: Simon and Schuster, 2003.

———. *Obama's Wars*. New York: Simon and Schuster, 2010.

Wright, Lawrence. *The Looming Tower: Al Qaeda and the Road to 9/11*. New York: Alfred A. Knopf, 2006.

Yousaf, Mohammad. *Silent Soldier: The Man behind the Afghan Jehad, General Akhtar Abdur Rahman Shaheed*. Lahore: Jang, 1991.

Yousaf, Mohammad, and Mark Adkin. *The Bear Trap: Afghanistan's Untold Story*. London: Leo Cooper, 1992.

Zaeef, Abdul Salam. *My Life with the Taliban*. Translated and edited by Alex Strick van Linschoten and Felix Kuehn. Columbia University Press, 2010.

Zakheim, Dov. *A Vulcan's Tale: How the Bush Administration Mismanaged the Reconstruction of Afghanistan*. Brookings, forthcoming 2011.

INDEX

Surnames starting with "al" or "al-" are alphabetized by the following part of the name.

Abdallah, Abdallah, 62
Abdulmutallab, Umar Farouk, 103
Afghanistan: al Qaeda in, 1, 81; communist government in, 27, 39; relationship with Pakistan, 22; U.S. military operations in, 2–3, 94, 121
Afghan Taliban: and ISI, 81, 129; and Musharraf, 62; red lines for, 129–30; resurgence of, 70–71; in syndicate of terrorists, 1
Ahmad, Mahmud, 40, 59, 64–66
Air India flight 814 hijacking (1999), 58–59, 70
Air mobility, 134–35
Akhtar Abdur Rahman, 21–22, 23
Ali, Chaudhary Rahmat, 4, 6
Al Jazeera, 98, 122
Al Qaeda: in Afghanistan, 1; arrests of operatives in Pakistan, 73, 98; and Azzam assassination, 34; and Bhutto assassination, 77, 82; and bin Laden's jihad, 78–85; franchises in Islamic world, 103–04; and Headley, 101; in Iraq, 94, 103, 104; and JeM, 70; and Musharraf,

63; in Pakistan, 1, 67, 94; resurgence of, 94; in Saudi Arabia, 33, 94; and Taliban, 3, 56, 81
Al Qaeda in Mesopotamia, 103
Al Qaeda in the Arabian Peninsula, 103
Al Qaeda in the Islamic Maghreb, 103
Al Zulfikar (group), 44
Arab-Israeli War (1947–48), 29
Arafat, Yasir, 20
Armitage, Richard, 65, 73
Arms sales. *See* Military aid
Army (Pakistan): Islamization of, 20–21; and LeT, 107–08; social status of, 21
As Sahab Foundation for Islamic Media Publication, 81, 98, 105
Assistance to Pakistan, 119–44; capacity building, 133–38; counterterrorism coordination, 125–27; engagement efforts, 127–33; and peace in South Asia, 138–43; trust-building, 121–25. *See also* Economic aid; Military aid
Ataturk, Mustafa Kemal, 63
Atlantic Council, 136

Australia, al Qaeda plots in, 102
Awami League, 10
Awlaki, Anwar al, 103, 105
Azad Kashmir, 9
Azhar, Maulana Masood, 40, 59, 69, 84
Azizi, Amir, 84
Azzam, Abdallah Yusuf Mustafa, 28–35, 102, 105
Azzam, Hutaifa, 55–56

Balawi, Human Khalil Abu Mulal al, 99
Bali, Indonesia, night club terrorist attacks (2002), 33
Baluchistan: and Afghanistan-Pakistan relations, 138; Afghan refugees in, 24; and jihadist Pakistan scenario, 110
Baradar, Mullah, 130
Bari, Maulana Abdul, 26
Batikhi, Samih, 57
The Bear Trap: Afghanistan's Untold Story (Yousaf), 25
Bengal province: absent from Ali's vision of Pakistan, 4; independence movement, 9–10, 26; and Jinnah, 6; and official language of Pakistan, 7
Berger, Sandy, 58
Bharatiya Janata Party (BJP, India), 115
Bhutto, Benazir: on al Qaeda, 107; assassination of, 1, 77, 82, 124; and CIA, 36–37; Clinton (H.) meeting with, 106; election of, 38–39, 43, 72; and Kashmir, 41, 46; and Musharraf, 75–77; ouster of, 44; and Pressler Amendment restrictions, 48; and Taliban, 43, 49; on Zarqawi and ISI, 57
Bhutto, Murtaza, 44

Bhutto, Zulfikar Ali, 10, 19, 20, 26–27
Biden, Joe, 1–2, 95
Bin Baz, Abdul Aziz, 30
Bin Laden, Osama, 60–85; in Afghanistan, 54–55; and Air India flight 814 hijacking (1999), 59, 70; and al Qaeda goals in Pakistan, 100–01; and Azzam, 30, 31, 32; and Bhutto (B.), 39; and Buddha statue destruction, 79; and mujahedin resistance, 32, 105; and Mumbai terrorist attacks, 89; and Musharraf, 62–72; and Omar, 53–57; in Pakistan, 67, 98; in Saudi Arabia, 54; and September 11, 2001, terrorist attacks, 79–80; and Sharif, 42, 51; in Sudan, 54; and Taliban, 50, 55–56
BJP (Bharatiya Janata Party, India), 115
Blair, Dennis, 95
Border stabilization, 138–43
Brigitte, Willie, 102
Brookings Institution, 2, 97
Brown, Hank, 47
Brown Amendment, 47
Brzezinski, Zbigniew, 27
Buddha statues destroyed by Taliban, 79
Bureau of Intelligence Research (U.S.), 14
Bush, George H. W., 41, 47, 48, 118
Bush, George W.: and drone attacks, 125; and Musharraf, 62, 72–78, 118; and trade policy, 136; and U.S.-India relations, 73, 122, 141
Butt, Ziauddin, 46

Capacity building, 133–38
Carter, Jimmy, 27
Casey, William, 17–18

Cawthorne, William, 8
Center for Proselytization and Preaching, 32
Central Intelligence Agency (CIA): and al Qaeda, 99; and Bhutto (B.), 36–37; establishment of relationship with Pakistan, 12; ISI relationship with, 13, 21, 73, 132; and millennium plots, 58; and mujahedin resistance, 23, 27; Northern Alliance support from, 67, 80; and Zubaydah, 64
Central Treaty Organization (CENTO), 13
Chamberlin, Wendy, 65
Cheney, Liz, 75
China: arms sales to Pakistan, 15; and Bhutto (Z.), 27; and jihadist Pakistan scenario, 111; nuclear program assistance from, 19, 138; and U.S.-Pakistan intelligence cooperation, 13
Churchill, Winston, 11
CIA. See Central Intelligence Agency
Clarke, Richard, 64–65
Clinton, Bill: and bin Laden, 51; and Kargil War, 51–52; and Musharraf, 60–61; Pakistani television address by, 61–62; and U.S.-India relations, 122, 141; and U.S.-Pakistan relations, 48–49, 128
Clinton, Hillary, 2, 95, 106
Cold Start approach, 115, 116
Committee for State Security (KGB, Soviet Union), 24
Comprehensive Test Ban Treaty, 51
Constitution (Pakistan), 7, 13, 127
Council on Foreign Relations, 136
Counterterrorism coordination, 62, 72–78, 125–27, 134–35
Crocker, Ryan, 76
Crossed Swords (Nawaz), 134

Dean, John Gunther, 35
Defense Intelligence Agency (U.S.), 51
The Defense of Muslim Territories (Azzam), 30
Democracy: and East-West Pakistan conflicts, 7–8; and jihads, 37–47; and Musharraf, 74–75; Pakistani public opinion on, 122
Demographics in Pakistan, 120, 135
Denmark, LeT plot against newspaper in, 101
Deobandi movement, 5
Donilon, Tom, 95
Dostam, Abdul Rashid, 42
Drone attacks, 125–27, 135
Dulles, Allen, 13
Dulles, John Foster, 12
Dulles, John Welsh, 12
Durand Line, 22, 138

East Pakistan: conflict with West Pakistan, 6–7; and democracy, 7–8; language conflict in, 7; vulnerability to Indian attacks, 9
Economic aid, 86–87, 123, 133–38
Education, 135
Egyptian Islamic Jihad, 98
Eisenhower, Dwight D., 12, 14
Elections (Pakistan): of 1988, 38; of 1993, 43; of 1997, 45; of 2002, 75; of 2008, 72, 77, 144; rigged, 8, 20, 75. See also Democracy
Emanuel, Rahm, 95
Embassy bombings in Tanzania and Kenya (1998), 51
Energy sector, 136
Engagement efforts, 127–33
European Islamic community, 104

Fahd (king of Saudi Arabia), 23
Fedayeen resistance, 29

Federally Administered Tribal Areas
(FATA): Afghan refugees in, 24; al
Qaeda in, 67, 68; counterterrorism
in, 87; drone attacks in, 125; and
jihadist Pakistan scenario, 114; and
Taliban, 92
Fertility rates, 120
55 Brigade, 56
First Indo-Pakistani War (1947), 8
Flournoy, Michelle, 1, 94, 119
Foreign Assistance Act of 1961, 47
Freedom Agenda, 75
Free trade agreement, 136

Gandhi, Indira, 15
Gandhi, Mahatma, 11
Gates, Robert, 2, 18, 41, 48, 95, 100
General Intelligence Directorate (Jor-
dan), 29–30, 34, 57, 58, 99
General Intelligence Directorate
(Saudi Arabia), 23, 27
Gilani, Daood Sayed. See Headley,
David Coleman
Gillani, Yousaf Raza, 2, 86–87, 129
Glenn Amendment of 1977, 51
Global Islamic Resistance Call
(al-Suri), 33
Global jihad, 86–105; and Azzam,
28–35; growth of, 97–105; and ISI,
38; and Mumbai terrorist attacks,
87–93, 114–18; and Musharraf,
63, 79; and Obama, 93–97; and
Pakistan, 106–18; regional impli-
cations of, 110–11; and Times
Square bombing (2010), 113–14;
U.S. policy options, 112–13
Government Information Agency
(KHAD, Afghanistan), 24
Grenier, Bob, 66
Gul, Hamid, 39, 41, 78, 107

Haass, Richard, 41, 48, 80
Hamas, 32, 34

Hambali, 33
Haqqani, Husain, 86, 119–20, 134
Harakat al-Muqawamat al-Islamiyyah
(Hamas), 32, 34
Harakat ul Mujahedin (HuM), 58
Hassan, Nidal Malik, 103
Hayden, Michael, 125
Hazari Shia, 54
Headley, David Coleman, 91–92, 97,
101, 104, 126, 131
Hekmatayar, Gulbudin, 42, 55, 67
Helicopters, 134–35
Hijacking of Air India flight 814
(1999), 58–59, 70
Hindus, 4, 5
Hizbul Mujahedeen, 40
Holbrooke, Richard, 1, 94, 119
HuM (Harakat ul Mujahedin), 58
Human Rights Commission of Paki-
stan, 108
Hydropower, 136

Illiteracy, 135
In Defense of Muslim Lands (Azzam),
102
Inderfurth, Karl Rick, 63, 64
India: and Bengal province, 6, 10; and
Cold Start approach, 115, 116; and
jihadist Pakistan scenario, 110–11;
and Jinnah, 5; and Kashmir region,
8–9, 40–41; and Musharraf, 71,
90; nuclear program of, 19, 45, 51,
136, 137; and Pakistani policy on
Taliban, 67; strategic review on, 1;
and supply depot explosion (1988),
38; and U.S. military operations
in Afghanistan, 66; U.S. relations
with, 14, 73, 122, 141–42. See also
Mumbai terrorist attacks
Indian mutiny of 1857, 5
Indian parliament terrorist attack
(2001), 68–69, 141
Indonesia, al Qaeda in, 124–25

Intelligence operations. *See specific intelligence agencies*

International Atomic Energy Agency (IAEA), 74, 136

International Security Assistance Force (ISAF), 96, 110, 139

Inter-Services Intelligence (ISI): and Afghan Taliban resurgence, 71, 81–82, 129, 130; and Air India flight 814 hijacking, 59; and Bhutto (B.), 38–39, 78; and bin Laden, 51, 55; CIA relationship with, 13; growth of, 8; and growth of global jihad, 19, 140; and Headley, 92; and Indian parliament terrorist attack, 69; jihadist training from, 32; and Kargil War, 46–47; and Kashmiri insurgency, 26, 40; leadership changes in, 38; and LeT, 83, 131; and mujahedin resistance, 23, 24; and Omar, 53; and Taliban, 43–44, 45, 67–68; and Zarqawi, 57; and Zia, 21–22

In the Line of Fire (Musharraf), 63

Iran: and jihadist Pakistan scenario, 110; nuclear program of, 73, 74; Shia revolution (1978), 22; and Taliban, 54

Iraq: al Qaeda in, 81, 94, 103, 104; Kuwait invasion by, 48; U.S. military operations in, 68

ISAF. *See* International Security Assistance Force

Isamuddin, Riduan, 33

ISI. *See* Inter-Services Intelligence

Islamic Association for Palestine, 31

Islamic Resistance Movement. *See* Harakat al-Muqawamat al-Islamiyyah (Hamas)

Islamization of army, 20–21

Israel: and Arab-Israeli War (1947–48), 29; and jihadist Pakistan scenario, 111

Jaish-e-Muhammad (JeM), 59, 69, 70, 73

Jamaah Islamiyah, 33

Jamaat-i-Islam Party, 6, 20, 23, 25–26, 39

Jamaat ud Dawa (JuD), 82–83. *See also* Lashkar-e-Tayyiba (LeT)

Jammu and Kashmir Liberation Front (JKLF), 26, 39–40

JeM. *See* Jaish-e-Muhammad

Jihad. *See* Global jihad; *specific leaders*

Jinnah, Fatima, 8

Jinnah, Muhammad Ali, 4–11

JKLF (Jammu and Kashmir Liberation Front), 26, 39–40

Johnson, Lyndon B., 14, 96

Jones, Jim, 2, 95

Jordan: al Qaeda in, 104, 124–25; and Azzam, 29–30; and Zarqawi, 57–58; Zia in, 20

Kalashnikov culture, 37

Kamal, Syed, 128

Karamat, Jehangir, 45, 128

Kargil War (1999): India's response to, 115; international response to, 141; and Lahore peace talks, 89–90; planning of, 46–47; political fallout from, 63; and U.S.-Pakistan relations, 51

Karzai, Hamid, 82, 138

Kashmir: border stabilization in, 138–43; and First Indo-Pakistani War (1947), 8; insurgency in, 39–41; and ISI supply depot explosion (1988), 38; and jihadist Pakistan scenario, 110–11; and Musharraf, 46–47, 71; Pakistani public opinion on, 124; partitioning of, 9; and Zia, 26

Kashmiri, Muhammad Ilyas: and Bhutto assassination, 77; drone attacks against, 126; and Headley, 101; and ISI, 40; and Taliban, 81

Kayani, Ashfaq Parvez: and bin Laden, 101; and counterterrorism cooperation, 87; and Musharraf, 72; and Taliban, 62, 70–71, 81, 92; and U.S.-Pakistan relations, 121, 129
Kennedy, John F., 14, 118
Kenya, embassy bombing in (1998), 51
Kerry, John, 123
Kerry-Lugar bill on Pakistan aid (2008), 86–87, 123–24, 135
KGB (Committee for State Security, Soviet Union), 24
KHAD (Government Information Agency, Afghanistan), 24
Khalis, Yunis, 55
Khan, A. Q., 19, 42, 73–74, 123, 136
Khan, Ayub, 8–9, 13, 14, 118
Khan, Ghulam Ishaq, 41
Khan, Liaquat Ali, 6, 12
Khan, Mohammed Daoud, 23
Khan, Yahya, 9–10, 15
Khorasani, Abu Dujannah al, 34, 99–100
Kissinger, Henry, 15
Kuwait, Iraq's invasion of, 48

Lahore Declaration (1999), 45, 89
Lakhvi, Azki Rehman, 88
Language, official, 7
Lashkar-e-Janghvi, 100
Lashkar-e-Tayyiba (LeT): and al Qaeda, 82–83; and Azzam, 32; and Brigitte, 102; goals of, 100; and Headley, 91–92, 101; and ISI, 73; and Kargil War, 90; in Kashmir, 39; and Mumbai terrorist attacks, 88–93, 129; and Musharraf, 62; and Pakistan army, 107–08; red lines for, 130–31, 141; in syndicate of terrorists, 1; and Zubaydah, 67
Levey, Stuart, 98, 126

Libya, nuclear program of, 73–74, 136
Limpert, Mark, 86
Line of Control (Kashmir), 47, 89, 140, 142
Literacy programs, 135
London bombings (2005), 83–84

Madrassas, 5, 21, 33, 82, 135
Madrid subway terrorist attack (2003), 84–85
Maktab al Khadamat, 31
Malik, Rehman, 100
Manhattan Raid. See September 11, 2001, terrorist attacks
Markaz-ud-Dawa-wal-Irshad (MDI), 32
Marshall, Charles Burton, 13
Massoud, Ahmad Shah, 42, 50, 57, 79, 102
Mawdudi, Mawlana Sayyid Abu A'ala, 5–6, 21, 25
McChrystal, Stanley, 96
MDI (Markaz-ud-Dawa-wal-Irshad), 32
Mehsud, Beitullah, 99, 126
Milam, William, 61, 64, 107, 142
Military aid: to India from U.S., 14; to Pakistan from China, 15; to Pakistan from U.S., 13, 14, 41, 72
Military coups: by Ayub Khan (1958), 8; by Musharraf, 52; and U.S. economic aid, 64; U.S. endorsement of, 118; by Zia (1977), 19
Military Inc. (Siddiqa), 128
Military operations: and jihadist Pakistan scenario, 112–13; Operation Fair Play, 19; Operation Genghis Khan, 10; Operation Gibraltar, 9; Operation Grand Slam, 9; Operation Searchlight, 10, 15. See also specific wars and conflicts
Mishal, Khalid, 32

The Morning and the Lamp (Zawahiri), 100
MQM (Muttahida Qaumi Movement), 109, 128
Muhammad, Khalid Sheikh, 32, 68, 103–04
Muhkabarat states, 74–75
Mujahedin: arms supplies to, 25, 32; and global jihad, 105; Pakistan support for, 18; support for, 23; and Taliban, 55
Mumbai terrorist attacks (2006), 90
Mumbai terrorist attacks (2008), 87–93, 114–18, 129
Al-Muqrin, 'Abd al-'Aziz, 33
Musharraf, Pervez: and bin Laden's jihad, 62–72; and Bush (G.W.), 72–78, 118; and counterterrorism cooperation, 70; and global jihad, 79; and India-Pakistan relations, 71, 73, 90; and Kargil War, 46–47, 51, 89; and Kashmiri, 40; and Kashmir peace process, 71; and Sharif, 45; and Taliban, 65, 66–67, 68; and U.S. military operations in Afghanistan, 65–66; on U.S. trade policy, 136
Muslim Brotherhood, 29, 30
Muslim League. *See* Pakistan Muslim League (PML)
Muttahida Qaumi Movement (MQM), 109, 128

Nasir, Javid, 42
National Counter Terrorism Center, 97
National Foreign Intelligence Board, 17
National Intelligence Estimate on Afghanistan, 17
National Security Agency (NSA), 13
NATO. *See* North Atlantic Treaty Organization
Naval blockade, 112, 116

Nawaz, Asif, 42–43
Nawaz, Shuja, 21, 35, 66, 134
Nehru, Jawaharlal, 8
Neuman, Ronald, 139
New America Foundation, 125, 126
9/11 Commission Report, 55, 59
Nixon, Richard, 13, 15, 118
North Atlantic Treaty Organization (NATO), 1, 80, 94
Northern Alliance: and Afghan civil war, 49, 80; and Taliban, 50, 67. *See also* Mujahedin
North Korea, nuclear program of, 73, 74
North-West Frontier Province, 24, 92
Norway, Pakistani diaspora in, 109
Nuclear power plants, 136
Nuclear proliferation, 64, 73, 109, 113, 136
Nuclear Suppliers Group (NSG), 136
Nuclear testing, 45, 47, 51, 116

Obama, Barack: and Afghanistan war, 2–3; and drone attacks, 125–26; on extremism in Pakistan, 124; Gillani meeting with, 2, 86–87; and global jihad, 93–97; on Pakistan's role in Afghanistan war, 133; and U.S.-India relations, 122, 141–42; and U.S.-Pakistan relations, 142
Omar, Mullah Muhammad: background of, 53–57; and bin Laden, 50, 66; and millennium terror plot, 57–59; and mujahedin, 24; in Pakistan, 67; and U.S. military operations in Afghanistan, 110
Operation Fair Play, 19
Operation Genghis Khan, 10
Operation Gibraltar, 9
Operation Grand Slam, 9
Operation Searchlight, 10, 15
Opium trade, 24

Pakistani Institute for Peace Studies, 92, 124

Pakistani Taliban: and al Qaeda, 3, 82; and Bhutto assassination, 77, 82; and Pashtuns, 83; in syndicate of terrorists, 1; and Times Square bombing (2010), 102, 113–14

Pakistan Muslim League (PML), 4, 6, 76, 108, 128

Pakistan Peoples Party (PPP), 10, 44, 72, 76

Palestinians, 20

Panetta, Leon, 95, 126

Pasha, Ahmad Shuja, 95, 120

Pashtuns: and Afghanistan-Pakistan relations, 22, 138; and ISI, 25; and Taliban, 54, 82, 83

Perry, William, 49

Petraeus, David, 1, 95, 134

PML. See Pakistan Muslim League

Population growth in Pakistan, 120, 135

Powell, Colin, 73

PPP. See Pakistan Peoples Party

A Practical Course for Guerrilla War (al-Muqrin), 33

Pressler, Larry Lee, 47

Pressler Amendment of 1985, 41, 47–48, 64, 143

Punjab province, 7, 83

Qasab, Mohammad Ajmal Amir, 88–89

Qatar, hosting of U.S. Islamic World Forum, 97

Qazi, Javad Ashraf, 43, 69

Qureshi, Makhdoom Shah Mehmood, 119

Qutb, Sayid, 104–05

Rabbani, Mullah, 52

Rahman, Akhtar Abdur, 21–22, 23

Rana, Tahawwur Hussain, 91–92

Raphel, Arnold, 34

Rashid, Ahmed, 54, 70

Rauf, Rashid, 84, 99, 126

Reagan, Ronald, 118

Red lines, 129–30

Refugees, 4, 24

Rehman, I. A., 108

Rehman, Sherry, 86

Ressam, Ahmed, 58

Rice, Condoleezza, 65

Richardson, Bill, 45, 50

Rigged elections, 8, 20, 75

Roosevelt, Franklin D., 11

Rose, Charlie, 95–96

Rumsfeld, Donald, 94

Saban Center for Middle East Policy, 2

Saeed, Amer Omar, 59

Saeed, Hafez, 32, 39, 83, 108, 121

Salih, Amarullah, 95, 130

Saudi Arabia: al Qaeda in, 33, 80–81, 94; Azzam in, 30; bin Laden in, 54; ISI relationship with, 21; and mujahedin resistance, 23; Pakistan troops in, 24; strategic review on, 1; and Taliban, 52

Schroen, Gary, 80

Scowcroft, Brent, 48, 133

The Search for al Qaeda (Riedel), 96

SEATO (Southeast Asia Treaty Organization), 13

Second Indo-Pakistani War (1965), 9, 63

Security Council (UN), 117

Selective counterterrorism, 70

Self-radicalization, 104

September 11, 2001, terrorist attacks, 65, 72, 79–80

Shahzad, Faisal, 102, 104, 113

Sharif, Nawaz: and Bhutto (B.), 106; and bin Laden, 51; election of, 45; and elections of 2008, 72; ISI support for, 41, 42; and Kargil War, 51–52; and Mumbai terrorist attacks, 89; and Musharraf, 63, 75–76, 77; and nuclear program, 45, 143; ouster of, 43; and Taliban, 50; and U.S.-Pakistan relations, 128

Sharif, Shahbaz, 63

Shia Muslims: and Iran's revolution (1978), 22; and jihadist Pakistan scenario, 109, 110, 112; and Taliban, 54

Siddiqa, Ayesha, 128

Siddiq Khan, Mohammad, 84

Sikhs, 4

Silent Soldier (Yousaf), 25

Singh, Jaswant, 5, 59, 69, 73

Singh, Manmohan, 71, 90, 91, 115

Sipah-e-Sohaba Pakistan, 22, 100

Six-Day War (1967), 20

Southeast Asia Treaty Organization (SEATO), 13

Soviet Union: Afghanistan occupation by, 18, 23, 24–25; and U.S.-Pakistan intelligence cooperation, 13; and U.S. policy in South Asia, 11–12

Special Services Group (SSG, Pakistan), 24, 25, 83

State Department (U.S.): and Freedom Agenda, 75; on military rule in Pakistan, 14; and U.S.-Pakistan relations, 132

Sunni Muslims, 22

Supply depot explosion (1988), 38

Al-Suri, Abu Mus'ad, 33

Sutphen, Mona, 50

Syrian Islamist movement, 33

Taj, Nadeem, 78

Tajiks, 54

Talbott, Strobe, 49, 51, 143

Taliban: and al Qaeda, 81; and Bhutto (B.), 49; Buddha statue destruction by, 79; ISI support for, 43–44, 45, 73; and Nawaz, 45; recognition of, 52; resurgence of, 94; rise of, 53–54; sanctions against, 61. *See also* Afghan Taliban; Pakistani Taliban

Tanweer, Shehzad, 84

Tanzania, embassy bombing in (1998), 51

Tenet, George, 58, 65, 73–74

Textiles trade, 136

Third Indo-Pakistani War (1971), 10, 63

313 Brigade, 40

Times Square bombing (2010), 102, 113–14

Trade policy, 136

Transparency International, 78

Truman, Harry, 11–12

Trust-building, 120, 121–25

Turki bin Faysal (prince), 23

UAVs (unmanned aerial vehicles), 125–27, 135

Union Oil Company of California (UNOCAL), 49

United Arab Emirates, 52

United Kingdom (UK): al Qaeda plots in, 84; and Bengal province, 6; and formation of Pakistan, 4; and Indian mutiny of 1857, 5; Pakistani diaspora in, 102, 109

United Nations: and Bhutto assassination, 77; Mumbai terrorist attack response by, 117; sanctions on Taliban, 61

United Nations Educational, Scientific and Cultural Organization (UNESCO), 79

University of Maryland, 122, 124

Unmanned aerial vehicles (UAVs), 125–27, 135

Urbanization, 120

Urdu as official language, 7
U.S.-India nuclear deal, 137, 141
U.S. Islamic World Forum, 97
U.S.-Pakistan relations: in 1990s, 47–53; and global jihad, 112–13; history of, 3–16; and Pressler Amendment, 41; and Zia, 26–28
USS *Cole* attack (2000), 58
U2 program, 13
Uzbeks, 54

Vajpayee, Atal Behari, 45, 89
Vietnam War, 96

Washington Post on U.S. military planning for jihadist Pakistan scenario, 114
Water resources, 120–21
West Pakistan: conflict with East Pakistan, 6–7; and democracy, 7–8; language conflict in, 7
Wilson, Charlie, 28
Wolpert, Stanley, 4
Woodward, Bob, 96

Yazid, Mustafa Muhammad Uthman abu, 98, 99, 126
Yousaf, Mohammad, 25, 35

Zaeef, Abdul Salam, 44
Zaid, Sharif Ali bin, 34
Zardari, Asif Ali: and bin Laden, 101; and counterterrorism, 90–91; election of, 72, 77; and India-Pakistan relations, 91; and Kayani, 129; and Murtaza Bhutto, 44; public opinion on, 127; and Taliban, 92; travels during monsoons and flooding in Pakistan, 121
Zargar, Mushtaq Ahmed, 59
Zarqawi, Abu Musaib al, 32, 57
Zawahiri, Ayman al: and al Qaeda goals in Pakistan, 100; and Azzam assassination, 34; and drone attacks, 126; on London bombings (2005), 83–84; and mujahedin resistance, 105; and Musharraf, 82; in Pakistan, 98; and September 11, 2001, terrorist attacks, 80
Zazi, Najibullah, 99
Zia ul-Haq, Muhammad, 17–35; and Azzam's jihad, 28–35; and Bhutto (B.), 106; coup by, 19; and global jihad, 18–19; and ISI, 19–26; and Kashmir, 46; and mujahedin resistance, 17–18; and nuclear program, 42; and U.S.–Pakistan relations, 26–28
Zubaydah, Abu, 57, 64, 67, 68